LIVE JESUS IN OUR HEARTS

JESUS CHRIST
AND NEW
THE
TESTAMENT

High School Framework Course 2

ALAN J. TALLEY

saint mary's press

Thanks and Dedication

A very special thank you to our student contributors: Viva from Cotter High School in Winona, MN; Casey and Ifeoluwa, both from Mater Dei High School in Santa Ana, CA; Matt from Providence Catholic High School in New Lenox, IL; and Vincent from De La Salle Collegiate High School in Warren, MI.

The Subcommittee on the Catechism, United States Conference of Catholic Bishops, has found that this catechetical high school text, copyright 2019, is in conformity with the *Catechism of the Catholic Church* and that it fulfills the requirements of Core Course II of the *Doctrinal Elements of a Curriculum Framework for the Development of Catechetical Materials for Young People of High School Age.*

Nihil Obstat: Dr. John Martens, PhD
                  Censor Librorum
                  November 15, 2018

Imprimatur: † Most Rev. Bernard A. Hebda
                  Archbishop of Saint Paul and Minneapolis
                  November 20, 2018

The nihil obstat and imprimatur are official declarations that a book or pamphlet is free of doctrinal or moral error. No implication is contained therein that those who have granted the nihil obstat or imprimatur agree with the contents, opinions, or statements expressed, nor do they assume any legal responsibility associated with publication.

The content in this resource was acquired, developed, and reviewed by the content engagement team at Saint Mary's Press. Content design and manufacturing were coordinated by the passionate team of creatives at Saint Mary's Press.

Printed in the United States of America

1166 (PO6318)

ISBN 978-1-59982-948-7

CONTENTS

UNIT 1
Jesus and Faith

WHAT DOES IT MEAN TO HAVE FAITH IN JESUS?

LOOKING AHEAD

To be honest, I don't agree with some of the Church teachings, but I do still believe in God because I see proof of God's love for us everywhere. Whenever I see a gorgeous sunset or the beautiful bluffs that surround my town, I see God's power reflected. Anytime I am around others who are happy, loving, generous people, I recognize the love of Jesus through them.

VIVA
Cotter High School

CHAPTER 1
Getting to Know Jesus

WHO IS JESUS?

SNAPSHOT

Article 1

Discovering Jesus: The Adventure Begins

"From the first day that I walked through those doors, those are magic doors . . . I saw kinship and love." These are the words of Mariana, recalling the first time she entered Homeboy Industries. Founded in 1988 by Jesuit priest Fr. Greg Boyle, Homeboy Industries is an organization that offers job training and free programs and support services. Homeboy works to help formerly gang-involved and previously incarcerated men and women in the Los Angeles area to change their lives for the better. Having been a drug user for seventeen years, Mariana never imagined her life could change, but she had a desire for something more. By responding to that desire and choosing to pass through those doors, she discovered the love of Jesus Christ. She also found a community of faith and support, and she worked to heal her own brokenness. Mariana has earned her GED, has finished the 18-month program at Homeboy, and has been promoted as a core member of the Homeboy staff. She will soon move on to a new job as a prison re-entry case manager.

courtesy Homeboy Industries

Fr. Greg Boyle works alongside formerly gang-involved and previously incarcerated men at Homeboy Industries.

Saint Paul's Shocking Transformation

It is amazing how discovering the love of Jesus Christ and placing your faith in him really does change lives. Mariana's story is definitely not unique. The Church's history is filled with stories of people who have turned their lives around after placing their faith in Jesus Christ. One dramatic example of this is Saul of Tarsus, better known now as Saint Paul. If you haven't done so already, take a moment to read the story of Saint Paul's conversion in Acts 7:54–8:3, 9:1–22. His story begins shortly after Jesus Christ had ascended into **Heaven**. Paul is first introduced as a threatening figure standing in the background, witnessing Saint Stephen being stoned to death. In that act, Paul actively approves of the death of the first **martyr** for the Christian faith. Paul goes on to hunt down many other followers of Jesus Christ and sees to it that they too suffer the same fate as Stephen (see Acts 8:3).

Then one day, it all changes for Paul when he meets the risen Jesus Christ. Even while Paul is "breathing murderous threats against the disciples of the Lord" (Acts 9:1), Jesus Christ reaches out to him on the road to Damascus. Through that encounter, Paul's heart and life are radically changed. Saint Paul not only becomes a Christian but also one of Christianity's most zealous advocates, spreading the saving message of Christ crucified and risen everywhere he goes.

When Paul encounters the Risen Christ, it is a life-transforming event.
He goes on to be one of Christianity's most zealous advocates.

Heaven ➤ A state of eternal life and union with God, in which one experiences full happiness and the satisfaction of the deepest human longings.

martyr ➤ A person who voluntarily suffers death because of his or her beliefs. The Church has canonized many martyrs as saints.

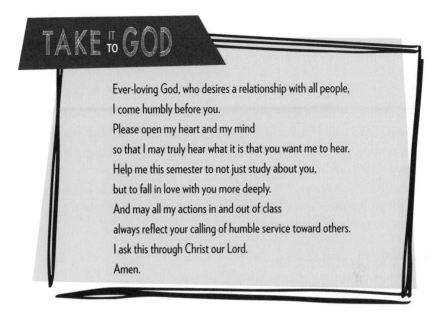

TAKE IT TO GOD

Ever-loving God, who desires a relationship with all people,

I come humbly before you.

Please open my heart and my mind

so that I may truly hear what it is that you want me to hear.

Help me this semester to not just study about you,

but to fall in love with you more deeply.

And may all my actions in and out of class

always reflect your calling of humble service toward others.

I ask this through Christ our Lord.

Amen.

Everyone Has Their Own Story

You may not have the same experiences as Mariana or be actively persecuting the Church like Paul, but Jesus Christ does call each one of us to **conversion**. Conversion is responding to Jesus' offer of love by turning away from sin and its effects and actively seeking to do God's will. Whether you are stopped on the road with a blinding light and a booming voice as was Saint Paul, or pulled by a desire for something more out of life like Mariana, Jesus is reaching out to you. Jesus initiates the relationship, inviting us to believe in him. Our role is to respond.

When we open our hearts to Jesus by inviting him in and saying we are sorry for our sins, we receive the gift of God's **grace** in our lives. Grace helps us in our efforts to avoid sin and live our lives as Jesus teaches. For Jesus is "the way and the truth and the life" (John 14:6). Just like Mariana, who finds the grace daily to fight her drug addiction, Jesus offers that same grace to all of us. His grace helps us discover and follow God's plan for our lives, avoid sin, and ultimately spend eternity with God, the Father, Son, and Holy Spirit, in Heaven. He is worthy of our belief, adoration, and love!

---

conversion ➤ A profound change of heart, turning away from sin and toward God.

grace ➤ The free and undeserved gift that God gives us to empower us to respond to his call and to live as his adopted sons and daughters. Grace restores our loving communion with the Holy Trinity, lost through sin.

We have to ask for God's grace to respond to Jesus' call to turn away from sin and live a life of holiness each day. These daily choices help us to be single-hearted in our love for God and to put aside things that lead us away from God.

Mariana could have chosen not to walk through those doors at Homeboy, but she did. Since that day, Mariana could have chosen to return to drugs, but she hasn't. Paul could have said no to Jesus, but he said yes. Paul could have quit spreading the Good News once he met resistance and things got difficult, but he didn't. Look at how God transformed both of their lives. Paul's life truly became an adventure, and Mariana is experiencing new joy and helping others find that joy for themselves. What great and wonderful things await you when you say yes to God's invitation!

What's So Great about Jesus?

Clearly, there is something powerful about the life and message of Jesus Christ. For two thousand years, he's been changing people's lives. Millions of people have found joy and hope after placing their faith in him. Tens of thousands of people, from the time of the first Christians to today, have willingly died rather than denounce God. People from other religions look up to Jesus as a great prophet and a spiritual leader. People who do not believe in God find his life and moral teachings admirable. He is indeed "the way and the truth and the life" (John 14:6).

How well do you know Jesus? This book is an introduction to his life and message. In the remainder of this chapter, we will explore the Gospel of Mark to learn some basics about his mission on Earth. In subsequent chapters, we will study what Scripture and Tradition reveal about him, especially through other **New Testament** writings. As you understand more deeply what it means to put your faith in Jesus, you will discover that God is calling you to a great adventure too. Are you ready for the adventure God has planned for you? ✳

HMMMMM. . . Why did Paul's encounter with Jesus Christ affect his life so profoundly?

New Testament ➤ The twenty-seven books of the Bible, which have the life, teachings, Passion, death, Resurrection, and Ascension of Jesus Christ and the beginnings of the Church as their central theme.

Article 2
The Life and Times of Jesus

Clarissa's grandma was telling her another story about what life was like when Grandma was a teen. "Here we go again," thought Clarissa, "another lecture on the evils of smartphones." Suddenly Grandma stopped and looked directly at her. "I'm sorry," Grandma said. "I know it must sound like I'm lecturing. But I just want you to know that the way we live today isn't the way people have always lived. And I thought you might better understand the things I love if you knew a little more about my life growing up."

What's true for Clarissa and her grandma is also true when it comes to reading about Jesus in the Gospels. The way we live today is different from the way people lived during Jesus' lifetime. If we understand some basic things about the way the people of his time lived, then many of the things Jesus said and did become clearer for us.

Daily Life during the Time of Jesus

Let's get some of the obvious things out of the way. People living in first-century Palestine (Jesus' time and country) had almost none of the technology we enjoy today. They didn't have electricity or gasoline engines, so there were no planes, trains, or automobiles. They didn't even have indoor plumbing (unless you were among the very wealthy). So, a large part of women's days was spent on things we take for granted: getting water, cooking food, making clothes, and so on.

There was little technology in first-century Palestine. Most things, such as planting, cooking, getting water, and making clothes, were done by hand.

Notice we said "women's days." The culture at that time was **patriarchal**. For the most part, men held the political, economic, and religious power. The primary social role of a woman was to be a wife and mother. Women took care of domestic tasks, and men were responsible for whatever economic livelihood sustained the family. Fathers made all the important decisions for the family, including arranging their daughter's marriages. Some of the ways Jesus interacted with women seemed to break these social norms.

What did the men do to make a living? Most of their work was agricultural. Many were farmers. Some raised sheep and goats. Some were fishermen. A few were craftsmen, like Jesus and his foster father, Joseph. Many of them didn't have their own land and would hire themselves out as **tenant farmers** to work the land of wealthy landowners. It is estimated that about 90 percent of the families at that time worked on farms or shepherded animals or both. This is why Jesus used so many farming, fishing, and shepherding examples in his parables.

If one primary cultural value defines life in first-century Palestine, it is commitment to family—and not just your father, mother, brothers, and sisters but your grandparents, uncles, aunts, great-uncles, great-aunts, and all your cousins. Probably you all lived together in the same village—there's a good chance everyone in your village was related to you by blood or marriage. You would think of your uncles and aunts as your other moms and dads and your cousins as your other brothers and sisters. You would probably even marry a second or third cousin! You would grow up and die in that village, always surrounded by your family. And you wouldn't do anything your family didn't approve of.

The Haves and the Have Nots

Another kind of work that ordinary people could do during the time of Jesus was to hire themselves out as **indentured servants**. The majority of the population we have been discussing was poor by our standards. They had just enough to feed themselves and provide the necessities of life. They lived in homes they built out of stone or dried mud. And if they fell on hard times, the only way some could survive was by essentially selling themselves as slaves to wealthy families.

---

patriarchal ➤ Describes a society, government, or religion in which the positions of power are held by men and important decisions are made by men.

tenant farmer ➤ A farmer who works someone else's land, paying the landowner a percentage of the crops or animals raised.

indentured servant ➤ A person who is under contract to work for another person for a period of time, usually without pay; often considered a form of slavery.

People could do this because a small percentage of the population was very wealthy and needed many servants to keep their estates running smoothly. Often called the elites, these families owned large, beautifully decorated homes in the big cities, with indoor plumbing and many rooms for entertaining. They owned the majority of the land in the countryside, which they leased out to tenant farmers. They ate and drank expensive wines and foods. They took advantage of the rest of the population through poor wages and heavy taxation.

This system of haves and have-nots is not God's vision for humankind as revealed in the Bible. God promises Abraham that there will be fertile land for all his descendants, not just a chosen few. When the Israelites move into the Promised Land, Joshua divides it up fairly between all the tribes. And the Old Law of the Old Testament even provided a way to redistribute the land every fifty years so that those who lost ownership of their family's land could have it restored (see Leviticus 25:8-17). It should not surprise us that Jesus has some challenging and even harsh words for the elites who ignore the needs of the less fortunate in their midst.

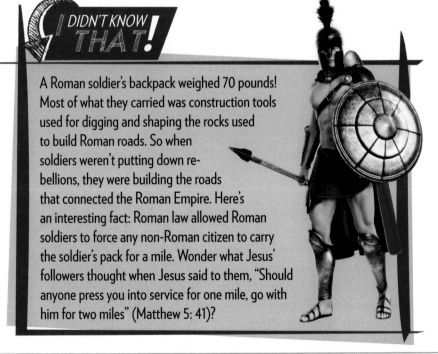

I DIDN'T KNOW THAT!

A Roman soldier's backpack weighed 70 pounds! Most of what they carried was construction tools used for digging and shaping the rocks used to build Roman roads. So when soldiers weren't putting down rebellions, they were building the roads that connected the Roman Empire. Here's an interesting fact: Roman law allowed Roman soldiers to force any non-Roman citizen to carry the soldier's pack for a mile. Wonder what Jesus' followers thought when Jesus said to them, "Should anyone press you into service for one mile, go with him for two miles" (Matthew 5: 41)?

elites ➤ A select group that has the most power and influence in a society, typically because of wealth and social status.

Old Law ➤ Divine Law revealed in the Old Testament, summarized in the Ten Commandments. Also call the Law of Moses.

Roman and Jewish Groups

First-century Palestine was part of the Roman Empire, but this wasn't by choice. The Romans took control of Palestine about sixty years before the birth of Christ (63 BC). The Romans typically allowed the lands they conquered to be overseen by local rulers as long as they pledged their allegiance to Rome. This led to a complex mix of Roman and Jewish political leaders in Palestine.

KEY PLAYERS AT THE TIME OF JESUS	
King Herod the Great	Herod was the Jewish (actually half-Jewish) king at the time Jesus was born. He was ambitious, brutal, and successful. He rebuilt the Temple in Jerusalem, enlarging it and making it a wonder of the ancient world.
Herod Antipas, Herod Archelaus, Philip Tetrarch, Salome, Herod Agrippa	The children and grandchildren of Herod the Great who ruled different parts of Palestine after Herod's death.
Pontius Pilate	The Roman governor who was sent by Rome to rule over Jerusalem after Herod's children proved to be poor rulers. He was ruthless, putting down several Jewish rebellions with mass crucifixions of Jews.
centurions	These men were commanders in the Roman army. A centurion commanded a group of eighty to one hundred soldiers and took his orders from a higher officer or the Roman governor.

As far as the religious side of things goes, several different Jewish groups existed during the life of Jesus. Each of these groups agreed on essential Jewish beliefs, but each group had its own take on what it meant to be a good Jew. Jesus encounters members of these groups throughout the Gospels. We can better understand his response to each group if we understand their philosophies.

© Paul Fearn / Alamy Stock Photo

Herod Archelaus ruled Palestine in the same brutal fashion as his father, Herod the Great.

GROUPS JESUS ENCOUNTERS AND THEIR PHILOSOPHIES

Chief priests and the High Priest	This group led the religious services and conducted the animal sacrifices held at the Temple in Jerusalem. At the time of Jesus, the High Priest was appointed by the Jewish king with the approval of the Roman governor. Both the king and the High Priest benefited from Roman rule and were seen by many as collaborators with Rome.
Pharisees	This group of Jews was known for its strict adherence to all the laws of the Old Testament. They believed in the resurrection of the dead.
Sadducees	This group of Jews consisted largely of the elite, wealthy class; many were chief priests. They did not believe in the resurrection of the dead.
Scribes	These people were scholars and teachers of the Jewish Law and Scripture. They were associated with both the chief priests and the Pharisees.
Zealots	These people believed that God wanted Israel to be an independent nation again, free from foreign rule. They preached a violent overthrow of the Roman occupiers.

Jesus told the crowds following him, "If any one comes to me without hating his father and mother, wife and children, brothers and sisters, and even his own life, he cannot be my disciple" (Luke 14:26). Given their cultural values, how do you think people would react after hearing this?

chief priest ➤ This person led the religious services and conducted animal sacrifices held at the Temple in Jerusalem.

High Priest ➤ This person led the religious services and conducted animal sacrifices held at the Temple in Jerusalem. The High Priest was appointed by the Jewish king with the approval of the Roman governor.

Pharisees ➤ This group of Jews was well known for its strict adherence to all the laws of the Old Testament. The Pharisees believed in the resurrection of the dead.

Sadducees ➤ This group of Jews consisted largely of the elite, wealthy class; many were chief priests. They did not believe in the resurrection of the dead.

scribes ➤ These people were scholars and teachers of the Jewish Law and Scripture. They were associated with both the chief priests and the Pharisees.

Zealots ➤ These people believed that God wanted Israel to be an independent nation again, free from foreign rule. They preached a violent overthrow of the Roman occupiers.

UNIT 1

Article 3

The Gospel of Mark, Part 1: The Human Face of God

Have you ever listened to a young child trying to tell a story they are really excited about? Usually it sounds something like this: "And then . . . (deep breath) and then . . . (deep breath) and then . . . " In many ways, the Gospel of Mark is like that excited young child. It's the shortest of the four Gospels and is told with the excitement of a child. For example, the words *and* and *immediately* appear frequently throughout the text. The first half of the Gospel moves rapidly from scene to scene, jumping months between events. Then it slows dramatically, counting down time by the hours as Jesus' Crucifixion approaches. Along the way, Mark gives us great insight into Jesus' humanity. So if you have never read a Gospel from beginning to end, Mark is a good Gospel to start with.

CATHOLICS **MAKING** A DIFFERENCE

Can you imagine a life with no arms? Do you think you would feel sorry for yourself and focus on the things that you could not do? Tony Melendez is a guitar player, composer, singer, and songwriter who was born without arms. His mother was prescribed Thalidomide while pregnant, which caused his disability. Tony did not feel sorry for himself or accept that there were just going to be things he could not do. He learned to play Frisbee, write, compose music, and play guitar—all with his feet! In high school, he became deeply involved in the Catholic Church. He even played one of his original songs for Pope Saint John Paul II! Tony has continued his music ministry by starting the Toe Jam Band and always reserves the front rows at his concerts for young people.

© AP Photo/Luis M. Alvarez

Who Was Mark's Audience?

To understand better some of the themes in the Gospel of Mark, it helps to know what was happening around the time the Gospel was written. Many scholars believe the Gospel of Mark was written around AD 70 for Christians living in Rome. Around this time, the people of Rome had experienced several disasters. In AD 64, fire broke out in Rome and burned for several days, destroying parts of the city. The emperor, Nero, blamed the fire on the Christians. This led to persecution of the Christians. It is even said that Nero burned Christians on crosses at night to help light the city. During this time, many Christians were so frightened that they denied their faith in an effort to escape persecution. Those who denied their faith, and perhaps even turned in their fellow Christians to save their own lives, were called **apostates**. This atmosphere of fear and betrayal is in part what Mark addresses in his Gospel.

Mark, Chapter 1: Setting the Stage

As followers of Jesus, we depend on our recognition and acceptance of him as the Son of God who died to save us from our sins. The first verse of the Gospel makes a bold proclamation: Jesus Christ is the Son of God. Mark then tells of John the Baptist's humility in heralding the coming of God's Son. Jesus' own Baptism follows, highlighted by God the Father's heavenly voice declaring to Jesus, "You are my beloved Son" (Mark 1:11). Jesus is immediately led into the desert, where he is tempted by the devil. From the beginning, we see that Jesus, the Son of God, though welcomed by some, will be in a battle against evil in his efforts to save us from our sins.

Why do you think Jesus wanted John to baptize him?

---

apostate ➤ One who denies or renounces one's faith.

Real Human Emotions

In the chapters that follow, numerous accounts of Jesus helping people reveal not only Jesus' power but also his humanity. One notable element of Jesus' human nature is his emotion and the way he chooses to respond to his feelings. Mark describes Jesus as having pity and compassion, as we see in his encounters with a leper (see Mark 1:40–45) or when seeing the crowds as "sheep without a shepherd" (6:34). In response, Jesus heals the leper and begins teaching the crowd.

Jesus, like all human beings, at times feels tired and hungry. Sometimes he is able to find rest, such as when he is asleep in the boat (see Mark 4:35–39). Other times, he has to actively seek solitude so he can have time to relax and eat. Yet in these instances, even Jesus' attempts to rest are interrupted by the needs of others. When he tries to sleep in the boat, he is awoken by the disciples. They are distressed because of a storm, and Jesus immediately comes to their aid by calming the storm. When seeking solitude, the crowds follow Jesus, so he multiplies the loaves and fish to feed them (see 6:30–44). In all these examples, we see Jesus' human nature and how he responds with his whole person—emotion, will, and reason—all contributing to his perfect response of love and compassion.

Jesus experienced real human emotions. His human nature allows him to respond to others with compassion.

© INTERFOTO / Alamy Stock Photo

Dealing with Rejection and Opposition

Jesus' human nature is also revealed in his response to the opposition he faces. If you have ever been misunderstood, do not worry. The Gospel of Mark reveals a Savior who definitely knows what it feels like to be misunderstood and even rejected. Throughout the first eight chapters, Jesus repeatedly runs into opposition, and Mark describes the variety of Jesus' emotions.

Let's look at one example in Mark 3:1–6. Jesus is about to heal a man with a withered hand, but the Pharisees are watching to see if Jesus breaks the Sabbath commandment by healing the man. They believe that healing is work, and the law says you cannot work on the **Sabbath**. Mark tells us Jesus is angry with the Pharisees and "grieved at their hardness of heart" (3:5).

Sabbath ➤ A day of religious observance and abstinence from work, kept by Jews from Friday evening to Saturday evening, and by most Christians on Sunday.

We call this type of anger "righteous indignation," because we are rightly upset over an injustice and the lack of compassion. Jesus cures the man, knowing that it will upset the Pharisees and even bring them one step closer to calling for his death. Sometimes doing the right thing can result in great personal sacrifice.

Jesus even experiences lack of support and understanding from his closest friends. In chapter 6, Jesus visits his hometown of Nazareth and is amazed by the people's lack of belief in him. Instead of arguing with them, Jesus heals a few of their sick and then moves on to the next town. Like many Old Testament prophets, Jesus is rejected by his own community. The prophet Micah is accused of being a false prophet (see Micah 2:6). Jeremiah is barred from entering the Temple because his preaching is considered inflammatory (see Jeremiah 36:5). Amos is told several times to be quiet (see Amos 2:12, 7:13). Jesus is aware of this history and understands that sometimes God's prophets— including Jesus himself—are rejected by those who most need to hear them.

Conclusion

From Mark's presentation of Jesus' ministry in the first half of the Gospel, we begin to see the humanity of Jesus. The difficulties we experience in our lives, and the emotions that come with them, are not unlike what Jesus himself experienced. It is reassuring to know we have a Savior who understands what it is like to be human. However, there are two important differences between Jesus and us. First, Jesus is fully human but also fully God. Second, Jesus is like us in all things except sin. Knowing that he has never sinned means we can look at how he reacts to situations and use those examples as the perfect model for how we should act in similar circumstances. ✳

OVERVIEW of the Gospel of Mark

- **Intended audience:** Christians living in Rome who were being persecuted.
- **Theme:** Jesus is the Son of God, the Messiah who suffered, died, and rose from the dead for us.
- **Reason for writing:** To show persecuted Christians that suffering is part of being a disciple of Jesus and that if they keep their faith in Jesus Christ, they will not suffer in vain.

HMMMMM. . . Think of an event that evokes a particularly strong emotion for you. Share the story of the event with a partner. Then discuss how Jesus might have responded in both circumstances.

Article 4

The Gospel of Mark, Part 2: Who Do You Say That I Am?

After eight chapters describing Jesus' teaching and powerful deeds, we arrive at the midpoint of the Gospel of Mark. Jesus turns to the **disciples** and asks them, "Who do people say that I am?" (Mark 8:27) and later, "Who do you say that I am?" (verse 29). The placement of these questions in the middle of the Gospel of Mark is an intentional literary technique used by the author of the Gospel. Everything that has happened so far leads up to Jesus' questions, and everything that happens in the second half of the Gospel flows from the answer to his questions.

Who Do People Say That I Am?

After Jesus asks the question "Who do people say that I am?" the disciples respond, "John the Baptist; and others, Elijah; and still others, one of the prophets" (Mark 8:28). If you were a first-century Jewish person, any of these three answers might seem reasonable. Like John the Baptist, Jesus calls people to repentance and preaches about the Kingdom of God. Elijah is a miracle worker who confronts authority. Jesus also works miracles and confronts authority, so many think he might be Elijah returned from Heaven. Finally, Jesus speaks for God like the prophets do, so it makes sense to think he might be a prophet. But Jesus is not John the Baptist, Elijah, or only a prophet. None of these answers captures Jesus' true identity as the Son of God, the Word of God Made Flesh.

The people in biblical times are like people of today. We often let our own ideas of who Jesus should be in our lives get in the way of his true identity. For example, we often bargain with Jesus, promising to change our behavior if we pass a test or to reform our ways if he helps us to escape the negative consequences of our actions. However, this is not how the saving power of Christ works in our lives. We don't need to bargain with Jesus for him to love us! He wants us to become his disciples and accept his love and grace. He will give us the courage and strength to take responsibility for our actions and choose daily to follow him.

---

disciple ➤ Follower of Jesus.

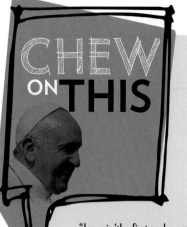

CHEW ON THIS

Contemplating the life of Jesus and looking at ourselves as pilgrims in this world with so many challenges, we feel the need of a profound conversion and the urgency to rekindle faith in him. Only then can we serve our neighbor in charity! Every day we are called to renew our trust in Christ and to draw inspiration from his life in order to fulfil our mission, because "Jesus is 'the first and greatest evangelizer." ("Address of His Holiness Pope Francis to Participants in the General Chapter of the Society of the Catholic Apostolate," October 10, 2016)

"Who Do You Say That I Am?"

Having heard these first responses, Jesus then asks his disciples the question that every person must ultimately answer: "Who do you say that I am?" (Mark 8:29). It seems that Jesus wants them to dig deeper and to answer for themselves. Peter gives the right answer: "You are the Messiah." So why does Jesus immediately instruct the disciples not to tell anyone about this (see verse 30)? It all has to do with the Jewish People's expectations.

At the time, many Jews believed the messiah would be an earthly military or political ruler, like King David in the Old Testament. They hoped the messiah would overthrow Rome's rule and return the Promised Land to the Jewish People.

However, Jesus was a very different Messiah than they were expecting. His Kingdom is not of this Earth, and human understandings of power do not apply to his spiritual realm. Instead, Jesus explains that the Messiah must suffer, die, and be raised from the dead to save the world from sin and death.

Messiah ➤ Hebrew word for "anointed one." The equivalent Greek term is *Christos*. Jesus is the Christ and the Messiah because he is the Anointed One.

Promised Land ➤ In the Bible, the land of Canaan, which was promised to Abraham and his descendants.

A suffering messiah is different from the strong military ruler people were expecting. One reason Jesus may have wanted the disciples to keep his identity secret is that he did not want the people to be confused. He wanted them to understand his real mission before they started calling him the Messiah.

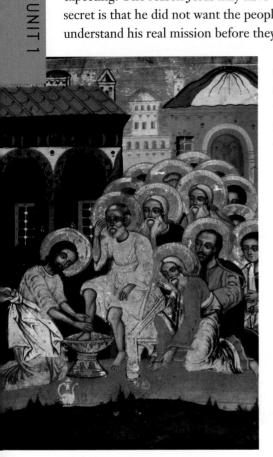

Jesus upset common expectations about the Messiah by humbling himself in actions like washing the feet of the Apostles.

Peter is the perfect example of this confusion over the role of the Messiah. He does not accept the idea that the Messiah must suffer and die, so he rebukes Jesus—that is, he tries to convince Jesus that he is wrong:

> He [Jesus] began to teach them that the Son of Man must suffer greatly and be rejected by the elders, the chief priests, and the scribes, and be killed, and rise after three days. He spoke this openly. Then Peter took him aside and began to rebuke him. At this he turned around and, looking at his disciples, rebuked Peter and said, "Get behind me, Satan. You are thinking not as God does, but as human beings do." (Mark 8:31–33)

It may sound harsh when Jesus tells Peter, "Get behind me, Satan," but Peter, and the other Apostles as well, were struggling to see how Jesus' suffering was necessary. Jesus has to help them see that God the Father's saving plan involves suffering; and Jesus, the Son of God, the Messiah, is here to fulfill it.

The Path of Discipleship

Because Jesus is a different type of messiah, it makes sense that he requires a different type of follower, or disciple. After explaining the he must suffer, Jesus teaches that his disciples must also be willing to put aside their own desires and follow God's will. He says to them, "Whoever wishes to come after me must deny himself, take up his cross, and follow me" (Mark 8:34). We quickly learn that if Jesus, the Messiah, is willing to suffer, his followers must be willing to suffer as well. This is a challenging call, to say the least.

Like Peter, we may not want ourselves or our loved ones to experience the sacrifice that comes with being a disciple of Christ. For example, we may not want to face the shame of admitting we have done something wrong. Or we may not want to experience the rejection that can happen when we choose not to participate in the sinful choices other people are making. However, sharing in Jesus' mission means accepting that sacrifice is sometimes part of that mission. Jesus gives us an example of the courage needed to accept the sacrifices we need to make, trusting that it will lead to healing in this life and eternal life with God after death.

Dropping Our Preconceived Ideas

From this crucial conversation in the middle of the Gospel of Mark, we learn that we too are called to trust in what Jesus reveals about himself. We learn that to truly live as one of Jesus' disciples we must accept our crosses—the hardships and sacrifices that can come with being faithful to God's will. Thanks be to God that he provides us the grace we need to do this. We do not become disciples by simply choosing it on our own. God takes the initiative in calling us. If we accept, God gives us the strength to persevere. What a blessed gift! What a wonderful call! ✳

What does it mean to you to live as a disciple of Jesus?

HMMMMM...

How surprised were you that Peter argued with Jesus? How might "arguing" with God be a good thing?

UNIT 1

Article 5
The Gospel of Mark, Part 3: The Empty Tomb Changes Everything

As the Gospel of Mark moves towards Jesus' **Passion**, death, and **Resurrection**—events that together form the **Paschal Mystery**—Jesus' identity as the Suffering Messiah comes into full view. The sense of Jesus' suffering is heightened as Mark tells how the disciples misunderstand and then completely abandon Jesus. It is hard to get through a difficult time even when you have the support of your friends and loved ones. Imagine how much harder it was for Jesus without their support.

The Lonely Path to the Cross

The disciples' misunderstanding and eventual abandonment of Jesus is highlighted more in Mark than in the other three Gospels. Recall that Peter rebukes Jesus right after Jesus tells the disciples that the Messiah must suffer and die. Unfortunately, the disciples' missteps continue. They try to turn away children brought to Jesus for a blessing. Jesus admonishes

© 2018 www.TheGloryStory.com

Though Jesus' Apostles and friends loved and followed him, Jesus ultimately faced his final hours suffering and alone.

Passion ➤ The suffering and death of Jesus during the final days of his life: his agony in the garden at Gethsemane, his trial, and his Crucifixion.

Resurrection ➤ The bodily rising of Jesus from the dead on the third day after his death on the cross; the heart of the Paschal Mystery and the basis of our hope in the resurrection of the dead.

Paschal Mystery ➤ The work of salvation accomplished by Jesus Christ mainly through his Passion, death, Resurrection, and Ascension.

them for doing this (see Mark 10:13–15). In another story, James and John seek a place of honor in Jesus' Kingdom, failing to understand discipleship in terms of suffering and self-sacrifice (see 10:35–45). Later, one of Jesus' closest followers, Judas, agrees to betray Jesus for money (see 14:10–11).

As Jesus' arrest and Crucifixion draw near, consider these events:

- While praying in the garden, Jesus is in emotional agony. Where are the disciples? They are asleep even though Jesus asked them to pray with him (see Matthew 25:36–46).

- When the crowd arrives to arrest Jesus, one of his disciples fights back and cuts off the ear of the High Priest's slave. The disciple still doesn't accept that Jesus needs to suffer and die, despite the fact that Jesus had told them three times that this must happen (see Mark 8:31, 9:32, 10:32–34).

- As Jesus is being interrogated by the High Priest, Peter denies being one of Jesus' disciples three times. The final time he even curses and swears that he is not, the ultimate denial (see Mark 14:66–72).

- As Jesus is dying in agony, having been whipped and nailed to the cross, none of his followers are with him. Only a few of the women are brave enough to look on from a distance (see Mark 15:40).

Taken together, these events create a dramatic picture of Jesus suffering a terrible death. He is in complete physical, mental, and emotional agony. But he is only one among thousands of people crucified by the Roman Empire. His story should have ended with his death. What led to Christ's dramatic impact on so many people over the last two thousand years?

MAKE IT SO

It is challenging to spread the Good News in today's society. Maybe part of the problem is that we need to share our beliefs in a way that is easy for others to encounter and understand. Today people communicate with short messages through social media. How can you use social media to encourage and inspire others? Share your faith in creative ways that invite people to believe in Jesus' saving work.

The Empty Tomb and Appearances

If Mark ended his account of Jesus' life with his death on the cross, it would be a depressing story. However, Jesus' suffering, abandonment, and death are not the final events of his life. In fact, they are just the beginning of something remarkable. Mark tells us that early Sunday morning, three women arrive at Jesus' tomb wondering who will roll away the large stone (see Mark 16:1–8). They come to find the stone has already been removed. It is amazing how God removes barriers when we are seeking Jesus. The women enter the tomb and to their shock, they find not Jesus' body, but a young man dressed in white. The young man announces the amazing news—Jesus is raised from the dead! He then instructs the women to go tell the disciples the Good News. However, the women do just the opposite, running away in fear and telling no one.

The original ending of the Gospel of Mark is a cliffhanger, ending with the empty tomb and no accounts of the resurrected Jesus. If this were a movie, this is where the screen would go black and the credits would begin to roll. The abrupt ending leaves us, the readers, with some important questions. Did you understand Jesus' message even though his disciples struggled to understand? Do you accept him as the suffering Messiah, the Son of God who saves us through his suffering and death on the cross? Will you share this Good News with others, even though the first witnesses were afraid to share it?

How do you think Jesus' close friends and followers feel when they discover that the tomb is empty?

You probably noticed that there is a longer ending to the Gospel (see Mark 16:9–20). The earliest manuscripts of the Gospel of Mark do not have this longer ending. No one is certain when the longer ending was added, nor are we sure who wrote it. Despite our uncertainty about its origins, we are certain that it is part of the canon of Scripture. It is the **inspired** Word of God and has something to reveal to us.

In the longer ending, the resurrected Jesus appears to his disciples three times. First, he appears to Mary Magdalene (see Mark 16:9–11; this also occurs in the Gospel of John). She goes and tell the others that she has seen the resurrected Jesus, but they do not believe her. They also do not believe the two disciples that meet Jesus while walking out of Jerusalem (see Mark 16:12–13). Mark gives us a brief version of this story, and Luke beautifully expands upon it, as you will see when you read Luke 24:13–35.

You may find it curious that the disciples do not believe their friends' testimony that Jesus really rose from the dead. But imagine being in their place. You would desperately want Jesus to be alive again, but it is just too incredible to believe that he has risen from the dead. You don't want your hopes dashed again, so you do not take the risk of believing in something so incredible. Jesus overcomes their lack of faith by appearing to all eleven Apostles (see Mark 16:14–18). This is a proof they cannot ignore, and we can only imagine their joy and surprise.

However, believing is not enough. Jesus sends them to the whole world to proclaim that he has risen from the dead. The one thing no human can escape, death, Jesus has overcome. Jesus tells the Apostles to baptize the new followers and to expect great things to happen. They will do wonders through Jesus Christ. Wonders can and will be done through us as his followers too.

The longer ending concludes with Jesus' Ascension. He is "taken up into heaven" and seated "at the right hand of God" (Mark 16:19). It ends by telling us that the disciples are no longer controlled by fear and doubt. They go forth proclaiming the Good News just as they are told. The fact that there are so many Christians today testifies to the success of their efforts in spreading the Gospel.

---

inspired ➤ Written by human beings with the guidance of the Holy Spirit to teach faithfully and without error the saving truth that God willed to give us.

What Difference Does the Resurrection Make?

So, what difference does Christ's Resurrection make? It makes all the difference in this world and the next. It is the proof that God's plan for salvation has been accomplished! Through the life, death, Resurrection, and Ascension of Jesus Christ, God has saved us from our sin. We call this amazing process of God's saving plan the Paschal Mystery. You will learn more about it in the next course. For now, understand that Jesus' passing over from death to life is the same process each one of us must follow as his disciples. We must die to self so that we too may rise with Christ.

The Resurrection also gives new meaning to suffering. Following Jesus does not mean that life will always be easy; there will be suffering involved. Jesus' life, especially as described in the Gospel of Mark, shows that God's plan sometimes involves sacrifice and suffering. Thankfully, God's plan is so much greater than just the suffering. When connected to God's plan, suffering for the sake of righteousness becomes something we as disciples can offer in imitation of Jesus. Sadly, our culture often encourages us to avoid suffering at all costs. Jesus shows us how to embrace suffering as a means to share in his saving mission. Imagine the hope this understanding gave to Mark's original audience as they suffered in Rome. Jesus' life, death, and Resurrection teach us that the way to salvation is to hold on to our faith even when things get difficult.

© Nice_Media_PRODUCTION / Shutterstock.com

We are often immune to the effects of war, famine, and disease in our world today. What are some ways in which modern culture distracts tries to distract you from suffering?

Jesus' Resurrection also radically transforms the meaning of the cross. What was viewed as a means of torture and humiliation has become a symbol of hope for Christians everywhere. We are a people of hope, knowing that suffering and death do not have the last word. Our Church community is a gathering of people committed to belief in Jesus Christ's Resurrection and the hope that he offers. As Jesus' disciples, we are called to actively participate in the Church community and to work tirelessly spreading the Good News of Jesus Christ by word and deed to all. We do this by offering hope, especially to those who are suffering the most.

Throughout this unit, we will be exploring the question "Why believe in Jesus?" After reading the Gospel of Mark, many reasons become apparent. We believe in him because as our Savior and God he has experienced the challenges of life just as we have. The Savior has shown us how God can take humility and self-sacrifice to transform suffering into something glorious. Discovering what it means to be a disciple is a journey. When we place our faith in Jesus Christ, we are also called to accept all that he teaches about what it means to be his disciple. ❋

HMMMMMM. . .   What effect does the empty tomb have on your understanding of Jesus' suffering, and what it means to be a disciple?

UNIT 1

1. What is the one aspect about Paul's conversion that makes it such a powerful example to others?

2. What type of messiah were some people expecting during Jesus' time?

3. Name one of the religious groups Jesus encountered and explain its philosophy.

4. Give three examples showing how Jesus' followers abandoned him when things got tough.

5. How does Jesus' Resurrection transform the meaning of the cross?

6. Why does Mark specifically focus on Jesus' challenges and suffering?

7. In the Gospel of Mark, Jesus says that whoever wants to be a disciple must "take up his cross, and follow me" (8:34). Why does Jesus say this?

© Renata Sedmakova / Shutterstock.com

ARTSTUDY

A CLASSICAL PAINTING OF JESUS' CRUCIFIXION

This classical painting gives us many clues about the culture during Jesus' life, as well as how the Crucifixion affected those around him.

1. How does this piece of artwork make you feel?

2. What elements of Jesus' life and culture are represented in this painting?

3. Why are images of Christ's Crucifixion so prominent in Catholic churches?

CHAPTER 2
Jesus Revealed

WHERE CAN I FIND THE TRUTH ABOUT JESUS?

SNAPSHOT

Article 6

How the Gospels Came to Be

Many of the world's religions testify to this important truth: As human beings, we experience a longing or a yearning that only God can fulfill. We may try to satisfy that longing with money, material goods, knowledge, sex, or even food. Saint Augustine experienced this longing and tried to satisfy it with many of these things. It wasn't until he had a momentous conversion experience that he came to understand that only God can satisfy this yearning. Later he wrote in his autobiography, "You have made us for yourself, O God, and our hearts are restless until they rest in you."

If this is true, how can we come to know God? How does God reveal himself to us? The most tangible way that God reveals himself to us is through the Person of Jesus Christ. By knowing Christ, we come to know God and his plan for our salvation. Jesus is the fullness of God's **Divine Revelation**, and the Gospels in the New Testament are a primary way to learn about Jesus' life and saving mission. To best understand the Gospels, it helps to first understand the rich history of how the Bible came to be.

TAKE IT TO GOD

Jesus,

Help me know you better

as I read about you in the Gospels.

Your teachings are so inspiring.

Your life is so amazing.

I want to love like you.

I want to help others like you.

Inspire me through your Holy Word,

to be better, to do better,

to imitate you in the way I live my life.

Divine Revelation ➤ God's self-communication through which he makes known the mystery of his divine plan. Divine Revelation is a gift accomplished by the Father, Son, and Holy Spirit through the words and deeds of salvation history. It is most fully realized in the Passion, death, Resurrection, and Ascension of Jesus Christ.

Write That Down

Imagine this: In chemistry class, a Bunsen burner malfunctions, causing a brief but large fireball. People scream and nearby lab papers catch on fire. No one is hurt, and the flames go out quickly. What do the students do? They begin talking about the accident of course. The story quickly spreads through the school. Now people who weren't even in the classroom at the time are telling others about the fireball. Sometimes they get the facts wrong, so the students who were there quickly correct them. By the end of the day, everyone knows about the chemistry lab fireball. Who knows, the event may even be remembered through references in the yearbook. In a similar way, the four Gospels in the New Testament went through several stages to become the sacred books we have today.

Word Spread

The first stage in the formation of the Gospels is the actual life and teachings of Jesus Christ. People are already talking about Jesus because of his miracles and his powerful teachings. Then, like the fireball in the lab, an exciting experience occurs. The Apostles and other disciples see Jesus Christ risen from the dead! They are walking, talking, and eating with the man who had brutally died on a cross days earlier. This is something people would definitely talk about! The disciples do just that. And not only do they describe these events but they also start preaching about the religious meaning of them. For example, they preach that the Resurrection is proof that Jesus Christ is the Messiah, the Son of God who came to save people from sin and death.

Many of these disciples become **missionaries**, traveling across the Roman Empire to share this Good News with others. Greek is their common language, and in Greek the word for "good news" is *gospel*, so their message becomes known as the **Gospel** (Good News) of Jesus Christ. This is the second stage in the formation of the Gospels, which is called the **oral tradition**. As the Gospel spreads by word of mouth, when questions arise, the Apostles and other eyewitnesses provide clarification.

---

missionary ❯ A person sent to preach the Gospel, or to help strengthen the faith already professed, among people in a given place or region.

Gospel ❯ Most basically, the "Good News" of the Revelation of God in and through the Word Made Flesh, Jesus Christ, proclaimed initially by him, then by the Apostles, and now by the Church; also refers to those four books of the New Testament that focus on the person, life, teachings, suffering, death, and Resurrection of Jesus.

oral tradition ❯ The stage in the formation of the Gospels by which the Good News was spread by "word of mouth" prior to being written down.

UNIT 1

The disciples traveled to the far reaches of the Roman Empire spreading the Good News of Jesus Christ.

Time to Write It Down

Why did the early Christian missionaries spread the Gospel by word of mouth instead of writing it down? One reason is that it was the most efficient way to spread the Gospel as quickly as possible. Most people couldn't read, and books were rare and expensive. There were no printing presses, so books had to be written and copied by hand. It could take years to make multiple copies of a single book available. So, for many years after Jesus' Ascension into Heaven, the oral tradition was the primary means for spreading the Good News.

Over time, something happened that prompted Church leaders to write down the stories they were telling about Jesus. The first Christians believed that Jesus Christ would return for the Last Judgment within their lifetime. So there was no need to have a permanent, written record of what Jesus said and did when you had plenty of eyewitnesses around. When the original eyewitnesses to Jesus' life, Death, and Resurrection started to pass away, they had to rethink things. To preserve the eyewitnesses' teaching and preaching about Jesus, they began to write down their accounts about the life of Christ.

We believe that's how the Gospels of Matthew, Mark, Luke, and John came to be written, under the inspiration of the Holy Spirit. Though we do not know the exact date each Gospel was written, many scholars believe the Gospel of Mark was written first, around AD 70. The Gospels of Matthew and Luke were probably written ten to fifteen years after Mark. It is possible that the Gospel of John was written around AD 100, nearly seventy years after Jesus' Resurrection. This third stage in the formation of the Gospels is the **written tradition**. Over time, the written Gospels were combined with the other writings now in the **canon of Scripture**, forming the New Testament.

Stage	Title	Description
	THE STAGES OF GOSPEL FORMATION	
1	The Life and Teaching of Jesus	Jesus lives and teaches among us until his Ascension.
2	The Oral Tradition	The Apostles hand on what Jesus has said and done, in that fuller understanding brought about by the Resurrection of Christ and the guidance of the Holy Spirit.
3	The Written Tradition	The inspired authors write the four Gospels, selecting from what has been handed on in either oral or written form, to bring us the truth about Jesus.

✳

---

written tradition ➤ The stage during the formation of the Gospels when the human authors, under the inspiration of the Holy Spirit, drew upon the oral tradition and earlier writings to create the four Gospels we have today in the Bible.

canon of Scripture ➤ The books of the Bible officially recognized by the Church as the inspired Word of God.

I DIDN'T KNOW THAT!

The Apostles were long-distance trekkers. They walked about 20 miles a day, and many traveled hundreds or even thousands of miles to share the Good News with new communities. They likely traveled in pairs or groups of three, taking only the clothes they wore, the sandals on their feet, and a walking staff. They relied on the hospitality of communities along the way for food and shelter. Think about that the next time you pack a suitcase and jump in your car for a vacation!

HMMMMM...

What motivated Jesus' first disciples to spread the Good News?

UNIT 1

Article 7

Four Gospels, Four Authors, Four Viewpoints

The four Gospels of Matthew, Mark, Luke, and John are central to Sacred Scripture because Jesus Christ is at their center. They are our primary source for all that is revealed in the life and teaching of Jesus. These events are worthy of our reflection and imitation. So why are there four Gospels instead of one? The answer has to do with each Gospel being written by different evangelists, in different historical situations, for different audiences.

Maybe this analogy will help. Have you ever noticed the many different cameras used to record a professional outdoor sporting event?

1.

Saint Mark, on the sideline near the play holding a camera and a clear sound disk to pick up the hard hits on the field.

2.

Saint Luke, in the far corner of the stadium taking the wide-angle view of the stadium.

3.

Saint Matthew, giving the traditional sideline view showing the field and the player's benches.

4.

Saint John, running the camera on the wire that moves all over the field of play from above.

Some cameras show the entire field, others show aerial views, and some can zoom in. All these different perspectives enhance our understanding of the game. The same can be said of the four Gospels. They each offer a different perspective on Jesus' life, Passion, death, Resurrection, and Ascension. By considering four different camera angles for a sports game, we can begin to understand the unique perspectives of the four Gospels.

The Traditional View

The sideline view of outdoor sporting events has been televised for decades. This traditional view shows the width of the field and often includes the players on the bench. The Gospel of Matthew is like the traditional view. It focuses on showing the connections between Jesus and the traditions found within the Old Testament. For example, Matthew's structure of five major discourses, or speeches of Jesus, would remind Jewish readers of the five books of the Torah, or Pentateuch, in the Old Testament.

The team on the bench is important for Matthew as well. Matthew is the Gospel that emphasizes Jesus' team, the Church. Matthew shows us how Jesus establishes the Church by giving his authority to his Apostles, as when he gives Saint Peter the keys to the Kingdom:

> He said to them, "But who do you say that I am?" Simon Peter said in reply, "you are the Messiah, the Son of the living God." Jesus said to him in reply, "Blessed are you, Simon son of Jonah. For flesh and blood has not revealed this to you, but my heavenly Father. And so I say to you, you are Peter, and upon this rock I will build my church, and the gate of the netherworld shall not prevail against it. I will give you the keys to the kingdom of heaven." (Matthew 16:15–19)

Torah ➤ A Hebrew word meaning "law," referring to the first five books of the Old Testament.

Up Close

During outdoor sporting events, there is usually a camera person who moves around on the sidelines. This camera angle captures all of the hard hits and gives us an eye-level view. It is almost as if we are with the players. We don't watch the entire game from this vantage point; we see just highlights and special plays from this view. This camera angle is similar to the Gospel of Mark. Mark's brevity and fast-paced presentation of Jesus' ministry is a little like watching highlights of a game. For example, the Gospel of Mark does not even mention Jesus' birth; it starts with him as an adult.

And just like focusing on the hard hits, Mark is the Gospel that gives us the most graphic details, like when he describes the boy possessed by a mute spirit. Only Mark tells us about the boy grinding his teeth or foaming at the mouth when Jesus goes to heal him (see Mark 9:14–29). We also get an eye-level perspective of the relationship between Jesus and his disciples. Mark shows the humanity of Jesus as he relates to his closest followers.

CATHOLICS MAKING A DIFFERENCE

Have you ever heard of "voluntourism"? Many people are looking for ways to travel, to get to know other cultures, to connect to the global community, but to also to be of service. Voluntourism allows people to do all of these things! The Apostles and Paul created relationships within the communities they established, and voluntourism allows us the opportunity to follow in their footsteps. Many organizations today encourage people to volunteer on their vacations. In fact, even the Ritz-Carlton has a program that provides opportunities for its guests to participate in half-day volunteer programs.

© Syda Productions / Shutterstock.com

From the Far Corner

Another camera angle is the fish-eye camera that is mounted way up in the corner of the stadium. It provides a unique wide-angle perspective. This camera shows not only the field but also most of the fans. It includes the people in the cheap seats who never even expect to be on television when they go to the game. The Gospel of Luke is kind of like this wide-angle view. In Luke, Jesus' life and mission are presented in a way that challenges society's limited perspectives. Luke presents the wider appeal of Jesus' message, recognizing that Jesus came to save everyone. Luke's Gospel includes stories about people who are not highly valued by society, like the poor and widows. Even the people in the "cheap seats" are part of the action.

Looking Down

Finally, there is the camera that moves around on a wire over the field of play. The other three cameras all show the game from a similar horizontal perspective, but this one shows us the view from high above, looking down. It also zooms in for incredible detail. Every blade of grass is visible, helping us see if a player's foot is in or out of bounds.

The Gospel of John is like this camera. It is unique when compared to the other three Gospels. It gives us a perspective from on high, with its soaring theology that focuses on Jesus' identity as God's Divine Son. Jesus' dialogue in the Gospel of John circles around just like the camera on a wire. Often Jesus begins the conversation on one topic and circles around to make several points ending on a different but related topic. John also zooms in to grass level. John focuses five chapters on the Last Supper, giving us an enormous amount of detail about Jesus relationships with his disciples, with God the Father, and with the Holy Spirit.

Just like different camera angles help us to better understand and enjoy a sporting event, the different perspectives of the Gospels help us to better understand and enjoy the life of Christ.

GOSPEL COMPARISONS

Gospel	Date Written (Approximate)	Audience	Theme	Organization
Mark	AD 65–70	persecuted Christians	Suffering and death lead to eternal life.	begins with baptism and public ministry, recounts acts of power and controversies with Pharisees
Matthew	AD 85	primarily Jewish Christians	Jesus is the Messiah who continues the Jewish tradition.	begins with infancy narrative, structured around five big speeches, places Jesus in the context of the Israelites' salvation history
Luke	AD 80–90	Gentile Christians	God's covenant of love is universal.	begins with infancy narrative, includes genealogy going back to Adam, and structures the Gospel around a journey to Jerusalem, the center of Jewish faith
John	AD 90–100	Jewish Christian community that may have included Gentiles and Samaritans	Jesus is the preexistent Word of God; salvation is available for all people who believe in him and commit their lives to him.	prologue, Book of Signs (organized around seven great signs performed by Jesus), Book of Glory (organized around Jesus' death and Resurrection), epilogue

HMMMMM. . .

How might our faith be different if there were only one Gospel in the Bible?

UNIT 1

Article 8
The Synoptics: Similar but Not the Same

Earlier we noted that the Gospel of John has a unique perspective when compared to the Gospels of Matthew, Mark, and Luke. Remember John's view was more from "above" and the others were more from the "side." Let's explore this further.

Imagine asking three people who are standing together looking at a famous piece of artwork to each describe what they see. It is reasonable to assume that there would be some similarities and some differences among their responses. They would all give you the same general description of what is taking place in the picture, but one person might notice the lighting depicted in the painting and emphasize that, and another person might focus more on the interaction of the people in the painting. As we put all three descriptions together, our understanding of the artwork becomes more complete. The same is true of the Gospels of Matthew, Mark, and Luke. They all tell the same story from a similar perspective. Together we call them the **synoptic Gospels**. The word *synoptic* comes from a Greek word meaning "seeing together."

© guruXOX / Shutterstock.com

Different perspectives on the same piece of artwork are similar to the different perspectives the Gospels offer on the life and teachings of Jesus.

synoptic Gospels ➤ From the Greek for "seeing together," the name given to the Gospels of Matthew, Mark, and Luke, because they are similar in style and content.

Similarities

As you read all three synoptic Gospels, it becomes apparent that they share a lot of common material. Most scholars believe that Mark was written first and that the authors of Matthew and Luke probably used the Gospel of Mark as a starting point for writing their own Gospels. Almost all of the Gospel of Mark appears in either Matthew or Luke in some way.

One thing the synoptic Gospels have in common are the many **parables** Jesus uses to teach (John has no parables!). The Parable of the Lost Sheep (see Matthew 18:9 and Luke 15:1) or the Parable of the Sower (see Matthew, chapter 13), for example, are short stories that teach a spiritual lesson. By using everyday objects like seeds, sheep, and coins, the people of Jesus' time can immediately relate to the topic in some way. Beyond being just a nice story, the parables cause the listener to think differently about God and the world they live in.

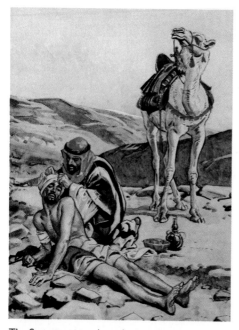

Parables often have a surprise twist in the end, like the Parable of the Good Samaritan (see Luke 10:29). In this parable, a Samaritan is the only person to help an injured Jew. Because the Jews and Samaritans generally despised each other, it is shocking for Jesus, a Jew, to declare a Samaritan the hero of the story. In the end, Jesus' parables challenge the listeners not only to think about their world differently but to act differently as well.

Jesus' many **miracles** are also central to the synoptic Gospels.

The Samaritan was the only one who stopped to help the injured man. This would have been shocking to those hearing the story at the time of Jesus, as Samaritans and Jews were sworn enemies.

---

parable ➤ Generally a short story that uses everyday images to communicate religious messages. Jesus used parables frequently in his teaching as a way of presenting the Good News of salvation.

miracle ➤ A special manifestation, or sign, of the presence and power of God active in human history.

As we will learn later, the Gospel of John has only a few miracles but calls them signs. A miracle is a special manifestation of the power and presence of God. It is a sign of the Kingdom of God, partially present in human history and fully realized in Heaven. We have many examples of Jesus miraculously curing illnesses, like blindness (see John, chapter 9) and leprosy (see Matthew 8:1–4). Jesus even brings his friend Lazarus back to life after he had been dead for three days (see John 11:1–44).

The miracles are not limited to healing. The synoptic Gospels also give us accounts of Jesus miraculously feeding thousands of people by multiplying a few fish and loaves of bread (see Matthew 14:13–21, Mark 6:34–44, Luke 9:10–17, John 6:1–15). Jesus even displays miraculous power over nature, calming a storm at sea (see Matthew 8:23–27, Mark 5:35–41). Perhaps the greatest miracle the synoptic Gospels all share is the Resurrection of Jesus Christ (see Matthew 28:1–10, Mark 16:1–14, Luke 24:1–44, John 20:1–29).

MIRACLES THAT APPEAR IN ALL THREE SYNOPTIC GOSPELS

Miracle	Matthew	Mark	Luke
Cure of Simon's (Peter's) Mother-in-Law	8:14	1:29–31	4:38–41
The Cleansing of a Leper	8:1–4	1:40–45	5:12–16
The Healing of a Paralytic	9:1–8	2:1–12	5:17–26
A Man with a Withered Hand	12:9–14	3:1–6	6:6–11
The Calming of a Storm at Sea	8:23–27	4:35–41	8:22–25
The Healing of the Gerasene Demoniac	8:28–34	5:1–20	8:26–39
Jairus's Daughter and the Woman with a Hemorrhage	9:18–26	5:21–43	8:40–56
The Feeding of the Five Thousand	14:13–21	6:34–44	9:10–17
The Transfiguration of Jesus	17:1–13	9:2–8	9:28–36
The Healing of a Boy with a Demon	17:14–21	9:14–29	9:37–43
Blind Bartimaeus	20:29–34	10:46–52	18:35–43

Why the Differences?

Just like the three people observing the artwork, each Gospel writer chose different elements of Jesus' life to emphasize. One reason for this could be that they were writing for different audiences. We alter how we present material based on our audience all the time. For example, if you are writing a paper for your English teacher, you probably write it one way. If you are writing on the same topic for your history teacher, you write your paper another way. Similarly, you may tell a particular story one way to your parents and slightly differently to a close friend.

As mentioned earlier, the author of Mark is writing to a community that is being persecuted. Some people are denying their faith in Jesus because of this. In response, Mark highlights Jesus' suffering and abandonment as an example to the community. If Jesus endured his suffering and later was raised from the dead, they should be confident that their suffering will bring them to new life.

Matthew's community is quite different. He is writing for a predominately Jewish Christian audience. They are struggling with their identity as Jews who have become followers of Christ. The author of Matthew emphasizes Jesus' connections to Judaism and uses those connections to present Jesus as the fulfillment of all that the Jewish Scriptures (the Christian Old Testament) foretell.

Finally, the author of Luke is writing for a predominantly Gentile (non-Jewish) Christian audience. They are influenced by Greek culture and are relatively unfamiliar with Judaism. The Gospel emphasizes the **universality** of Jesus' message. Luke's accounts focus on how Jesus' offer of salvation is extended to all people, especially the outcast and marginalized.

We are blessed to have all three of the synoptic Gospels. Together they give us a well-rounded understanding of Jesus' life, death and Resurrection. One Gospel by itself cannot hope to capture the complete picture of the greatest event in human history. ✳

HMMMMMM. . . Which Gospel do you most closely identify with? Why?

---

universality ➤ Jesus' offer of salvation is extended to all people, especially the outcast and marginalized.

Article 9

Scripture and Tradition: Why We Need Both

Tyler was talking to his friend Mandy. "I don't get you Catholics," Tyler was saying. "Why do you have all these rules and documents and bishops and the Pope? Isn't the Bible enough? Why all this other stuff?" Mandy's eyes lit up, because they had just been discussing this in religion class. "The Bible is great," she responded, "and we read it a lot. But there is also this important thing called Tradition. . . ."

What Is Sacred Tradition?

Through Jesus Christ, the Eternal Son, God the Father revealed himself to humanity. He entrusted this Revelation to the Apostles. Christ commanded the Apostles to preach the Gospel to the ends of the Earth, to share the fullness of his revealed truth so that all might be saved (see Matthew 28:19–20). Inspired by the Holy Spirit, the Apostles did this, in both preaching and writing. The Apostles' teaching authority was passed on to the popes and bishops who succeeded them so that the apostolic teaching would be handed down to all generations until Christ comes again in glory. This living transmission of the Gospel in the Church is called **Sacred Tradition**, or sometimes the Apostolic Tradition.

Some Christians rely on only Sacred Scripture to understand Divine Revelation. Catholics, however, recognize the authority of both Sacred Scripture and Sacred Tradition. It is through both that God is fully revealed and his truth is made known to us. Sacred Scripture and Sacred Tradition both come from God. They are not separate or contradictory; rather, they are two ways of transmitting Divine Revelation.

Sacred Tradition ➤ This word (from the Latin meaning "to hand on") refers to the process of passing on the Gospel message. Tradition, which began with the oral communication of the Gospel by the Apostles, was written down in Scripture, is handed down and lived out in the life of the Church, and is interpreted by the Magisterium under the guidance of the Holy Spirit.

The **Deposit of Faith** is a term used to describe the heritage of faith contained in Sacred Scripture and Sacred Tradition. Tradition and Scripture are inseparable. "Sacred Tradition and Sacred Scripture make up a single sacred deposit of the Word of God, which is entrusted to the Church" (*Dogmatic Constitution on Divine Revelation* [*Dei Verbum*, 1965], number 10). They work together to achieve the same goal of handing down the Gospel. Scripture and Tradition help to maintain the purity of the Gospel message. Scripture and Tradition support and reinforce each other and will never be in contradiction.

Here's an example. Through Scripture we know that Mary courageously said yes to God's plan, agreeing to become the mother of Jesus. But only through Tradition do we know that Mary herself was conceived without Original Sin and remained free from sin throughout her life. These two teachings do not contradict each other and, in fact, they work to shed light on each other. It makes great sense that the woman who would give birth to the Son of God would herself be free from all sin.

CHEW ON THIS

By caring for the spiritual growth of our communities, by forming minds and hearts in the truths and values taught by our religious traditions, we become a blessing to the communities in which our people live. (Pope Francis, "Ecumenical and Interreligious Meeting Address," November 26, 2015)

Which Catholic traditions (lowercase *t*) provide the most nourishment for your spiritual life?

Deposit of Faith ➤ The heritage of faith contained in Sacred Scripture and Sacred Tradition. It has been passed on from the time of the Apostles. The Magisterium takes from it all that it teaches as revealed truth.

Tradition versus tradition?

So what's the difference between Tradition with a capital *T* and tradition with a lowercase *t*? Tradition with a capital *T* refers to Sacred Tradition. It is the process of sharing God's authoritative Revelation through the Church. Sacred Tradition is a living process. New generations always need to hear the Gospel message, so it is always ongoing.

In contrast, tradition with a lowercase *t* refers to a custom. For example, does your parish community sing "Silent Night" at Midnight Mass on Christmas? Do you wear a medal of your patron saint or pray the Rosary during the month of October? These are all examples of Catholic traditions. They are not part of God's authoritative Revelation, so they can be changed or altered to suit different circumstances, time periods, and cultures. In other words, because singing "Silent Night" is a tradition—rather than part of Tradition—it is okay to sing a different song at Christmas Mass. ✳

Tradition with a lowercase *t* can include songs, meals, and rituals with our families or faith communities.

HMMMMM. . .
How would you describe the relationship between Scripture and Tradition to a non-Catholic friend?

Article 10

The Magisterium: Passing On God's Revelation

Have you ever played the game "telephone"? It's a party game where the first person in a line whispers something in the ear of the next person and that person whispers it to the next person and so on. Usually, by the end of the line, the message has changed and is often unrecognizable from the original message.

As the Church's Tradition is passed from one generation to the next, what keeps it from changing like the messages in the telephone game? The answer is the Holy Spirit. During the Last Supper, Jesus promised the help of the Advocate, or Holy Spirit, to keep the Church firmly grounded in the truths God has revealed. "The Advocate, the holy Spirit that the Father will send in my name—he will teach you everything and remind you of all that I told you" (John 14:26).

The First Steps in a Long History

When Jesus chose the Apostles, he commissioned them to share in his ministry of preaching the truth and proclaiming the Reign of God. As we read in Mark's Gospel, Jesus "went up the mountain and summoned those whom he wanted and they came to him. He appointed twelve [whom he also named apostles] that they might be with him and he might send them forth to preach and to have authority to drive out demons" (3:13–15).

Jesus said to the disciples, while they were gathered on the mountain in Galilee: "All power in heaven and on earth has been given to me. Go, therefore, and make disciples of all nations, baptizing them in the name of the Father, and of the Son, and of the holy Spirit, teaching them to observe all that I have commanded you. And behold, I am with you always, until the end of the age" (Matthew 28:18–20). This command is called the Great Commission, and it continues to apply to us today.

The Apostles, in turn, shared the mission that Christ had entrusted to them with their designated successors. We have a record of this process early in the Church's history. Recall Paul telling Timothy in Second Timothy, "And what you heard from me through many witnesses entrust to faithful people who will have the ability to teach others as well" (2:2). Paul tells Timothy to pass this on to others. Those individuals will then pass it on to the next generation. This faithful handing on of the Tradition under the guidance of the Holy Spirit has continued to the present day. The Pope, who is the bishop of Rome, and all the bishops of the Church, are the modern-day successors of the Apostles. Together

UNIT 1

they are called the **Magisterium**, the official teaching authority of the Church. Christ continues to teach us through the Magisterium. This entire process is called **Apostolic Succession**.

An Awesome Assurance

Jesus has guaranteed that all his followers—everywhere and throughout time—will have access to the truths required for salvation. Guided by the Holy Spirit, the Magisterium teaches God's revealed truth without error. They can do this because Christ gives the Church a share in his own infallibility. *Infallible* means "without error."

The Magisterium is the official teaching authority of the Church and includes the Pope and all of the bishops of the Church.

Catholics believed in the **infallibility** of the Church for many centuries, but it wasn't formally declared a **doctrine** of the Church until the First Vatican Council in 1870. The Church has defined the following three levels of infallibility and magisterial authority.

Level 1: Infallibility of the Deposit of Faith. The divinely revealed truths that are part of the Deposit of Faith, and handed down through Scripture and Tradition, are always true. These can be defined and explained by the Pope "ex cathedra" (from the chair) or by the college of bishops when gathered at an Ecumenical Council. This level of infallibility also applies to individual bishops when they are teaching about the Deposit of Faith and their teaching is in union with the college of bishops and the Pope. We, the faithful, are required to give our assent and obedience to these teachings.

Magisterium ➤ The Church's living teaching office, which consists of all bishops, in communion with the Pope, the bishop of Rome. Their task is to interpret and preserve the truths revealed in both Sacred Scripture and Sacred Tradition.

Apostolic Succession ➤ The uninterrupted passing on of authority from the Apostles directly to all bishops. It is accomplished through the laying on of hands when a bishop is ordained in the Sacrament of Holy Orders as instituted by Christ.

infallibility ➤ The gift given by the Holy Spirit to the Church whereby the Magisterium of the Church, the Pope, and the bishops in union with the him, can definitively proclaim a doctrine of faith and morals without error.

doctrine ➤ An official, authoritative teaching of the Church based on the Revelation of God.

Level 2: Infallibility of Teaching on the Deposit of Faith. The Church's infallibility also extends to the doctrines that are necessary to explain and safeguard the truths contained in the Deposit of Faith. The doctrine of infallibility is one these necessary teachings. Similar to the first level, infallible doctrines in this level can be declared by the Pope or by the bishops in an Ecumenical Council, or they can be taught by individual bishops. We are required to give our assent and obedience to these teachings too.

Level 3: Other Authentic Teaching by the Magisterium. The Pope and bishops regularly release other teachings to deepen our understanding of Revelation in regard to faith and morals. These can be papal encyclicals, apostolic exhortations, teaching documents from Ecumenical Councils, teaching documents released by bishops' conferences, and teaching documents by individual bishops. These documents can cover a wide range of concerns and not only deepen our understanding on the revealed truths of faith but also safeguard us from false teaching and ideas. Though these teachings are not infallible and may further develop over time, we should give them our most serious consideration and presume their truth out of respect for the teaching office of the Church.

Because of Apostolic Succession and papal infallibility, Catholics throughout all time share one faith, a faith that goes directly back to Christ himself. These two gifts guarantee that all of us continue to have access to God's revealed truth until Christ comes again in glory.

Seeking Unity While Being True to Ourselves

Doctrines such as Apostolic Succession and papal infallibility can be hard for non-Catholics to understand. Despite this, the Church places great value on

MAKE IT SO

Just as the Magisterium hands on the Sacred Tradition of the Church under the guidance of the Holy Spirit, we can also "pay it forward" with the Good News. Which of these would you be willing to try?

- Pray for those who haven't heard the Gospel message.
- Volunteer at your local soup kitchen.
- Collect non-perishable food items for your local food pantry.
- Take the time to listen to your grandparents or an elderly relative or neighbor who might be lonely.
- Include a classmate who seems to be shy or alone in your group for a project or at your lunch table.

UNIT 1

seeking unity among Christians and with all people of good will. We seek unity without compromising the truths of our faith. Here are some examples of how the Catholic Church has built bridges with other Christians and with people of other faiths:

- The Vatican Council II *Decree on Ecumenism* (*Unitatis Redintegratio*, 1964) stresses that the Sacrament of Baptism unites all Christians.
- Also among the writings of Vatican Council II is the *Declaration on the Relation of the Church to Non-Christian Religions* (*Nostra Aetate*, 1965). It speaks of the high regard in which the Catholic Church holds other faiths.
- Saint Pope John Paul II began **interreligious dialogue** with the Jewish community. He was the first pope since Saint Peter to visit a **synagogue**. He was also the first pope to pray at the Western (Wailing) Wall in Jerusalem.
- During his papacy, Pope Benedict XVI visited Jewish communities throughout the world. He also dialogued with Muslims.
- Pope Francis has also increased the signs of interreligious understanding and tolerance. At a Holy Thursday liturgy he washed the feet of twelve juvenile inmates. Among the children were a Muslim boy and girl. In addition, when Pope Francis was installed as pontiff, many leaders of the Islamic world attended the installation Mass.

Efforts to dialogue with people of other religions do not alter or water down the Catholic Church's mission. Rather, these efforts are an essential part of our mission. As Catholics, we are called to be channels of unity, makers of peace. We must witness to the truth in every time and place. ✳

The Pope models the example of Jesus by washing the feet of inmates on Holy Thursday.

© WENN US / Alamy Stock Photo

HMMMMM. . . . What assurances do we have that the Gospel message we hear is the same as the one proclaimed by the original Apostles?

interreligious dialogue ➤ The efforts to build cooperative and constructive interaction with other world religions.

synagogue ➤ The building where a Jewish assembly or congregation meets for religious worship and instruction.

1. When questions of accuracy arose during the time of the oral tradition, to whom did the community turn for clarification?

2. What makes the Gospel of Mark like the camera on the sideline of a game?

3. Why is the Gospel of John similar to the camera up on a wire above the playing field?

4. Why are the Gospels the "heart" of the New Testament?

5. What is the difference between *Tradition* and *tradition?*

6. How are Sacred Scripture and Sacred Tradition connected?

7. To whom does Jesus entrust the preaching of the Gospel message? Whom do they hand it on to?

8. When are a pope's statements taken to be infallible?

Comparing the Gospels

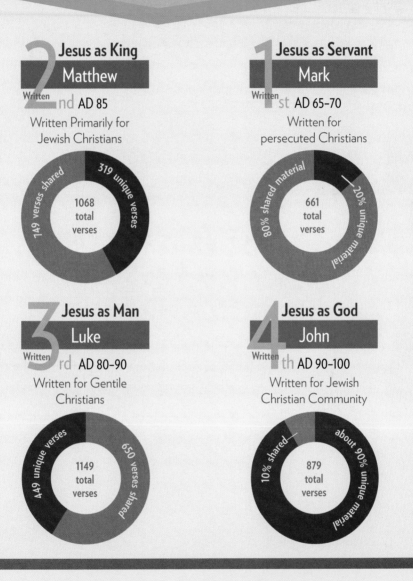

2 Jesus as King
Matthew
Written **2nd** AD 85
Written Primarily for
Jewish Christians

149 verses shared
319 unique verses
1068
total
verses

1 Jesus as Servant
Mark
Written **1st** AD 65–70
Written for
persecuted Christians

80% shared material
20% unique material
661
total
verses

3 Jesus as Man
Luke
Written **3rd** AD 80–90
Written for Gentile
Christians

449 unique verses
650 verses shared
1149
total
verses

4 Jesus as God
John
Written **4th** AD 90–100
Written for Jewish
Christian Community

10% shared
about 90% unique material
879
total
verses

1. Find which Gospel was written first. How much material from this Gospel is used in the others?

2. Find the intended audience for each Gospel. How do you think this influenced the focus of each Gospel?

CHAPTER 3
The Two Natures of Jesus

WHAT DOES IT MEAN
TO SAY THAT JESUS IS
TRUE GOD AND TRUE MAN?

SNAPSHOT

Article 11

True Man

A baby born in a manger. A twelve-year-old teaching in the Temple. A carpenter. A teacher. A friend to the sick and marginalized. A prophet who challenged the political and religious norms of his society. Suffering Servant. Messiah. Savior. Who is Jesus?

There are two dominant perspectives of Jesus Christ that we can use as our starting points in getting to know him: Jesus in the fullness of his human nature and Jesus in the fullness of his divine nature. It has been revealed through Scripture and Tradition that Jesus Christ is both true God and true man. This means that even though he is one Divine Person, he has two natures—his human nature and his divine nature. **Christology** is the study of Jesus Christ—the Son of God and the Second Divine Person of the Trinity—and his earthly ministry and eternal mission. In this chapter, we examine Christ's human nature and divine nature, and try to better understand how Jesus Christ is at all times one Divine Person with two distinct natures.

TAKE IT TO GOD

God,

Every day when I wake up, I try to be a good person and make good choices.

Sometimes it seems as if I have failed at this before I even leave my house.

Thank you for loving me even when I'm tired and short-tempered.

Thank you for loving me when I yell at my mom for no reason, or shut out my
    friends and family when I really want them close to me.

Thank you for not condemning me when I fail to do what is just or right.

Please give me the strength to be the person that you wish me to be, and help me
    to recognize that I don't have to be perfect to be deserving of your love.

Amen.

Christology ➤ Literally the study of Christ; the systematic statement of Christian beliefs about Jesus Christ, including his identity, mission, and saving work on Earth.

Jesus' Human Nature

Think about a time when you had to make a tough moral choice. Maybe you had the opportunity to cheat when you didn't study, or maybe someone told you a secret that you really wanted to tell your friends. These would be good times to apply the question, "What would Jesus do?" This question is a simple reminder that Jesus took on a human nature and experienced the same joys and challenges that we do. In tough situations, Jesus chose to do that which is right and just. Knowing that Jesus, having a true human nature, still chose to do what is right, helps to guide our own actions. Like us, the Eternal Son of God worked with human hands, thought with a human mind, acted with a human will, and loved with a human heart. Our creator became one of us; the perfection of who we were created to be. Because Jesus shows his humanity in every event of his life on Earth, we see plenty of examples of Jesus' human nature in Sacred Scripture.

Jesus is not just God appearing to look human. He has a physical, human body. This is clear in the Gospels. Jesus uses his hands when he takes the little girl by the hand as he raises her from the dead (see Matthew 9:18–19,23–25). Sacred Scripture mentions Jesus' eyes as he looks up to deliver the Sermon on the Plain (see Luke 6:20). Mark mentions Jesus using his arms to hug a child (see 9:36).

Jesus thought with a human mind. In Luke 2:52, we learn that the twelve-year-old Jesus grew in wisdom. Jesus also learned from experiences, just as we do. He had to ask questions to learn information, like when he asked how many loaves and fish were available before feeding the five thousand (see Mark 6:38). On the other hand, because of Jesus' divine nature, his knowledge of God and of God's will was perfect and complete.

One characteristic that defines what it means to be human is our **free will**. Our ability to know right from wrong and to intentionally choose between doing right and doing wrong separates us from the rest of creation. In his human nature, Jesus too had a free human will. We see this when Jesus is in the garden right before he is arrested. His prayer, "My Father, if it is possible, let this cup pass from me; yet, not as I will, but as you will" (Matthew 26:39), reveals his human will. The difference between our will and Jesus' will is that Jesus' human will is in complete harmony with his divine will. He chooses to live "in obedience to his Father all that he had decided with the Father and the Holy Spirit for our salvation" (*CCC*, number 475). In other words, Jesus never

---

free will ➤ The gift from God that allows human beings to choose from among various actions, for which we are held accountable. It is the basis for moral responsibility.

sinned. His freedom is shown in his perfect love for us, in his choosing to suffer and die for our salvation. Jesus shows us what it looks like when our human will perfectly submits to God's will.

The Human Experience

Jesus had close friends and family members with whom he developed genuine relationships. The Gospels tell us that he shared meals and celebrations with those people. He attended the wedding feast at Cana (see John 2:1–11). He had dinner at the home of Martha, Mary, and Lazarus (see Luke 10:38–42). He also enjoyed visiting the homes of those who were misunderstood or cast out by society, such as Simon the Pharisee (see Luke 7:36–50) and Zacchaeus the tax collector (see 19:1–10). Just as we attend celebrations, have dinner at our best friends' houses, and form relationships with those who are on the margins of our group, Jesus also delighted in these friendships.

It may be difficult to understand that the same person who offers us salvation also experienced hunger, pain, fatigue, suffering and sorrow. Consider Celia's story and see if you can draw some comparisons to Jesus' experience.

When Celia was eleven, she fell while riding her bike. Though it didn't seem like a bad fall, she broke her leg. The doctor said she was lucky, because the X-ray of the broken bone in her leg showed that she also had a tumor. Unfortunately, the tumor was cancerous. Celia underwent treatment, and for a long time she was too weak to go to school or play with her friends. She made friends with other patients and wept when they died. Often Celia was in great pain. Sometimes she even prayed to God and asked him to let her die so she wouldn't be in pain anymore. But Celia did not die. Her story is not over.

Because of Jesus' truly human nature, he forms and fosters deep friendships with many, including Martha, Mary, and Lazarus.

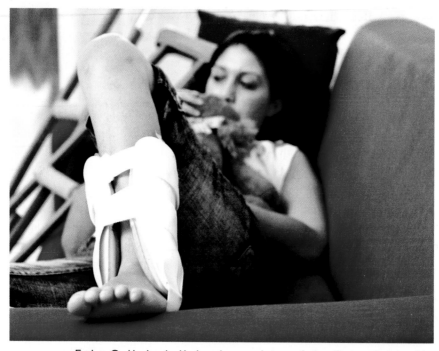

Faith in God looks a lot like love. In surrendering to faith in God, we find ourselves wanting to more about God, to please God, and to share our faith with others.

Can you remember a story from Scripture when Jesus was physically weak or in pain? Right after his Baptism, Jesus goes into the desert and fasts for forty days. Satan tempts Jesus with food because he is so painfully hungry from fasting (see Matthew 4:1–11). When Jesus is arrested, the Roman governor has him whipped with forty lashes, a torture so painful that many people who received this punishment passed out from the pain.

Was Jesus ever angry? Do you recall Jesus entering the Temple courtyard and overturning the tables of the money changers? Jesus definitely experienced righteous indignation that they had turned the Temple into a marketplace (see Matthew 32:12–13).

Can you recall Jesus weeping for the loss of a friend? Jesus had friends with whom he shared his life. In the Gospel of John, we read a story about his dear friend Lazarus who had fallen ill. When Jesus arrives at the home of his friends, Lazarus has died and been in the tomb for four days! Confronted with the deep sorrow of Lazarus's sisters, Mary and Martha, Jesus weeps. As any other human being would do, he grieves for his friend (see John 11:1–37).

Did Jesus experience fear? In the Gospel of Matthew, we hear the story of Jesus praying in the garden before his arrest. It actually says that Jesus feels sorrow and distress. He asks his heavenly Father if the situation can be changed. He agonizes over his impending suffering and death (see 26:36–39).

Like Celia, Jesus lived the deepest experience of being human. And though Jesus died, his story is not over. We cannot focus on the human nature of Jesus alone. Jesus rose from the dead, and through his Resurrection, we come to know his divine nature. We come to know Jesus Christ, Savior and Messiah.

© Holmes Garden Photos / Alamy Stock Photo

In what ways can it help you to know that Jesus also experienced sorrow, distress, and suffering?

Don't Forget His Divinity

Getting to know Jesus from the perspective of his human nature has its strengths, but it also has its limitations. It is wonderful to focus on Jesus' human nature, because it reminds us that every aspect of Jesus' life is important, and it can make relating to Jesus easy. However, we must be sure not to overlook his divine nature. If we forget his divine nature, then we reduce Jesus to just another good moral person or great teacher. If we begin our understanding of Jesus by focusing on his human nature, we must move toward an understanding of his divine nature as well. ✳

HMMMMMM. . . How does focusing on Jesus' human nature help us to know God better?

UNIT 1

Article 12
True God

Think about the people in your community—at home, at school, in your extracurricular activities. You likely look up to and admire many of them. You could probably think of several stories about people you know who have gone out of their way to help others or have taken a strong stance on a moral issue. Perhaps a teacher, coach, scout leader, youth minister, or other adult in your life has provided you with guidance and good advice. Think about the impact this person has had on you. Yet, this person can't go any further than being a role model or mentor. He or she cannot satisfy your deepest longing or offer you salvation. No one but Jesus can do that. When we call Jesus the Second Person of the Blessed Trinity, we are affirming that he is God, and there are numerous places in Sacred Scripture that reveal and affirm Jesus' divine nature.

The Annunciation refers to the visit of the angel Gabriel to the Virgin Mary to announce that she had been chosen to bear the Son of God.

The Son and the Father

Sacred Scripture is clear that Jesus Christ is the Son of God who existed before all time. The Gospel of Matthew hints at Jesus' divine nature in the first chapter. Matthew includes this quote from Isaiah: "Behold, the virgin shall be with child and bear a son, and they shall name him Emmanuel" (1:23). Emmanuel is a Hebrew name meaning, "God is with us." The Gospel of John reveals that Christ was with God the Father at the dawn of creation (see 1:1–18). Paul's Letter to the Galatians also affirms Christ's preexistence: "When the fullness of time had come, God sent his Son, born of a woman, born under the law, to ransom those under the law, so that we might receive adoption" (4:4–5).

Jesus himself elaborates on the relationship between himself and the Father, especially in the Gospel of John. For example, when Jesus is speaking to the crowds about being the Good Shepherd he explains that "the Father and I are one" (John 10:30). It is clear that Jesus is declaring himself equal to God the Father, because the crowds immediately pick up stones preparing to kill him for making this claim. The Father and the Son are Divine Persons distinct from one another, yet they are One God, a mystery we will explore more deeply when we examine the Trinity in chapter 9.

Divine Powers Revealed

Throughout the Gospels, Jesus displays powers that only God possesses. On several occasions, he displays divine knowledge. For example, in the synoptic Gospels, he accurately predicts the details of his own Passion and death three different times. On a less intense subject, Jesus uses his divine foreknowledge to pay the Temple tax. He tells Peter to catch a fish from the Sea of Galilee and pull out the two coins he will find within its mouth to pay their taxes (see Matthew 17:24–27). We can only wonder what Peter was thinking as he set out to find this fish!

I DIDN'T KNOW THAT!

One way we show reverence for Jesus Christ is through certain gestures we make at church. Genuflection is one example. When we genuflect before the cross or tabernacle, that is bend our right knee to the ground, we are humbling ourselves in acknowledgment of Christ's glory as God. We are fulfilling what Paul wrote in the Letter to the Philippians, "that at the name of Jesus / every knee should bend" (2:10). Next time you are at Mass, watch to see when the presider genuflects, and then take a moment to realize you truly are in God's presence.

genuflect ➤ To kneel on one knee as a sign of reverence for the Blessed Sacrament.

Jesus' divine knowledge also enables him to know people's hearts and minds. The Gospel of Matthew tells us that "Jesus knew what they were thinking" (9:4) when describing an encounter between Jesus and the scribes. Jesus also knows that Judas has decided to betray him and mentions it at the Last Supper (see John 13:2, 21–30). Finally, Jesus possesses knowledge of God the Father that no one else has: "Not that anyone has seen the Father except the one who is from God; he has seen the Father" (John 6:46). In the Gospel of John, we learn that it is this knowledge of the Father, known to Jesus through his divine nature, that he has come to share with us.

Acknowledged as God by Others

During Jesus' earthly life, others recognized and acknowledged that he is the Divine Son of God. Twice God the Father's booming voice from the heavens declares Jesus as his Son. It first happens when Jesus comes out of the water after John the Baptist baptizes him. As Jesus rises, we hear God the Father declaring, "This is my beloved Son" (Matthew 3:17). Later, when Jesus is trans-

figured before Peter, James, and John, the Father's voice once again proclaims, "This is my beloved Son" (17:5).

There are also human beings who make this connection. At the foot of the cross, an unnamed centurion (a Roman guard) realizes that Jesus is divine after seeing him die. Interestingly, this is not a moment in which Jesus displays great power. Instead, it is a moment of apparent weakness, yet the guard proclaims, "Truly this was the Son of God" (Matthew 27:54). After the Resurrection, even the doubting Apostle, Thomas, acknowledges that Jesus is God. After seeing the resurrected Jesus' wounds, he declares, "My Lord and my God!" (John 20:28). Jesus responds by praising those who believe in him as Lord and God without seeing him in the flesh. He's talking about us!

The Transfiguration gave the Apostles a preview of Jesus' divine nature. What do you see in this painting that points to this reality?

Perhaps you don't identify with the concept of "believing without seeing." Like Doubting Thomas, many people find it hard to believe in a God that is not tangible. If we can't hear his voice or see his face, then why should we believe he exists? Yet in our daily lives, we often believe in things we cannot see or touch or verify existence of. Certainly you have taken your parents at their word without proof or accepted as fact things you have heard in class without questioning their validity. What is holding us back from believing that Jesus is God incarnate? If we take the risk of believing the Gospel claims, we might be able to see the awesome impact that belief in Jesus' divine nature can have on our life.

Keep It Balanced

Focusing on Christ's divine nature is important for our own prayer life and relationship with God. It helps us to have as deep and profound a reverence for Jesus Christ as we do for God the Father. Believing in Jesus' divine nature gives us hope that salvation is attainable despite our sins and flaws. It helps us believe that everything Jesus taught is true. It motivates us to put our faith in Christ as the source of our salvation.

However, our belief in Jesus' divine nature must be balanced with our belief in his human nature. We find hope in the truth that the Son of God became human, became our brother, while remaining our Lord and God. Let's say you are struggling with the loss of a good friend or family member. Knowing that Jesus wept when his good friend Lazarus passed away comforts us, for we know he experienced the same emotions we do. If we did not believe that Jesus shared our human nature, we would have a harder time believing that God understands our human sorrows and struggles. Yet, because he is also fully God, we can be confident that he will provide the grace we need to live through our grief. The author of the Letter to the Hebrews captures this balance well:

> Therefore, since we have a great high priest who has passed through the heavens, Jesus, the Son of God, let us hold fast to our confession. For we do not have a high priest who is unable to sympathize with our weaknesses, but one who has similarly been tested in every way, yet without sin. So let us confidently approach the throne of grace to receive mercy and to find grace for timely help." (4:14–16) ✳

HMMMMMMM. . . In what ways does Jesus' divine nature offer hope for people who are weak and sinful?

UNIT 1

Article 13

True God and True Man

Ashanti's family is Catholic. She attends church with her family on Sundays, and her family is actively involved in many parish activities. Ashanti never questioned her religious beliefs until she met Ben. Ben confided in Ashanti that he isn't sure what he believes about God, but the idea that God would become man seems ridiculous to him. "Why would you become human if you are an almighty, all-powerful, all-knowing being?" he asked her. Ben's question sounded valid to her, and it made her question what she really believed about Jesus. Because Ashanti's dad liked to talk about religious things, she decided to talk to him about Ben's question.

CATHOLICS **MAKING** A DIFFERENCE

Saint Mother Teresa, as famous as she was, was committed to humility. She had a practical list of activities anyone can try in order to live humbly, and thus be close to Christ. Here are some of the things she tried to live by:

- Speak as little as possible about yourself.
- Keep busy with your own affairs and not those of others.
- Do not interfere in the affairs of others.
- Accept small irritations with good humor.
- Do not dwell on the faults of others.
- Accept insults and injuries.
- Be courteous and delicate even when provoked by someone.
- Do not seek to be admired and loved.
- Give in, in discussions, even when you are right.
- Choose always the more difficult task.

Ashanti's dad told her that the correct term for God taking on flesh and becoming man is called the **Incarnation**. He told her that Christ could have remained in Heaven, but he willingly accepted a human nature to help us. Jesus did not take on flesh as an act of power or a show of importance. He humbled himself and without ceasing to be God, took on our human nature in order to offer us salvation. He endured humiliation, torture, and death to bring us salvation. Ashanti's dad said this is one of the big mysteries of faith that he believes in with all his heart because of the testimony of Scripture and Tradition.

An Act of Humility

In Saint Paul's Letter to the Philippians, there is a hymn that gives us great insight into the Incarnation. In Philippians 2:5–11, Paul reflects on the humility of Christ, who even though he was God, willingly took on our human nature. This amazing display of humility should inspire us to be humble as well. Reflect on this list of spiritual practices that can help you grow in humility:

© mimagephotography / Shutterstock.com

- Recognize your limitations.
- Work to address your flaws. Never quit trying to grow and improve.
- Be grateful for what you have.
- Almost every person has something to teach you, so listen with openness to every person you encounter.
- Admit your mistakes and practice apologizing.
- Be considerate of others' opinions and viewpoints.
- Give recognition to those who have helped you.

What are some spiritual practices that you are willing to try?

Incarnation ➤ From the Latin, meaning "to become flesh," referring to the mystery of Jesus Christ, the Divine Son of God, becoming man. In the Incarnation, Jesus Christ became truly man while remaining truly God.

UNIT 1

Both Fully God and Fully Man

Scripture and Tradition testify that when the Incarnation happened, the Son of God, the Second Person of the Trinity, did not stop being God in order to become the man Jesus of Nazareth. In other words, the humble child in the manger at Christmas is the All-Powerful God. Christ was at all times *one* Divine Person with *two* natures. The theological term for this mystery of the two natures in one Divine Person is **hypostatic union**. The two natures of Jesus Christ do not simply exist one alongside the other; instead, they are joined so completely that both are always fully present.

A good example of this is when Jesus approaches his death. Jesus has divine knowledge of his death and Resurrection. Remember, he predicted it in detail three times. However, this does not mean that he is unafraid. In the garden, he is sweating blood, asking God the Father to let this cup pass (see Matthew 26:36–39).

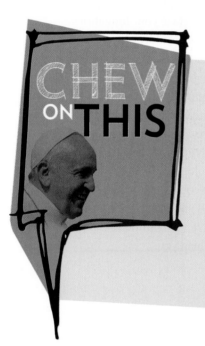

CHEW ON THIS

Jesus came to serve, not to be served. And hope is the virtue of the humble. I believe that this could be the way. I tell you with sincerity: nothing else comes to my mind to say. Humility and service: these two things guard the little hope, the most humble virtue, but the one that life gives you. (Pope Francis, "Address to the Community of Christian Life (CVX)–Missionary Students' League of Italy," April 30, 2015)

---

hypostatic union ➤ The union of Jesus Christ's divine and human natures in one Divine Person.

Why the Hypostatic Union Matters

Because Jesus is one Divine Person, a union of a fully human nature and a fully divine nature, we know and experience Jesus' divinity *through* his humanity. We come to know Jesus as God Made Flesh among us, through knowing Jesus the man. The whole of Jesus' earthly life, including his emotions, friendships, values, and priorities, reveals God to us in a unique and powerful way.

A good way to understand how Jesus' human nature reveals God's true nature is to compare the images of God that come through the Old Testament to the image of God revealed through Jesus in the New Testament. For example, from the Old Testament, you might think that you can win God's love and approval only by following his Law. But Jesus' compassion reveals that the Law is just a guide and that God loves us without any conditions. From the Old Testament, you might get the impression that God's justice is all about punishment for wrongdoing. Jesus, however, makes it clear that God's justice is focused on mercy and forgiveness. From the Old Testament, you might even get the impression that God's saving power is manifested through winning wars and conflicts. Jesus' humanity makes it clear that God's saving power comes through sacrificial love. ✻

Jesus' sacrifice is the most powerful example of God's saving love.

HMMMMM. . . Why does studying the life and teachings of Jesus Christ help you better understand who God is?

Article 14

Why Does the Incarnation Matter?

Think back to Ben's question to Ashanti: "Why would you become human if you are an almighty, all-powerful, all-knowing being?" The question is so powerful and simple that even Ashanti, who had been raised with a strong religious background, had difficulty answering the question. Ashanti's dad tried to help her understand by explaining that Jesus took on human form in order to offer us salvation. Perhaps Ben would have countered that explanation with, "Why would an all-powerful being need to become human in order to offer us salvation?"

Ashanti needs only to look in the mirror to answer Ben. Each one of us is the answer. God takes on human form because God is beyond our human understanding. In order to have any concept of God, grace, or salvation, God has to approach us in a way that we can understand. Think of it this way: We can imagine what life is like on Mars only by comparing what we know about Mars with something we know through our experience on Earth. Astronomers tell us that a solar day on Mars is 24 hours and 39 minutes in "Earth time." We are able to better understand what a day is like on Mars by framing it with something we already experience: a day on Earth. In a similar way, we can understand God better by framing our understanding of God with something we already know through human experience. God's taking on human form in the Person of Jesus provides the frame needed to understand more fully God and his saving love for us.

MAKE IT SO

Think about how you picture these spiritual realities: God the Father, God the Son, God the Holy Spirit, Heaven, Hell, and the Kingdom of God. Where do your images come from? your parents and grandparents? your culture? your life experiences? You are part of a *catholic* church, a *universal* church. Take some time to explore how Catholics of other cultures depict these spiritual realities. How can their images and experiences deepen your understanding of our faith?

Speaking Our Language

Our western culture has ingrained in many people an image of God the Father as a wise old man or a gentle father. Little children might say that God is an old man with a long white beard, wearing a long white robe. If you take a moment to do a quick search on the internet for "images of Jesus," what you find may surprise you. Based on cultural and societal norms, some people's image of God the Son is a white man with shoulder-length brown hair and a bright smile. Others portray Jesus as a wiry, dark-skinned man of Middle Eastern descent. Israel is not far from Egypt and the surrounding countries of Africa, so some people picture Jesus as having the skin tone and facial features of a person from one of these countries. Artists portray Jesus as a reflection of their own culture so that we can identify more closely with him.

God became flesh in the Person of Jesus Christ because he is identifying with our humanity. He wants to be as relatable to us as possible. By reading the stories of Jesus' struggles and triumphs, we have something to identify with. God humbles himself and becomes man because he wants to be sure that we understand his message of salvation. What better way to communicate to us as human beings than through the humanity of Jesus Christ? ✳

How do you imagine Jesus?

UNIT 1

1. What is Christology?

2. Explain the problems that can arise if we overemphasize either Jesus' divine nature or his human nature.

3. In what ways does Jesus show his divine knowledge in the Gospels?

4. Where does the word *incarnation* come from?

5. What do we mean when we use the term *hypostatic union*?

6. Explain why God would humble himself to take on flesh and live among us.

7. What difference does it make that Jesus is true God and true man?

EXPLORING YOUR APPROACH TO JESUS

This painting of Jesus washing the feet of the Apostles was painted in a style unique to native Ethiopian artists.

1. What do you see in the picture that represents Jesus' human nature?

2. What do you see in the picture that represents Jesus' divine nature?

3. How does this image speak to you about who Jesus is?

CHAPTER 4
It Comes Down to Faith

WHY PUT MY FAITH IN JESUS?

SNAPSHOT

Article 15

The Gift of Faith

Have you ever noticed people holding up signs at major sporting events that simply read, "John 3:16"? This is their way to remind people of the greatest gift in the world. John 3:16 states, "For God so loved the world that he gave his only Son, so that everyone who believes in him might not perish but might have eternal life." God's love is so great that he sent his only Son to die for us and offers us eternal life. What are we asked in return? To put our faith in Jesus Christ and believe his Gospel message.

Faith Is a Gift

Through faith, we come to accept and believe the truth God has revealed to us. God knows that believing in him can be challenging. None of us can maintain faith completely on our own. That is why faith is a supernatural gift, a grace, that God freely offers to us. God's grace makes it possible for us to say yes to God with our mind, heart, and will. It helps us grow in our relationship with the Holy Trinity—Father, Son, and Holy Spirit. However, believing in and loving God is ultimately our choice. We cannot force someone to love us. Love has to be freely given. God has given us the gift of free will; he does not force us to believe in him or love him. The Holy Spirit is there to help us but does not contradict our human freedom. We must be willing to believe and trust in what Jesus teaches us about God, about ourselves, and about how we should live.

We Don't Have to Understand Everything!

Choosing to believe in God and to have faith does not mean that we have everything all figured out. Sometimes the truths of Revelation may not make complete sense to us. Having faith sometimes means that we must trust those truths because we trust the One who has revealed them. We regularly trust what others—friends, family members, or classmates—tell us. Shouldn't we also trust what God—the source of all life and love—tells us?

Often when we encounter truths that we struggle to accept, these are the very areas of our faith that God is calling us to dig deeper to understand. It would be easier to just throw up our hands and say, "I don't care" or "I just don't believe in this part of the faith." For example, although Jana says she would never have an abortion herself, she's not sure that society has the right to tell other women what they can or can't do with their body. Jana's youth minister tells her that she's overlooking a big piece of the picture. It isn't just about a woman's body; there is another life to think about as well. The youth minister challenges Jana to dig deeper and take time to study what the Church teaches about abortion. She asks Jana thought-provoking questions, encourages her to back up her answers, and asks her to spend time with it in prayer. As Jana does this, she becomes convinced that life begins at conception and that abortion is a sin for everyone. Her commitment to seeking the truth not only makes her more confident of the Church's teaching but also brings her closer to God.

Life Behind the Wheel

A life of faith means trusting that God wants what is best for us. Some people call this "surrendering to God's will." Think of it like getting the keys to the family car. When you first get behind the wheel, you feel free. You can choose to stop at a friend's house or go through the fast-food drive-through. The idea of being able to go anywhere is exhilarating!

But there's another side to this. When your parents trust you with the keys to the car, they expect you to take that responsibility seriously. They expect you to use the freedom the car gives you to go to school, drive to sports and play practices, and go to safe places to have fun with your friends. You might say this is their "will" for, or expectation of, you. A similar thing is true in your relationship with God. God also gives you the freedom to make your own choices. He wants you to use that freedom to make choices that will lead to your true happiness and the happiness of others. This is his will for you. When we have faith, we trust that God knows what is best for us. So we continually strive to surrender ourselves to God's will and allow God's truth to direct our lives and to guide our choices. In a way, Saint Paul writes about this in his Letter to the Romans when he discusses the "obedience of faith" (1:5). The word *obedience* comes from a Latin root, meaning "to hear, listen, or pay attention to." Through faith, we learn to listen to the Holy Spirit as it gently guides us toward holiness and eternal life.

© Sergey Furtaev / Shutterstock.com

What connection do you see between freedom and responsibility?

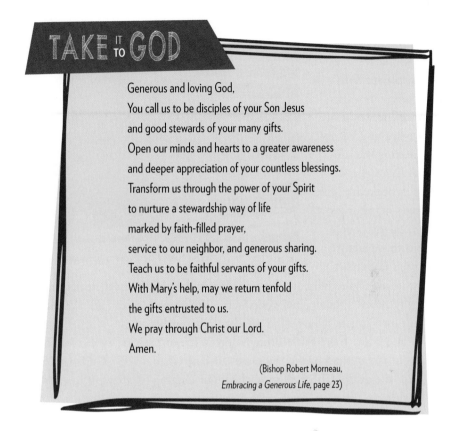

TAKE IT TO GOD

Generous and loving God,
You call us to be disciples of your Son Jesus
and good stewards of your many gifts.
Open our minds and hearts to a greater awareness
and deeper appreciation of your countless blessings.
Transform us through the power of your Spirit
to nurture a stewardship way of life
marked by faith-filled prayer,
service to our neighbor, and generous sharing.
Teach us to be faithful servants of your gifts.
With Mary's help, may we return tenfold
the gifts entrusted to us.
We pray through Christ our Lord.
Amen.

(Bishop Robert Morneau,
Embracing a Generous Life, page 23)

Faith Needs Nourishment

It is possible to lose the gift of faith if we do not nourish it and help it to grow. What can we do to strengthen and nourish our faith? One way to grow in faith is to read Sacred Scripture regularly and prayerfully. As we grow familiar with the different people and events in the Bible, they become part of the way we view the world and events in our own lives. For example, imagine hurrying to class and seeing a student struggling with papers all over the floor due to a broken backpack. Do you stop to help, or do you hurry to class? Knowing the Parable of the Good Samaritan (see Luke 10:29–37) may help shape how you respond to the situation. The Bible is full of timeless wisdom that we can use daily to make good decisions and grow in faith.

Spending quality time with other people is another way we can nourish our faith. Participating in works of service and works of justice helps us grow in faith. Seeking the support of other believers to help us deal with life's challenges helps us grow in faith. Asking people whose faith we admire about their faith helps

Who has helped you to grow in your faith?

us grow in faith. We might ask them to share a moment when their faith in God really affected them. This works both ways, so we also should take time to share our own stories of how God is working in our life.

We also nourish our faith through prayer. In our prayers, we can join the Apostles in asking the Lord to "increase our faith" (Luke 17:5). God, who first granted us the gift of faith, will surely hear our longing for that gift to grow and flourish.

A Home for Nourishment

Jesus founded the Catholic Church knowing that our personal faith thrives best in a community of faith. He gave us a community that reflects Jesus' own life and teachings; we can rely on the Church's life and teachings to reflect the fullness of Revelation. We find strength and support in the Church, knowing that we share one faith, in one Lord, through one Baptism with people around the world. We even have God's promise to guide the Church so that our faith will not get off track. With the guidance of the Holy Spirit, the Magisterium guards, interprets, and hands on God's revealed truths. If our personal faith thrives best in community, then as a faith community, we should unite to be the Body of Christ at work in the world. ✳

HMMMMM. . . In your opinion, why does faith need to be nourished? What are some ways your own faith has been nourished?

Article 16

Learning about Faith from Paul's Letters

The power that faith in Jesus Christ has to change our lives is amazing. Look at Saint Paul. Before his conversion, he actively hunted down Jewish Christians. After his conversion, he traveled even more—over 10,000 miles, mostly by foot—spreading the Good News throughout the Roman Empire. He started numerous churches in cities he had never seen before. Under the guidance of the Holy Spirit, he worked with Peter and the other Apostles to guide the first Christians on issues of faith and morality. Once these communities were established, he would move on, continuing to spread the Good News. Oh, and he wrote lots of letters! In his letters, we can see the importance of faith in Paul's life and in the life of the early Church.

Paul Pens Encouraging Letters

We are fortunate that during Paul's travels to spread the Gospel, he wrote many letters. Some of his letters were addressed to specific people, and others were addressed to entire communities. Some letters he even wrote while he was in prison. Many of them became part of the New Testament. This means that they are no ordinary letters. They are inspired by God, meaning that the Holy Spirit guided Paul to share the eternal truths that God wanted all people to know about God himself and our salvation.

PATTERN OF PAUL'S LETTERS	
Part 1: Greeting	Paul introduces himself, often by mentioning he is an Apostle of Jesus Christ, in order to establish his authority. The greeting offers grace and peace to the recipient.
Part 2: Prayer	This is usually a prayer of thanksgiving. Paul sometimes mentions the good works of individuals or the communities' ability to hold on to their faith during difficult times.
Part 3: Body	Under the guidance of the Holy Spirit, Paul addresses the problems and questions that have come to his attention.
Part 4: Final Blessing	The letters usually close with greetings and a final blessing. The greetings are either Paul saying hello to a specific member of the community or passing along greetings from other Christians.

A Time Long, Long Ago

Understanding Paul's letters can be challenging. The problems and questions that Paul is addressing are not always obvious to us because we have only Paul's half of the communication. It's kind of like sitting in a room and listening to someone talk on the telephone. You hear only one side of the discussion, so you must use logic and reasoning to determine the topic of the conversation.

© pathdoc / Shutterstock.com

How much can we learn from essentially reading one side of a conversation through Paul's letters?

Another challenge is that Paul lived and wrote in a time very different from our own. To help us understand what Paul is trying to communicate and ultimately what God is trying to communicate to us through Paul's words, we must seek to understand the culture and ways of communicating used at the time. As Catholics, we are blessed to have the Magisterium, which is the official teaching authority of the Church. Their responsibility is to interpret and preserve the truths of the Church found in both Scripture and Tradition. Through the guidance of the Holy Spirit, the Magisterium helps us better understand the truths that God wanted to convey to us through not only Paul's letters but all of Scripture.

We can acquire great insight from reading Paul's letters. One of the most interesting things we learn is the variety of ways Paul calls others to faith. Sometimes we see Paul as a fatherly guide giving advice, as he does in his

I DIDN'T KNOW THAT!

Some of the most famous authors in the world have actually not written every word in the books attributed to them! Tom Clancy and James Patterson are among many authors who have used ghost-writers, people who write all or part of the book in the author's name, using the author's style. The practice of writing under someone else's name isn't new. It seems quite probable that Paul did not write five or six of the letters attributed to him in the New Testament. Why, then, are these letters accepted as part of the New Testament canon? The reason is that this was a morally acceptable way for a disciple to apply his teacher's thought to new situations. In other words, writing under the name of Paul was a way of honoring Paul's memory and teaching.

Letter to Philemon. Other times, he is like a learned rabbi, giving scholarly arguments for having faith in Jesus, as he does in his Letter to the Romans. Still other times, we see Paul utterly frustrated and challenging individuals who are leading others astray, as he does in his Letter to the Galatians. Yet, no matter what means Paul uses, his passion for the Gospel and his desire for others to put their faith in Jesus is always clear. The rest of this chapter focuses on three of Paul's letters and what they can teach us about faith. ✳

© aluxum / iStockphoto.com

What are the benefits of writing or receiving a handwritten letter?

HMMMMMM. . .
Why were Paul's letters such an important part of his ministry?

Article 17

Galatians and Ephesians: Faith and Unity

It must have been incredibly difficult to spread the Good News in cities that were a melting pot of people from all over the Roman Empire. Given this situation, why was Paul so successful at establishing Christian communities?

One reason is that Paul was willing to embrace people's differences and diversity. To Paul, it did not matter if they were **Gentiles** or Jews, rich or poor, slave or free. The message of salvation was for everyone! He didn't try to force each community to fit into the same mold. He met people where they were and addressed their specific struggles. Imagine his distress when he heard that the Christian community in Galatia had abandoned this teaching after new missionaries told them they had to follow Jewish Law before they could become Christians!

The Galatians Lose Faith in Paul and His Message

"O stupid Galatians!" (Galatians 3:1). Wow! Probably not what you expected to read in the Bible from Saint Paul to a Christian community. Sometimes the journey to faith has bumps along the way, and the Galatians apparently hit one of those bumps. This bump must have been serious to get Saint Paul so upset. Fortunately, his Letter to the Galatians provides the clues we need to figure out what was happening.

The Christians in Galatia were predominately Gentiles who, before meeting Paul, worshipped pagan gods. However, when they heard Paul's message calling them to put their faith in Jesus Christ, many responded and became Christians. Paul mentions that they received the Holy Spirit, and mighty works were done among them (see Galatians 3:5). Additionally, their love for Paul was overwhelming. Paul says they would have plucked their eyes out for him, if it would have helped him (see 4:15).

But something changed. After Paul left, other missionaries started spreading a different message about Jesus Christ (see Galatians 1:6–7). Unlike Paul, these missionaries taught that the Galatians had to become full Jews—including being circumcised and obeying all the Jewish laws—in order to become Christians. Not only did this contradict Paul's teaching, but these missionaries

---

Gentile ➤ A non-Jewish person. In Sacred Scripture, the Gentiles were the uncircumcised, those who did not honor the God of the Torah. Saint Paul and other evangelists reached out to the Gentiles, baptizing them into the family of God.

also questioned his authority as an Apostle. Unfortunately, the Galatians were being swayed by these visitors and began to doubt Paul and his Gospel message (see 1:6–12).

Make a U-turn! Make a U-turn!

Somehow, word of this got back to Paul and he was not happy. In his letter, he asks the Galatians, "You were running well, who hindered you from following [the] truth?" (Galatians 5:7). Paul defends his authority as an Apostle by mentioning that Jesus himself appeared to him and sent him on mission (see 1:11–12). He even mentions confronting Saint Peter and winning an argument over how to treat Gentile Christians (see 2:11–14).

As Paul goes on to defend the Gospel message, we learn more about faith in Jesus. Paul asks the Galatians to remember their own initial conversion. He reminds them of the amazing things the Holy Spirit did among them when they first believed (see Galatians 3:1–5). Paul then asks them if they experienced the power of the Holy Spirit without following the Jewish Law, then why now rely on the Law (see 3:7–14)? He explains that faith in Jesus Christ is sufficient for justification.

Justification is a word Paul uses to explain how faith in Christ saves us from sin and death. It refers to God's act of bringing sinful human beings into right relationship with him. Justification flows from God's forgiveness of our sin and the gift of God's sanctifying grace to renew our holiness. Paul's message to the Galatians is that they have been deceived into believing they can be justified with God by following the Old Law. The truth Paul proclaims is that the Old Law brings judgment only; only faith in Jesus Christ brings justification and our salvation.

Saint Paul urges the Galatians to turn away from the false belief that their salvation depends on following the Old Law and turn back to faith in Christ.

justification ➤ God's act of bringing a sinful human being into right relationship with him. It involves removal of sin and the gift of God's sanctifying grace to renew holiness.

salvation ➤From the Latin *salvare*, meaning "to save," referring to the forgiveness of sins and assurance of permanent union with God, attained for us through the Paschal Mystery—Christ's work of redemption accomplished through his Passion, death, Resurrection, and Ascension. Only at the time of judgment can a person be certain of salvation, which is a gift of God.

Stop the Hypocrisy!

Have you ever met someone who says one thing but does another? Hypocrisy can be frustrating. Apparently, in Ephesus the Jewish Christians were not getting along with the Gentile Christians. The divisions were going against Christ's teachings and had the potential to hinder the spreading of the Gospel. The Letter to the Ephesians addresses the hypocrisy of Christians who are divided among themselves. In doing so, it gives us further insight into faith in Jesus Christ as well as faith's unifying effects.

As you read the Letter to the Ephesians, you hear Paul's explanation of how God chose us to be in relationship with him before the creation of the world (see 1:3–6). Then Paul speaks about our **redemption** in Christ (see 1:7–14). *Redemption* is another word used to describe how God's saving plan works. It is the process by which one is brought back from slavery to sin into right relationship with God.

Amazingly, God's offer of redemption is a gift:

> For by grace you have been saved through faith, and this is not from you; it is the gift of God; it is not from works, so no one may boast. For we are his handiwork, created in Christ Jesus for the good works that God has prepared in advance, that we should live in them. (2:8–10)

The offer of salvation is a gift from God.
What does accepting that gift mean to you?

---

redemption ➤ From the Latin *redemptio*, meaning "a buying back," referring, in the Old Testament, to Yahweh's deliverance of Israel and, in the New Testament, to Christ's deliverance of all Christians from the forces of sin. As the agent of redemption, Jesus is called the Redeemer.

We need only accept God's gift of salvation in faith. At the heart of this gift is Jesus Christ's self-sacrifice on the cross. Through his sacrifice, Jesus is able to make right the relationship between God and humankind. When believers put their faith in Jesus Christ, they are sealed and transformed by the Holy Spirit, the Third Person of the Blessed Trinity (see Ephesians 1:13, 2:22). Once transformed, believers are called to live holy lives that reflect the restored unity between God and humankind. They are also called to be united with one another in peace and love (see 4:1–6). By treating one another with dignity and respect, Christians are a sign of the unity that God desires for all people.

CATHOLICS **MAKING** A DIFFERENCE

How you live your life matters! Your words and actions can draw others into the Church community or turn them away. If you tell a friend that you can't spend the night on a Saturday because you have to go to Mass the next morning, you are making a statement about your priorities. If you volunteer for service projects at your school or parish, you are sending a strong message about what you believe in. Have you ever thought of yourself as making a difference by being a good example to others in the way you live your life?

What Do Galatians and Ephesians Teach Us?

These ancient letters are not dead, dusty, meaningless words. The issues that Paul writes about are still with us today. Most important, these letters reveal that faith begins with God. God initiates the offer of salvation to each one of us. It is our responsibility to respond to that offer. Unlike the Galatians, who failed to trust Paul when the other missionaries came with false teachings, we are called to believe and trust what God has communicated to us through both Scripture and Tradition. We have to open our hearts and be willing to believe all that Jesus taught us about God—the Father, Son, and Holy Spirit—and the amazing love God has for each one of us.

We also are reminded that it is easy to be drawn away from the true focus of our faith. We can be tempted by false teachers who promise to save us by something other than our faith in Jesus Christ. Like the Galatians, we too must ask ourselves, "What hinders me from following the truth God has revealed?" Do we allow teachings that contradict what the Church teaches to influence our faith as the Galatians did?

Finally, Ephesians reminds us that faith in Christ should transform our lives. By receiving the gift of faith, we are called to live a life that reflects our new status as adopted sons and daughters of God our Father. A main characteristic of our new life is how we love and treat everyone we encounter each day. Are we a sign of the love and unity God desires, or do we contribute to divisions among our families, classmates, friends, or parish community? ✳

OVERVIEW of the Letter to the Galatians

- **Intended audience:** Gentile Christians living in the region of Galatia.
- **Themes:** The correct understanding of what it means to be saved through faith in Jesus Christ.
- **Reason for writing:** Missionaries with false teaching about Christ have led the Galatians astray, and Paul is writing to set them straight.

OVERVIEW of the Letter to the Ephesians

- **Intended audience:** Both Jewish Christians and Gentile Christians living in and around the city of Ephesus.
- **Themes:** Jews and Gentiles have both been chosen by God and justified through their faith in Jesus Christ. They are to be a sign of unity to the world.
- **Reason for writing:** To address disagreements that arose between Jewish Christians and Gentile Christians causing disunity and hindering others from believing in Jesus.

HMMMMMM. . . How might division among Christians affect the way people look at the Church?

Article 18

First Corinthians: Faith Overcomes Division

Tension filled the air at the first meeting for the parish mission trip. Most of the students who gathered didn't know one another. The youth director wanted to discuss the reasons behind poverty as part of the trip preparation. One student immediately spoke up and said it was basically because people were lazy and wanted to live off the government. This caused another person to react and say it was because of poor wages and the lack of jobs. Several other people took sides, and voices were raised. Finally, the youth director stepped in and said: "Let's calm down a bit. There are many causes. This isn't about who's right and who's wrong. Let's look at some Scripture for direction, especially the Letter to the Corinthians and how Paul responded to conflicts in the community."

Corinth was a crossroads for travelers from all over the world, making it the ideal location for Paul to preach.

© Lefteris / iStockphoto.com

During Paul's time, Corinth was a bustling seaport city, which meant it was a crossroads for travelers from all over the world. Paul's work as a tent-maker meant he would have many potential customers. This made Corinth a good place for Paul to preach to travelers so his message could be carried far and wide. Like most large first-century Roman cities, Corinth was a mix of cultures and religions. There was a Jewish synagogue and several temples dedicated to pagan gods and goddesses. Corinth also had a reputation for prostitution and sexual promiscuity.

Cliques Harm the Corinthians' Unity

According to Acts of the Apostles 18:11, Paul spent about a year and a half living, working, and preaching in Corinth. Sometime after he left Corinth, scholars estimate around AD 56, Paul sent his first letter to the church in Corinth. In this letter, it is apparent that the Corinthians are figuring out exactly how to follow Jesus and live as a community of faith. Unfortunately, instead of focusing on Jesus, they have divided themselves into cliques. Some groups say they are followers of Paul, and others are following a preacher named Apollos. It is no surprise that right at the beginning of the letter (see Corinthians 1:4–9), Paul mentions Christ five times. Paul is reminding the Corinthians that they are followers of Jesus Christ, not a particular Church leader (see 1:10–13).

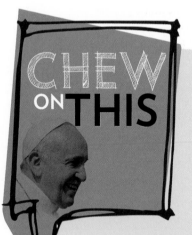

CHEW ON THIS

Just as Christ gathers to himself all those who believe and makes them his body, so the Christian comes to see himself as a member of this body, in an essential relationship with all other believers. The image of a body does not imply that the believer is simply one part of an anonymous whole, a mere cog in a great machine; rather, it brings out the vital union of Christ with believers and of believers among themselves (cf. Rom 12:4–5). Christians are 'one' (cf. Gal 3:28), yet in a way which does not make them lose their individuality; in service to others, they come into their own in the highest degree. (Pope Francis, "The Light of Faith" ["Lumen Fidei," 2013], number 22)

Sadly, the divisions among the Corinthians have also shown up at worship. Some wealthy people bring food to eat before the celebration while others in the community go hungry. This emphasizes the divisions between the rich and the poor (see 1 Corinthians 11:17–22). Paul reminds them of their unity in faith. They should celebrate the Lord's Supper as one. Paul directs the Corinthians to eat their meals at home to avoid any divisions. Here and throughout the letter, Paul continually reminds the Corinthians of how having faith in Jesus Christ must be demonstrated by the way they act toward one another in community.

What We Do Matters

For Paul, even what a person eats can affect the faith of the community. Apparently, Paul was asked if Christians were morally allowed to eat meat that had been offered as a sacrifice to an idol, or pagan god (see 1 Corinthians 10:23–33). In the letter, Paul says the answer is both yes and no. On one hand, Christians would be fine to eat it, knowing that there are no gods besides the one, true God. (At the time, almost all the meat sold in the Corinthian marketplaces was first offered as a sacrifice to a pagan god.) Paul is basically saying that it isn't a big deal to eat food sacrificed to gods that don't exist. It's just food.

Paul's letters addressed day-to-day issues for early Christian communities, such as the morality of eating meat that had been offered as sacrifice to an idol.

On the other hand, Paul also cautions that it is not okay to eat this meat if another Christian whose faith is weak or uncertain would be offended by your behavior. In this situation, it is better to not eat the meat and avoid causing division within the Christian community. For Paul, "being right" is not as important as preserving the unity that we have with other Christians. When we focus on Christ, we move out of our own egoism and find solutions to the things that would otherwise divide us.

So what does this have to do with us today? You probably do not run into the issue of whether to eat meat that has been sacrificed to idols. But there are plenty of other issues that can divide Christians. Let's return to the students who were preparing for the mission trip. Listening to their youth leader, they committed to serving people in need with respect and compassion. They could all agree that this is what their faith in Jesus called them to do. During their week of service, they continued to talk and pray about their common experiences. In the process, they learned to respect and even appreciate opinions different from theirs. Paul's reminder to keep our focus on Jesus Christ really does help us to respect and appreciate one another. ✳

OVERVIEW of the Book of First Corinthians

- **Intended audience:** The Church in Corinth that Paul helped found. It was made up of mostly Gentile Christians.
- **Themes:** All are one in the faith, and Christ is our head. General and specific instructions on how to live their faith as individuals and as a community.
- **Reason for writing:** Paul writes to this young Church that was struggling with divisions and had many questions about living the faith.

 HMMMMMM. . . Why is Paul's answer to the Corinthians' question about eating meat sacrificed to idols important to us today?

Article 19

We Celebrate Our Faith in Community

This unit began with a big question: Who is Jesus? Previous chapters have discussed how God reveals himself through natural and Divine Revelation, how Jesus is the fulfillment of Revelation and is the focus of all Scripture especially the Gospels, how Jesus is presented in the Gospel of Mark, and how Jesus is true God and true man. But the most important question is the one only you can answer: Who is Jesus for you?

One way to think about this question is to look at what believing in Jesus Christ has meant to other people. For example, Tradition tells us that all but one of the Apostles were martyred; that is, they were killed because of their Christian faith. Noncanonical written records and oral history tell us the Apostles suffered beheadings, crucifixion, stabbings, stoning, burning, flaying, and more! What made them willing to die just to tell people about Jesus Christ?

This isn't just ancient history. In March 2016, four sisters from the Missionaries of Charity were serving at a nursing home in Yemen. Even though they knew they might be in danger, the nuns and Fr. Tom Uzhunnalil continued to tend to the elderly there. Then a terrible act of hatred occurred. According to news reports, jihadists tied the nuns up, shot them, and smashed their heads. Father Tom's whereabouts are unknown, but there is speculation that he was crucified on Good Friday. Yes, even today, those committed to serving Christ are willing to sacrifice everything and even be killed in order to spread the Gospel and serve the poor.

© Godong / Alamy Stock Photo

Many early Christians were martyred for their faith. Unfortunately, Christians in some parts of the world today still face the possibility of martyrdom for their beliefs.

UNIT 1

Giving It Our All

What is so powerful about believing in Jesus that for two thousand years people have been willing to give up their lives to follow him? The answer is **faith**. What exactly is faith? More than anything else, faith is a relationship with God, the Father, Son, and Holy Spirit. God desires a personal relationship with each of us. To make this relationship possible, God offers us the gift of faith. Faith makes it possible for us to believe in all that he has revealed about himself and to respond to his revealed truth with our whole heart, mind, and will. Faith makes us want to share this Good News with others.

Faith is more than just agreeing to a set of beliefs. Our intellect is part of it, but faith involves our entire self. Having faith in God can be likened to falling in love. When we love someone, we don't just believe certain things about that person. When we fall in love, our whole life is changed. We say and do things differently. We find ourselves thinking about and longing to be with the other person. We even enjoy telling others about our newfound love.

Faith in God is like that. It is a relationship that transforms us. In freely surrendering our whole selves to the truth God has revealed to us, we find ourselves wanting to learn more about God. We are compelled to say and do things differently to please God. We want to share our faith with others, hoping they too will find the same peace and joy we have found. Ultimately, we may even find the courage to surrender our lives for God as the Apostles and Missionaries of Charity did for their faith.

© Mauricio Graiki / Shutterstock.com

Faith in God is like falling love. It can be scary to have our whole lives change. but when we surrender our fears, much like these skydivers, we will find peace and joy!

---

faith ➤ In general, the belief in the existence of God. For Christians, the gift of God by which one freely accepts his full Revelation in Jesus Christ. It is a matter of both the head (acceptance of Church teaching regarding the Revelation of God) and the heart (love of God and neighbor as a response to God's first loving us); also, one of the three Theological Virtues.

Because faith is ultimately a relationship with God, here are some daily ideas for helping build that relationship:

- Pray in the morning while you brush your teeth.
- Dedicate your schoolwork to God.
- Show your faith through your kindness to other people.
- Tell others about your faith.
- Use an app that helps you read the Bible daily.
- At bedtime, reflect on ways you saw God working in your life that day.

There are so many ways to get to know God better. What other ideas do you have?

Expressing Our Faith

You may hear people say, "I have faith, but I don't do religion." Unfortunately, they have made a wrong assumption that the two things can be split. Although they are different from each other, true faith is intimately connected with authentic religious practice. In faith, we accept God's Revelation; we have a willingness to believe and trust in what God has communicated to us. Religion is the set of beliefs and practices followed by people committed to the service and worship of God. We commit to our faith as individuals and then express our faith together in our religious beliefs and practices. Expressing our faith in community involves prayer, worship, and service—in other words, religious practices.

Faith and religion are so closely connected that we cannot truly have one without the other. If we try to sustain our faith without expressing it through religion, it will eventually lose its power in our life and fade away. True faith is always nurtured and sustained by our participation in a religion, by being part of a community of faith. On the other hand, if we participate in religious practices without having real faith, religion loses its power to transform our life. Our religion becomes an empty ritual, a meaningless collection of words, gestures, and actions.

Worship and Adoration

When the triune God is the focus of our faith, it is impossible to overlook the importance of the religious practices of worship and adoration. When Jesus was confronted and tempted by the Devil in the desert, he quoted the Book of Deuteronomy: "You shall worship the Lord, your God, / and him alone shall you serve" (Luke 4:8). Worship of God is a key component of religion; without it, we cannot say we are truly practicing our faith. Because God, the Father, Son, and Holy Spirit, is the Source of all that we are, worship of God is our duty. In religious worship, we acknowledge our utter dependence on God and offer grateful thanks for all God's works. It is through worship that we give back to God all that we, as his creation, owe him. As Catholics, our most powerful way of worshipping God is through the celebration of the Mass.

In **adoration**, we lift our mind toward God and celebrate his endless mercy and love. Through both private and communal prayer, we praise the One whose goodness and mercy holds us in life, recalling that every blessing we enjoy is a gracious gift from our kind and gentle God. When we truly adore God, we acknowledge him as our Savior and as the Creator of all that we know and will ever know.

© Thoom / Shutterstock.com

Service and Sacrifice

Though participating in the Mass is the source and summit of our faith lives, it often seems that getting up to go to church is even harder than getting up to be on time for school! Just like we know that if we hit the gym or choose a salad over fries we will feel better, it can take

The consecrated host is placed in a monstrance during Eucharistic adoration. How do you express your grateful appreciation for God and God's gifts?

adoration ➤ The prayerful acknowledgment that God is God and creator of all that is.

all of our willpower to get off the couch or make ourselves a healthy lunch. Our relationship with God also needs attention in order to be healthy. We cannot expect to have a deep, intimate relationship with God while putting the Eucharist, prayer, and service low on our priority list. We have to make God a priority and be present with our entire selves.

What exactly does it mean to be "present with our entire selves"? It means that it isn't enough just to put our body in the pew on Sundays. We have to live out our faith by loving and serving our neighbors. It isn't enough to pray for the poor and needy. Our faith requires us to seek out physical ways to be in service to them.

Think of the three *T*'s: time, talent, and treasure. Think of how you spend your time. Do you volunteer? Do you spend time with those who are less fortunate? Are you willing to listen to someone who is sad or lonely? Do you carve more than an hour out of your week to be present to those who are needy? Giving of your time is part of what it means to "be the face of Christ" for others.

What are your talents? Can you tutor someone who needs help in a specific subject area? Can you cook, clean, or mend? Are you handy at repairing things? Could you sing or play an instrument to perform at a nursing home or be part of the choir at your parish? Could you drive someone to the store or pharmacy? Could you shop for someone who is sick or housebound? Could you give a manicure or a shampoo to someone who has debilitating arthritis? Think outside the box about how to use your talents to serve others!

The last *T* is a challenge for many teens because your funds are limited. However, you could always set aside a small portion of your babysitting or tutoring money to donate to a charity. You can save a small percentage of monetary gifts to give in the collection. Maybe you could even have a garage sale and donate the profits to an organization that helps a crisis pregnancy center or a sports program for youth who are underprivileged.

In sacrificing our time, money, or other resources for the good of others, we unite ourselves more fully with the sacrifice Christ offered on the cross and make our whole lives a sacrifice to God. ✳

HMMMMM. . . Why is participating in a religious community essential to increasing our faith?

1. How does faith in Christ help us to make choices that are right and just?

2. Why do we need both faith and religion in order to grow a deep and intimate relationship with God?

3. What makes Paul's Letters different from ordinary letters?

4. What is the Magisterium and what is its role in the Catholic Church?

5. What role does the Galatians' initial conversion experience play in Paul's attempts to help them make a U-turn?

6. According to the Letter to the Ephesians, what two ways are believers a sign of unity?

7. How does Paul make a living? Why is that job particularly useful in Corinth?

8. In First Corinthians, what does Paul say about Christians eating meat that has been sacrificed to idols?

Faith Rooted in Christ

As Catholics, our faith is rooted in both Scripture and Tradition.

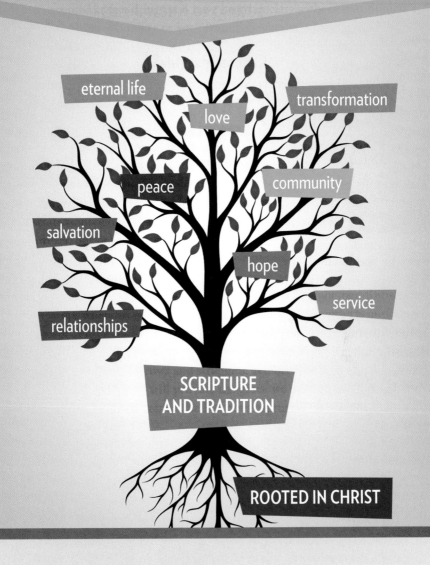

eternal life

love

transformation

peace

community

salvation

hope

service

relationships

SCRIPTURE AND TRADITION

ROOTED IN CHRIST

1. Why are both Scripture and Tradition important to fully developing our faith?

2. What are some other words you would use to describe what faith in Christ produces in us?

UNIT 1

UNIT 1 HIGHLIGHTS

CHAPTER 1 Getting to Know Jesus

Chapter Main Idea

We can come to know the person of Jesus through his life and teachings as presented in the Gospels.

Detail

If we understand the culture and daily life of the people during Jesus' life, we can better understand the things he said and did.

Detail

Jesus experienced joy, rejection, hunger, temptation, and compassion.

Detail

The Gospel of Mark shows Jesus as a messiah who must suffer, die, and be raised for our salvation.

Suffering and Resurrection

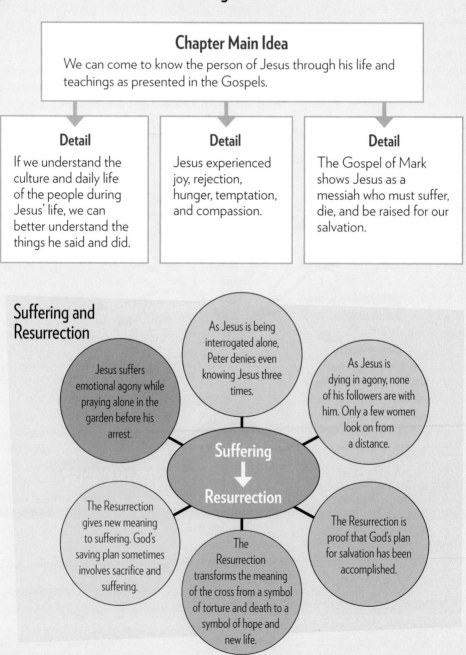

As Jesus is being interrogated alone, Peter denies even knowing Jesus three times.

Jesus suffers emotional agony while praying alone in the garden before his arrest.

As Jesus is dying in agony, none of his followers are with him. Only a few women look on from a distance.

Suffering → Resurrection

The Resurrection gives new meaning to suffering. God's saving plan sometimes involves sacrifice and suffering.

The Resurrection transforms the meaning of the cross from a symbol of torture and death to a symbol of hope and new life.

The Resurrection is proof that God's plan for salvation has been accomplished.

CHAPTER 2   Jesus Revealed

Scripture, Tradition, and the Magisterium

Scripture

- Scripture comes from God.
- Scripture is inseparable from Tradition.
- Scripture and Tradition work together to hand down the Gospel.

Tradition

- Scripture and Tradition are both ways of transmitting God's Divine Revelation.
- Scripture and Tradition help to maintain the purity of the Gospel message.
- Interpretation of Scripture must not go against Tradition, and Tradition must not contradict what is found in Scripture.

Magisterium

- Christ gives a mission to the Apostles to make disciples and share the Good News.
- The message is passed on to each new generation of bishops, under the guidance of the Holy Spirit.
- The Pope and all the bishops of the Church, called the Magisterium, are the modern-day successors of the Apostles, who protect and share Divine Revelation.

Stages of Gospel Formation

Step 1
The Life and Teaching of Jesus

Step 2
Oral Tradition

Step 3
Written Tradition

CHAPTER 2 Jesus Revealed

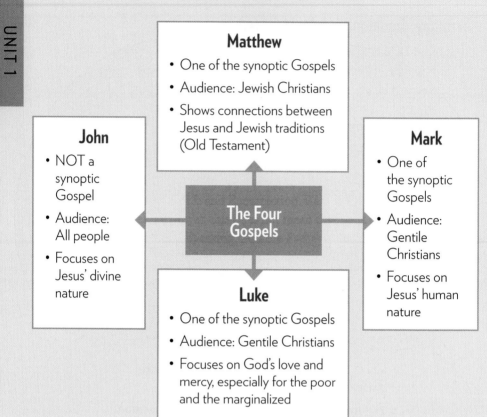

Matthew
- One of the synoptic Gospels
- Audience: Jewish Christians
- Shows connections between Jesus and Jewish traditions (Old Testament)

John
- NOT a synoptic Gospel
- Audience: All people
- Focuses on Jesus' divine nature

The Four Gospels

Mark
- One of the synoptic Gospels
- Audience: Gentile Christians
- Focuses on Jesus' human nature

Luke
- One of the synoptic Gospels
- Audience: Gentile Christians
- Focuses on God's love and mercy, especially for the poor and the marginalized

CHAPTER 3 The Two Natures of Jesus

Jesus Christ: One Divine Person, Two Natures

Examples of Human Nature	Examples of Divine Nature	Incarnation	Why It Makes a Difference
• Jesus has a physical, human body. • Jesus thinks with a human mind. • Jesus has close friends and family members.	• Jesus speaks to the crowd and says, "The Father and I are one" (John 10:30). • Jesus uses his divine foreknowledge. • Jesus knows Judas will betray him. • God the Father declares Jesus as his son.	• The Incarnation, or hypostatic union, describes the union of Jesus Christ's divine and human natures in one Divine Person. • Jesus Christ becomes truly man while remaining truly God.	• We come to know Jesus' divinity through his humanity. Jesus' emotions, friendships, values, and priorities reveal God to us in a unique and powerful way.

CHAPTER 4   It Comes Down to Faith

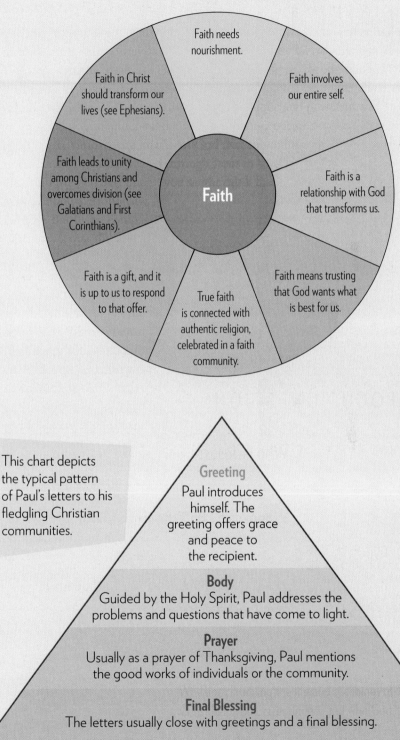

Faith

Faith needs nourishment.

Faith in Christ should transform our lives (see Ephesians).

Faith involves our entire self.

Faith leads to unity among Christians and overcomes division (see Galatians and First Corinthians).

Faith is a relationship with God that transforms us.

Faith is a gift, and it is up to us to respond to that offer.

True faith is connected with authentic religion, celebrated in a faith community.

Faith means trusting that God wants what is best for us.

This chart depicts the typical pattern of Paul's letters to his fledgling Christian communities.

Greeting
Paul introduces himself. The greeting offers grace and peace to the recipient.

Body
Guided by the Holy Spirit, Paul addresses the problems and questions that have come to light.

Prayer
Usually as a prayer of Thanksgiving, Paul mentions the good works of individuals or the community.

Final Blessing
The letters usually close with greetings and a final blessing.

UNIT 1

BRING IT HOME

WHAT DOES IT MEAN TO HAVE FAITH IN JESUS?

FOCUS QUESTIONS

CHAPTER 1   Who is Jesus?

CHAPTER 2   Where can I find the truth about Jesus?

CHAPTER 3   What does it mean to say that Jesus is true God and true man?

CHAPTER 4   Why put my faith in Jesus?

VIVA
Cotter High School

Faith in Jesus is also about how we see Jesus in our daily lives and recognizing when we need to draw on our faith to support us as we are faced with difficulties. It can get difficult for me to constantly look at the suffering and death in the world and still see God's love for everyone, but my faith comes from the good I see in the world and in other people.

REFLECT

Take some time to read and reflect on the unit and chapter focus questions listed on the facing page.

- What question or section did you identify most closely with?

- What did you find within the unit that was comforting or challenging?

UNIT 2
Exploring Jesus' Divinity

WAS JESUS CHRIST REALLY DIVINE?

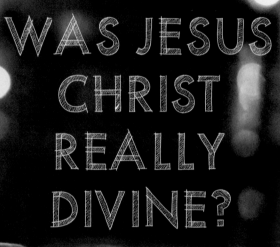

LOOKING AHEAD

UNIT 2

When I hear the word *divine*, I think of something that is completely and totally pure and beautiful. I believe that Jesus is fully divine, but I do understand that not everyone feels this way, and I know that I shouldn't push it on anyone. This was one hard thing about going from a completely Catholic school to a school where the students have mixed and diverse religious backgrounds.

CASEY
Mater Dei High School

CHAPTER 5
The Gospel of John:
The Book of Signs

WHO IS JESUS, REALLY?

SNAPSHOT

Article 20

The Gospel of John: Not a Synoptic

Have you ever come home from school and found a plate of freshly baked cookies on the counter? You can hear your stomach grumble, so you grab a handful and take them to your room. Oh! Chocolate chip, your favorite! As you throw down your backpack and check your messages, you eat those cookies without really thinking. Now there is only one left, and as you put it in your mouth, something totally unexpected happens. You have a mouthful of oatmeal raisin cookie. How did this happen? It looked just like all the others. It smelled like the others. But it is definitely not the same.

All of the Gospels complement one another, and all four are true accounts of the life of Jesus Christ. In essence, at a glance, they all "look" the same, just like the cookies. Yet John's Gospel is quite different from Matthew, Mark, and Luke. It is still a Gospel, but it is as different from the synoptic Gospels as oatmeal raisin cookies are from chocolate chip cookies. So as we dig in to the Gospel of John, let's consider two important questions: What makes John's Gospel so different from the other three? Why is it different?

Like an oatmeal cookie is different from a chocolate chip cookie, but both are still cookies, so the Gospel of John is different from Matthew, Mark, and Luke, but all four are still Gospels..

One of These Books Is Not Like the Others!

You may have noticed three important differences as you read the first eleven chapters of John's Gospel. First, John portrays Jesus' divinity far more prominently than the synoptic Gospels do. From the beginning, John describes Jesus as "the Word became flesh" (1:14). John refers to Jesus with divine titles, such as Lamb of God, Son of God, and Savior.

UNIT 2

UNIT 2

Second, the Gospel of John is structured differently from the synoptic Gospels. John is essentially divided into two halves. The first half is called the Book of Signs and focuses on seven miracles (the synoptic Gospels contain many more), using them as signs to point to Jesus' divinity. The second half focuses on Jesus' Passion, death, and Resurrection. The second half of John is called the Book of Glory (more on this in chapter 6), and it starts with Jesus washing the disciples' feet and then delivering several long talks at the Last Supper. These events are not included in the synoptic Gospels. Jesus also begins the events of his last days with a confidence and control not seen in Matthew, Mark, and Luke.

Third, the Gospel of John uses Greek philosophical categories and terms to help describe Jesus' identity more fully. These categories and terms are not used in the other three Gospels. These three elements—the focus on the divine nature of Jesus, the unique structure, and the influence of Greek language and philosophy—are important differences between John and the synoptic Gospels.

Why does the author of John give us this bold depiction of Jesus with his language of signs, wonders, and "God-like" statements? Let's remember that when we interpret Scripture, we need to consider what the human author was communicating, and what God wants to reveal through the human author's words. To understand what the human author is addressing, let's look at the historical and cultural situation at the time the Gospel was written.

TAKE IT TO GOD

Jesus,

We call you Lord and Messiah.

We call you Beloved Son and Logos.

We call you the Second Person of the Blessed Trinity.

We call you Savior and Redeemer.

Jesus, even when I find these names for you hard to understand,

  help me to remember that you ultimately want me

    to have a relationship with you,

    to call you friend.

I want to build that relationship.

I want to turn all my cares over to you.

I want to be called a Christian.

Amen.

Timing Is Everything

The author of John most likely wrote his Gospel ten to thirty years after Matthew, Mark, and Luke were written, between AD 90 and AD 100. The author probably knew these Gospels and did not need to create another Gospel like them. He had a different reality to address.

The author of John lived when there may have been a growing tension between the Jews who believed that Jesus was the Messiah and the Jews who did not believe Jesus was the Messiah. For Jewish Christians, this would mean strained relationships with friends, relatives, and the religion they had grown up with. It is easy to see why some of these believers might waver in their faith. The author of the Gospel of John wanted to assure them that their belief in Jesus as the Divine Messiah, the Son of God, was accurate and justified.

John's Names for Jesus

The Gospel opens with a section of eighteen verses called the Prologue. Over the course of the Prologue, the Son of God is slowly revealed using different titles. It is here that John first refers to Jesus as the Word. We learn that the Word (*logos* in Greek) is uncreated and existed with God prior to all creation. We learn that the Word played a role in creation: "All things came to be through him, / and without him nothing came to be" (1:3). We also learn that the "Word was God" (1:1).

The Gospel of John was most likely written between AD 90 and AD 100.

UNIT 2

The Prologue then uses a different title to describe Jesus: the light. What does it mean to call Jesus the light? It means that he illuminates and reveals his divine plan. Not everyone will accept Jesus (the light), but the message conveyed through Jesus will prevail. "The light shines in the darkness / and the darkness has not overcome it" (1:5). This is the first hint that not everyone will accept Jesus as the Messiah, the Second Person of the Trinity.

At the very beginning of the Gospel, the author of John reveals how the eternal Word of God broke into history by becoming flesh (see 1:14), the great mystery called the Incarnation. Before we learn anything about Jesus' earthly ministry, the Gospel has already revealed Jesus Christ's divine identity as the Son of God. He is the fulfillment of God's promise to Adam and Eve and the people of ancient Israel. John tells us that it is Jesus' role to reveal his Father to the world. Who better to tell us about the Father than the Divine Son, come down from Heaven, who has been with the Father for all eternity? ✳

OVERVIEW of the Gospel of John

- **Intended audience:** A community initially composed of Jewish Christians who had been expelled from the synagogues and who are also familiar with Greek culture.

- **Theme:** John focuses on the divinity of Jesus, the Divine Son of God, who reveals God the Father and fulfills his Father's saving plan.

- **Reason for writing:** To strengthen the faith of early Christians by giving proof that Jesus is the Son of God come down from Heaven.

HMMMMMM. . . Why is it important that the Gospel of John is different from the other three Gospels?

Article 21

The Gospel of John: The Book of Signs

When we think of Jesus, we often think of his many miracles. We are amazed by his power over nature: walking on water and multiplying loaves and fish. The author of John calls us to think about these events from a different perspective. It is not so much about the miracles themselves as it is about the One who performed them. To emphasize this, the Gospel refers to them not as miracles but as signs. These signs point to the true identity of Jesus. To put it simply, since only God can perform miracles, Jesus is God.

This is why the first half of the Gospel of John is called the Book of Signs. In these chapters, the author of John tells us about Christ's public ministry and the seven signs that reveal Christ's true identity as the Divine Son of God. With each sign, Jesus gives a speech reflecting on his role in the plan for our salvation.

UNIT 2

CATHOLICS **MAKING** A DIFFERENCE

© UrCon Collection / Alamy Stock Photo

Saint Oscar Romero, pictured here with Pope Paul VI, broke social barriers to spread the Good News. He was not a controversial person when he was first appointed as Archbishop of San Salvador. This soon changed. After spending time with the people in his archdiocese, he realized how much they were suffering from government-supported violence and oppression. After a Jesuit priest and friend of his was assassinated, Archbishop Romero began to speak out against the poverty, torture, and killings; condemning the unjust treatment of the citizens by the government. His humanitarian efforts gained international recognition, making him an embarrassment to the government. Archbishop Romero was executed while celebrating Mass on March 24, 1980, most likely by a government-supported group. He is an example of how one person can bring about change by choosing to stand up for their beliefs.

Jesus' "Hour": His Mission Is Put in Motion

The first sign in the Gospel of John is Jesus turning water into wine at the wedding feast at Cana. Recall from John, chapter 2, that Jesus and his mother are attending a wedding feast. At that time, the celebration of a marriage could go on for several days! Imagine the stress of the wedding couple as they run out of wine at their wedding feast. It would be an embarrassing and quick end to the celebration. As Mary turns to Jesus for a solution, he makes an interesting comment: "My hour has not yet come" (John 2:4). What is this "hour" Jesus is talking about? It is not a 60-minute period of time; rather, Jesus is using symbolic language to refer to the time his mission is accomplished. Jesus isn't saying that he doesn't want to help the newly married couple, but he knows that by revealing his power, the journey to his hour will be in motion. Yet he does as his mother requests, accepting that the plan has been put in motion.

Later in the Gospel, Jesus relates his hour to Moses lifting the serpent on the staff in the desert. In the Book of Numbers, when the Israelites were being bitten by serpents while wandering in the desert, God tells Moses to put a serpent on the top of his staff. All who are bitten are to look upon the serpent and be healed (see 21:4–9). Similarly, Jesus' elevation on the cross is when all humanity will look upon him and be saved (see John 3:14–15). Throughout the Gospel, we see a building toward the hour of his Crucifixion and Resurrection. With this first sign, turning water into wine, the path toward Jesus' hour is in full motion.

Turning water into wine is the first sign in John's Gospel.

© Lanmas / Alamy Stock Photo

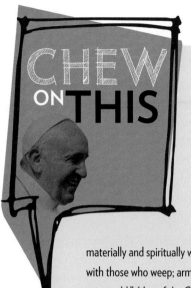

Pope Francis reminds us that Jesus' sacrifice on the cross represents the way he lived his entire life:

Jesus' sacrifice on the cross is nothing less than the culmination of the way he lived his entire life. Moved by his example, we want to enter fully into the fabric of society, sharing the lives of all, listening to their concerns, helping them materially and spiritually with their needs, rejoicing when they rejoice, weeping with those who weep; arm in arm with others, we are committed to building a new world." (*Joy of the Gospel [Evangelii Gaudium],* 2013, number 269)

UNIT 2

In the Dark

Just as signs point to something beyond themselves that we may not initially understand, John's Gospel contains conversations that involve some confusion. These conversations often lead to clarification of Jesus' identity. Have you ever had a conversation with a friend, only to realize at some point that you were not talking about the same thing?

We see a similar confusion at times in the Gospel of John. Jesus is speaking about spiritual realities while the person he is speaking to is talking about earthly realities. Sometimes the other person catches on to Jesus' meaning and even Jesus' true identity, but sometimes not. Jesus' conversation with a Pharisee named Nicodemus shows this type of misunderstanding.

The author of John sets the scene by pointing out that the conversation takes place at night (see 3:2). This light versus dark theme introduced in the Prologue appears again and again throughout the Gospel. When people come to Jesus at night, or in darkness, it is John's way of saying that they do not understand. In particular, they do not understand Jesus' true identity. Because Nicodemus's conversation with Jesus happens at night, we know that Nicodemus comes with a lack of understanding.

As the conversation evolves, it is clear that Nicodemus is confused about being "born again" because he is thinking in earthly realities. He even asks how to return to a mother's womb. However, Jesus is speaking in spiritual terms about being born again. This rebirth involves a belief in the identity and words of the One Sent by God. John does not tell us how Nicodemus responds to the conversation, but Nicodemus does appear later in the Gospel. When the Pharisees are seeking to kill Jesus, it is Nicodemus who pushes for a fair hearing (see John 7:50). Then after Jesus' death, Nicodemus brings an extravagant amount of myrrh to help bury Jesus (see 19:39). It seems in the end that Nicodemus may have understood Jesus' true identity.

Breaking Social Barriers

Jesus' discussion with the Samaritan woman at the well in John, chapter 4, also shows us a person slowly coming to understand Jesus' true identity. Over the course of the encounter, the Samaritan woman goes from not knowing who Jesus is at all to telling others about him and bringing them to faith in Jesus. One way John shows her growth in understanding is through the names and titles she uses for Jesus.

First, the woman calls Jesus a Jew (see John 4:9), pointing out how her race, the Samaritans, and the Jews do not get along. Next, she calls him Sir (see 4:11), which shows her first sign of respect for Jesus. After Jesus reveals his knowledge of her marriage issues, she calls him a prophet (see 4:19). She is getting closer to his true identity, but she is still not quite there. Finally, she mentions the coming of the Messiah. Jesus tells her that she is speaking with him (see 4:25–26). She finally understands his identity and rushes to tell others about him.

© jorisvo / Shutterstock.com

In what way does Jesus break social barriers by talking to the Samaritan woman at the well?

The turning point in their conversation comes when Jesus asks the Samaritan woman for a drink of water. It is here that the author of the Gospel of John helps us to recall the promise of our Baptism and to open the eyes of the Samaritan woman at the same time. Jesus says, "If you knew the gift of God and who is saying to you, 'Give me a drink,' you would have asked him and he would have given you living water" (4:10). Even though she is confused, she tells Jesus she wants this living water. Jesus reveals that our Baptism not only begins our faith journey but also washes away the sins of the past. The woman hears the rewards that Jesus offers, and she desires to share in them.

This conversation also teaches us about Jesus' willingness to go against social expectations. To interpret this properly, we need to consider the ways people spoke and acted at the time. In first-century Israel, men did not talk to women, especially strangers, in public places. Further, Jews did not associate with Samaritans. So Jesus was breaking several societal rules by talking publicly with this woman. But talk to her he does! Even his disciples are amazed (and probably shocked!) to return and find him speaking to her. John reminds us that we are called to share God's love and mercy with all people, even those on the margins of society and shunned by others. ✳

UNIT 2

HMMMMM. . . . What are the ways the Gospel of John points to Jesus' divinity? Which of these ways do you find most convincing?

Article 22

Revealing Jesus' Divine Nature

In addition to turning water into wine during the wedding feast, Jesus performs six other signs in the Book of Signs. Each sign, in its own way, reveals that Jesus is the Divine Son of God, the Messiah.

Sign	Location in the Gospel
Wedding at Cana	John 2:1–12
Cure of Royal Official's Son	John 4:46–54
Cure of Man at Pool of Bethesda	John 5:1–18
Multiplication of Loaves	John 6:1–15
Walking on the Water	John 6:16–21
Cure of the Man Born Blind	John 9:1–41
Raising of Lazarus	John 11:1–44

MAKE IT SO

Despite the threat of opposition and rejection, Jesus boldly continues to reveal his true identity through the use of his miraculous abilities. As followers of Jesus, we too are called to be bold in following God's call. God has given each of us unique gifts and talents to use and share with others. So, if you are a good singer, don't be shy about singing out loud. If you love drawing, don't be afraid to share your work with your friends. If you are a good writer, don't hide your papers when others want to read your stories. What gifts are you hiding that God is calling you to boldly share with the world?

Some of the signs show Jesus' divine identity by calling to mind God's works in the Old Testament. For example, consider the cure of the royal official's son. Recall that in Genesis, God the Father creates the universe by merely speaking (see chapter 1). In John, Jesus shows himself equal to the Father by curing the royal official's son without even seeing the boy. Jesus simply speaks the words, "Your son will live" (4:50). When Jesus walks on the sea while the disciples are in the boat battling a storm (see 6:16–24), it calls to mind Psalm 77.

> The waters saw you, God;
>> the waters saw you and lashed about,
>> even the deeps of the sea trembled.
> The clouds poured down their rains;
>> the thunderheads rumbled;
>> your arrows flashed back and forth. . . .
> Through the sea was your way;
>> your path, through the mighty waters,
>> though your footsteps were unseen.
>> (Psalm 77:17–18,20)

The most powerful sign of Jesus' divine nature is when Jesus raises his friend Lazarus from the dead (see John 11:1–54). Mary and Martha send for Jesus, pleading, "Master, the one you love is ill" (verse 3). They trust that Jesus will come for the sake of their brother, whom he loves. When Jesus hears their message, he says: "This illness is not to end in death, but is for the glory of God, that the Son may be glorified through it" (verse 4). The raising of Lazarus reveals the power of the Son of God over life and death, a power only God possesses.

The most powerful sign of Jesus' divine nature in John's Gospel is the raising of Lazarus.

UNIT 2

As Jesus prepares to set out to Bethany, his disciples are highly aware that returning to this area will put Jesus in harm's way. Earlier, his Jewish opponents had tried to have him stoned there (see John 11:8). The Jewish leaders see Jesus' rising popularity as a threat to their security and power. After word gets back to the Pharisees that Jesus has raised Lazarus from the dead, they call a meeting of the **Sanhedrin**. They plot to kill Jesus, bringing his hour ever closer. Ironically, this final miracle not only points dramatically toward Jesus, divinity but also leads to his death on the cross.

The Hour Arrives

The Book of Signs closes with the arrival of Jesus' hour at the end of chapter 12. The Pharisees, seeing the crowd welcoming Jesus, complain: "Look, the whole world has gone after him" (verse 19). Then a group of Greeks, who are not Jews, approach Philip, one of the disciples. They ask to see Jesus. When Philip tells Jesus of their request, Jesus make a profound statement, "The hour has come for the Son of Man to be glorified" (verse 23).

These Greeks symbolically represent that the whole world, Jews and Gentiles alike, are now seeking out Jesus Christ, the Word of God. It is time for Christ's glorious hour, when he is lifted upon the cross, drawing all people to himself. ✳

HMMMMM. . . Explain how Jesus' miracles are also signs.

Sanhedrin ➤ The highest council of the ancient Jews, consisting of seventy-one members exercising authority in religious matters.

Article 23

The Power of "I AM"

A young woman was on a date at a restaurant when her date started to berate her and even threaten her. She was visibly upset, and some people at nearby tables were wondering if they should step in. An older man walked over and sat down at the table with them. A few minutes later, the abusive young man, noticeably subdued, got up, paid for their meal, and quietly left the restaurant. Later someone asked the older man, "What did you say to him?" The older man smiled and said, "I told them I was an off-duty cop, showed him my badge, and asked if I needed to call my partners on duty."

Words have power. Late in the Gospel of John, Jesus utters two words, and men with swords immediately fall to the ground (see 18:4–6). What two words had such power for Jesus? "I AM." Jesus uses this phrase many times in the Gospel of John, and only in the Gospel of John. Each time, it points us toward his divinity and teaches us something about who Jesus is and what he does. We call these the "I AM" statements.

"I AM" Statements	Location in the Gospel of John
"I am the bread of life; whoever comes to me will never hunger, and whoever believes in me will never thirst."	John 6:35
"I am the light of the world. Whoever follows me will not walk in darkness, but will have the light of life."	John 8:12
"Amen, Amen, I say to you, before Abraham came to be, I AM."	John 8:58
"I am the gate. Whoever enters through me will be saved, and will come in and go out and find pasture."	John 10:9
"I am the good shepherd. A good shepherd lays down his life for the sheep."	John 10:11
"I am the resurrection and the life; whoever believes in me, even if he dies, will live."	John 11:25,26
"I am the way and the truth and the life. No one comes to the Father except through me."	John 14:6
"I am the vine, you are the branches."	John 15:5

UNIT 2

Back to the Burning Bush

To understand why these statements are so powerful, we first must recall the account of Moses and the burning bush from Exodus 2:23–4:9. In this story, God calls Moses to go to **Pharaoh** and insist that Pharaoh let the Israelites go free. Moses is reluctant and asks God several questions. One of his questions is what he should tell the Israelites when they ask about God's name. God answers Moses: "I am who I am. Then he added: This is what you tell the Israelites: I AM has sent me to you" (Exodus 3:14). "I AM" is pronounced "*Yahweh*" in Hebrew.

This mysterious name seems to have several meanings. It points to God as the origin and source of all things. It also implies that God is present through all of creation. By revealing his sacred name to Moses, God gives us insight into his nature as well as opening the door to a deeper relationship with us. We must keep this account in mind as we read the Gospel of John and hear Jesus say the words, "I AM." By using the same words that God spoke to Moses, the author of John is clearly implying Jesus' divine nature.

God identifies himself to Moses by saying, "I am who I am." In the Gospel of John, Jesus uses this same phrase to identify himself, "I AM."

pharaoh ➤ A ruler in ancient Egypt.

UNIT 2

I DIDN'T KNOW THAT!

Can you imagine seeing sheep grazing on the White House lawn? During World War I, President Woodrow Wilson actually kept over forty sheep at the White House. At a time when all Americans were being asked to make personal sacrifices to help support the troops, these sheep became a sign of everyone doing their part. The President raised over fifty thousand dollars for the Red Cross by auctioning off the sheep's wool. Additionally, he saved money and manpower on grass cutting. The president literally became a shepherd to help lead the people of this country.

UNIT 2

Jesus Is the Source of Life and Wisdom

The first instance of Jesus using an "I AM" statement reveals Jesus' abiding presence and his spiritual support for those who believe in him. After Jesus feeds a large group by multiplying a few loaves and fish at the beginning of John, chapter 6, the crowds seek Jesus out the next day (see verses 1–24). In what is called the Bread of Life Discourse (see verses 22–59), Jesus offers them not ordinary bread, but the bread of eternal life. They ask for this bread and Jesus states, "I am the bread of life; whoever comes to me will never hunger and whoever believes in me will never thirst" (6:35). From this statement, we learn that Jesus is the one who spiritually nourishes and sustains us. As the discourse continues, we learn that Jesus is speaking not of bread but of his own flesh and blood, the Eucharist.

The next "I AM" statement shows John's flair for the dramatic. Imagine the joyful atmosphere of the annual Feast of Tabernacles celebrated at the Temple. During this fall festival, Jews from all around would gather in Jerusalem at the Temple to celebrate the end of the harvest, thanking God for the rains. The celebratory feast included the lighting of huge bowls, which were so big that ladders were required to climb up them to put in the wood and oil. In the evening, these bowls would be lit, and it is said they would light all of Jerusalem. With this dramatic backdrop, Jesus stands up and proclaims: "I am the light of the world. Whoever follows me will not walk in darkness, but will have the light of life" (John 8:12).

In Jewish tradition, the Torah was often referred to as the light, the source of divine wisdom. By calling himself "the light of the world," Jesus presents himself as the new Torah, the divine source of wisdom for humankind. He is calling all people to follow him and walk in his ways.

The Gate and Good Shepherd

As the source of wisdom for humankind, Jesus is often referred to as "the Good Shepherd." What is the significance of Jesus as shepherd? Being a shepherd in the first century was a difficult and dangerous job. Keeping an eye on wandering sheep and protecting them from hungry wolves required constant vigilance and bravery. At night, the shepherd would bring his sheep into a circular pen for safekeeping. The walls of the pen would have small branches sticking out along the top to prevent wolves from jumping over it. The only way in or out of the pen was an opening in the walls about four feet across. On many of these pens, there was no door, so the shepherd would lay across the opening and sleep there, serving as the door. Any sheep wanting out would have to walk on the shepherd, thus waking him. Any animal wanting in to eat the sheep would have to go through the shepherd.

How can the image of Jesus as the Good Shepherd help you to understand the depth of God's love for you?

When we visualize the sheep pen, Jesus' words in John, chapter 10, are all the more powerful. Jesus uses two "I AM" statements when talking about sheep. The first is when he states, "I am the gate" (John 10:9). Jesus is revealing that he is the one to lead them to safety inside the pen, to show people the way leading to salvation. Jesus continues by explaining that he is the one true leader of God's people. Other false prophets have tried to lead God's people astray.

The second "I AM" statement then follows: "I am the good shepherd. A good shepherd lays down his life for the sheep" (John 10:11). This "I AM" statement recalls the many

© Nancy Bauer / Shutterstock.com

times God is referred to as a good shepherd in the Old Testament. For example, consider Psalm 23:1, "The Lord is my shepherd"; Jeremiah chapter 23:3, "I myself will gather the remnant of my flock"; and Ezekiel 34:15, "I myself will pasture my sheep." By applying this statement to himself, Jesus is equating himself with the God of the Old Testament. He indicates he is willing to lay down his life for his sheep. This statement becomes a reality on the cross as Jesus willingly offers himself up to save humanity.

Leading Us to the Father and Heaven

In three other "I AM" statements, we learn of Jesus' divine role as the one who leads us to the Father and eternal life. Recall when Jesus is speaking to Martha about Lazarus before raising Lazarus, Jesus says to her, "I am the resurrection and the life" (John 11:25). By bringing Lazarus back to life, Jesus proves his divinity and affirms that he is the one to lead us to eternal life.

In a similar way, Jesus reveals his role in leading us to the Father when he tells the disciples at the Last Supper: "I am the way and the truth and the life. No one comes to the Father except through me" (John 14:6). Jesus later talks about his role in connecting believers with his heavenly Father: "I am the vine, you are the branches" (15:5). Jesus describes his role as the one who unites all believers and enables them to produce good fruit, that is, good works.

Jesus Knocks Them off Their Feet

The Gospel of John's numerous "I AM" statements point us toward Christ's divinity. They give us insight into his role as Son of God, Savior. But it is his final "I AM" statement, as he is surrounded by men ready to arrest him, in which Jesus most clearly echoes God at the burning bush. The men ask if he is Jesus of Nazareth and Jesus responds, "I AM" (John 18:5). The men literally fall to the ground in response to the full revelation that Jesus is God.

If you were to ask Jesus if he truly is God, and he answered, "I AM," how would you react? Would you sit down and catch your breath? Would you fall to the ground? Would you praise God? Would you even be able to speak? Throughout Scripture, Jesus does in fact reveal himself to us. How are you going to respond? ✳

HMMMMM. . . Why are the "I AM" statements of Jesus such powerful signs of his divinity?

1. What are three important differences between the Gospel of John and the synoptic Gospels?

2. Why did the early Christians begin worshipping separately from the Jews who did not believe Jesus was the Messiah?

3. Name one of the titles the author of the Gospel of John uses to describe Jesus in the Prologue, and describe how this title implies that Jesus is God.

4. Why does John call miracles "signs"?

5. What is Jesus referring to when he mentions his hour?

6. What incident causes Jesus to declare that his hour has arrived?

7. What Old Testament occurrence do the "I AM" statements allude to?

8. Name two of Jesus Christ's "I AM" statements in the Gospel of John, and explain how they are related to Christ's Divine Personhood.

Who Is? I AM?

In the Gospel of John, Christ uses variations of the phrase "I AM"
to reveal his equality with God the Father.

UNIT 2

1. Why do you think the author of John uses the "I AM" statements and the other Gospel writers do not?

2. How do these statements help you to better know about Jesus?

CHAPTER 6
The Gospel of John: The Book of Glory

HOW CAN JESUS' DEATH BE GLORIOUS?

SNAPSHOT

Article 24

Jesus' Final Evening with His Disciples

The first followers of Jesus had a marketing problem. It wasn't that Jesus' teachings weren't meaningful or his miracles weren't powerful and moving. No, it was that he died as a criminal. Even the way he died was a problem. Crucifixion was the death sentence for the worst of the worst. It was reserved for people the Romans considered murders, terrorists, and insurrectionists. How do you convince others to put their faith in a person who died a common criminal on a cross?

The author of the Gospel of John tackles this problem head-on. Rather than apologize for the way Jesus died, he makes it the centerpiece of his Gospel account. The Book of Glory (chapters 13–20) is the climactic conclusion of the Gospel. Everything in the Book of Signs has been building up to the Divine Son's glorious "hour," his Passion, death, and Resurrection.

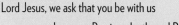

TAKE IT TO GOD

Lord Jesus, we ask that you be with us
   as we explore your Passion, death, and Resurrection.
As you gave the example of humility by washing the disciples' feet,
   help us to always be humble in service of others.
As you stayed true to yourself during the stress of your arrest and trial,
   help us to be true to our calling whenever the stresses of life overwhelm us.
As you transformed the cross from a sign of death to our sign of hope,
   help us to always look upon your cross as a reminder of the great sacrifice
   you made for each one of us.
As you brought peace to those you encountered after your glorious Resurrection,
   help us to seek your presence in our life so we too may live a life pleasing
   our Heavenly Father.
Amen.

Foot Washing

On the eve of his death, Jesus chooses to spend his final hours sharing a meal with his closest friends. You may have noticed that in the Gospel of John this meal is not the Passover meal, as it is in the synoptic Gospels. In John, the Last Supper takes place the evening before the day of **Passover**. The difference in timing will be important when Jesus is on the cross (more on that later). Instead of having Jesus share bread and wine with his disciples during the Last Supper (the institution of the Eucharist), John goes in a completely different direction.

As you read in John, chapter 13, during supper Jesus takes off his outer garment and begins washing the feet of the disciples. Sweaty, stinky, dust covered feet in the first century were as unappealing as you can imagine. Foot washing was work done only by the lowest class of slaves and servants. So, when Peter protests, saying that he will not let Jesus wash his feet, he is reacting as any first-century disciple would have reacted to his master. For the readers of the Gospel, Peter's concern is heightened because we know it

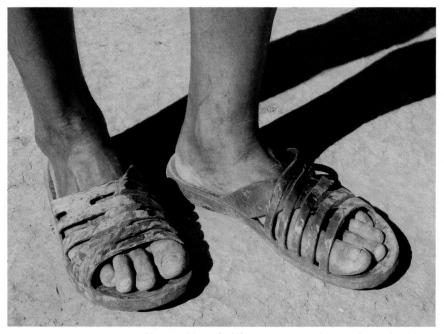

© Denis Pogostin / Shutterstock.com

How would you feel if your parent, teacher, coach, youth minister, or mentor got on his or her knees to wash your feet?

Passover ➤ The night the Lord passed over the houses of the Israelites marked by the blood of the lamb, and spared the firstborn sons from death. It also is the feast that celebrates the deliverance of the Chosen People from bondage in Egypt and the Exodus from Egypt to the Promised Land.

is Jesus Christ, the Divine Son of God, who is humbling himself to wash the disciples' feet. This makes Jesus' actions even more amazing. Imagine God stooping down to wipe the grime off your feet.

The Gospel of John provides a conversation between Jesus and Peter that explains why he washes the disciples' feet (see 13:1–20). First, Jesus makes a symbolic reference to Baptism: "Unless I wash you, you will have no inheritance with me" (verse 8). Jesus' foot washing points to the washing away of our sins through the sacramental graces of Baptism. Then Jesus explains to the disciples that he is giving them an example to follow (see verses 12–16). If Jesus is so humble in his service of others, his followers should do the same. Jesus shows us that honor comes from humility and self-sacrifice.

Jesus' humble, loving act of faithful service is contrasted with Judas's lack of faith. We learn that Jesus knows that Judas will betray him and still allows the plan to continue—a sign that Jesus has complete trust in his Father's plan, even as events are leading to his death. As you recall, the Prologue introduces us to the battle between light and darkness. It is no surprise that when Judas leaves supper to betray Jesus, John tells us, "And it was night" (John 13:30).

UNIT 2

CATHOLICS MAKING A DIFFERENCE

As a gesture of service toward marginalized communities, Pope Francis humbled himself to wash the feet of twelve prison inmates at the Holy Thursday Mass on April 13, 2017. The inmates included three women and nine men, one of whom was converting from Islam to Catholicism. Pope Francis reiterated the sentiments of Jesus, saying: "He (Jesus) came into the world to serve us. He came to make himself a slave for us, to give his life for us and to love us to the end." He added: "The Pope is merely the image of Jesus, and I want to do the same as he did. In this ceremony, the pastor washes the feet of the faithful. The one who seems to be the greatest must do the work of a slave."

Final Thoughts for the Disciples and a Prayer

The next three chapters of John, 14–16, are called the "Last Supper **Discourses**." They are long speeches given by Jesus to his disciples. In these speeches, Jesus makes several points unique to John's Gospel. He reiterates his unique oneness with the Father (**consubstantial** with the Father in Church language) and talks about returning to the Father to prepare a place for those who believe in him (see 14:2–3). He encourages the disciples to do and say what he has done and said while with them (see verses 12–14). Jesus also tells them he is sending the Advocate, or Holy Spirit (see verses 16–20). Jesus does not want to leave them on their own, so the Holy Spirit will be there to teach and guide them.

© Adam Jan Figel / Shutterstock.com

Finally, Jesus notes that the world did not receive him, so the disciples should not expect the world to receive them. (Keep in mind that the author of John uses sharp contrasts to make his points, so when he says the "world" he doesn't literally mean everyone in the world.) Opposition to Jesus' message is to be expected. In the face of this opposition, Jesus promises that if the disciples ask his Father for something in Jesus' name, the Father will grant it to them (see John 15:18–27). We still act on this today when we say, "In Jesus' name we pray." At the end of these

In the Gospel of John, Jesus gives several long speeches to the disciples. They are called the Last Supper Discourses.

---

discourse ➤ An authoritative speech or presentation.

consubstantial ➤ Having the same nature or essence.

speeches, the disciples finally declare, "We believe that you came from God" (16:30). Jesus warns that their faith will be tested and they will soon be scattered (see verse 32).

The Last Supper closes with Jesus praying, which reminds us of what has taken place thus far in the Gospel:

> He raised his eyes to heaven and said, "Father, the hour has come. Give glory to your son, so that your son may glorify you, just as you gave him authority over all people, so that he may give eternal life to all you gave him. Now this is eternal life that they shall know you, the only true God, and the one you sent, Jesus Christ. I glorified you on earth by accomplishing the work you gave me to do. Now glorify me, Father, with you, with the glory that I had with you before the world began. (John 17:1-5)

There are echoes of the Prologue throughout the prayer as Jesus asks the Father to glorify him since he has done what he was sent to do. He has revealed God to the world. Jesus prays for the disciples, asking the Father keep them safe. Jesus even prays for those who will come to believe in him as a result of the disciples preaching the Good News. This means that at the Last Supper Jesus was praying for us too! ✳

HMMMMM. . . Through his words and actions at the Last Supper, what does Jesus teach us about being a disciple?

Article 25

Jesus' Suffering and Death Reveal His Divine Dignity

Imagine wearing a replica of an electric chair or hangman's noose on a necklace as a sign of your religion. Well, that's essentially what we do when we wear a cross, because crosses were the means used to execute criminals at the time of Christ. However, we wear them with reverence because God's Revelation, especially in the Gospel of John, helps us to see the cross as a sign of Christ's victory over sin and death.

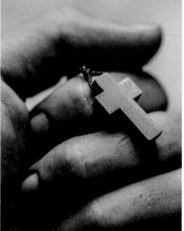

© ChristianChan / iStockphoto.com

In John, chapters 18 and 19, the identity of Jesus Christ as the One sent by the Father, and the choice each person must make to either accept or reject him, comes into full focus. The cosmic battle between light and darkness first spelled out in the Prologue comes to completion with Jesus' death on the cross and his Resurrection. John refers to Jesus as the Lamb of God, and his sacrificial death is necessary for God's triumph over sin and death.

The author of John continues to emphasize Jesus' divine nature by portraying Christ in control of every event and encounter—even in his Passion and death.

Do you have a piece of jewelry with a cross? What does it represent to you?

He is allowing—even directing—things to happen according to the Father's plan. Here are some examples:

- Judas does not leave in secret to betray Jesus; Jesus sends him out (see 13:27).
- At Jesus' arrest, the soldiers and guards don't make demands; Jesus goes out to them and asks them who they are looking for (see 18:4).
- Jesus orders the soldiers to let his disciples go free, and they do (see 18:8–9).
- When brought before Pilate, Jesus interrogates Pilate and lectures him on the truth; Pilate even finds Jesus innocent (see 18:33–38).
- On the cross, Jesus continues to give directions to his disciples (see 19:26–27) and purposely speaks so the Scriptures are fulfilled (see verse 28). He decides the moment of his death and hands over his spirit—it is not taken from him (see verse 30).

Let's look at some of these events more closely.

I DIDN'T KNOW THAT!

Simon of Cyrene was the man compelled by the Romans to carry the cross of Jesus as Jesus was taken to his Crucifixion, according to all three synoptic Gospels. Cyrene was located in northern Africa and there was a Jewish community there. Even though Simon was forced  into this service, many think he willingly accepted it as an act of sympathetic generosity. The service of Simon has become the basis for a movement in the United Kingdom and Ireland called "The Cyrenians." Their guiding principle is "sharing the burden," which explains the Cyrenians, approach to providing services to homeless and other disadvantaged groups in society.

Arrest and Trial

The enormous crowds that flood into Jerusalem during Passover overflow into the Kidron Valley and fill the area with their tents. It is no wonder that the people coming to arrest Jesus need an insider, like Judas, to find him in that crowd. The soldiers come at night to avoid stirring up the crowds and starting a riot. This gives John yet another opportunity to bring up the theme of light versus darkness. The Temple and Roman guards, along with the chief priests and Pharisees, have lanterns and torches. They are in darkness, seeking the Light of the World.

When they find Jesus, he does not cower. He is not afraid. Jesus remains in full control of the situation. He demands the release of his followers, and though Peter has cut off the ear of one of the soldiers, they comply. The disciples are free as Jesus willingly leaves the garden with the guards.

Peter doesn't go too far. As the Jewish authorities question Jesus, Peter remains nearby. The author of John purposefully alternates back and forth between the questioning of Jesus and the questioning of Peter. Inside, Jesus is courageously declaring his true identity. Outside, Peter is in the darkness denying his identity as a follower of Christ. As the rooster crows and Peter realizes he has denied knowing Jesus three times, we are reminded that when Jesus says something will happen, it always does.

As Jesus' hour of glorification on the cross approaches, he is brought to trial before Pontius Pilate. The trial is filled with ironic situations and statements, as those in darkness fail to understand the identity of the man before them. For example, John tells how the Jewish leaders took Jesus to the praetorium, which is the home of the Roman royal governor, Pontius Pilate. Because Pilate is a Gentile, Jews would be ritually unclean if they entered his house. So, the chief priest and elders remain outside because they do not want to be made unclean before the Passover celebration the next day. How ironic that they are seeking to kill the Son of God, but are so careful not to break God's Law in the process.

After Jesus' arrest, Peter denies even knowing Jesus on three separate occasions.

MAKE IT SO

During the arrest, Jesus and Peter respond to the stress in two opposite ways. Jesus remains calm and trusts in God's plan. Peter allows his anger to take control, and he lashes out with violence. How do you respond to stressful situations? When you feel you are under a lot of stress, due to family situations or schoolwork, do you remain calm and talk through it, or do you lash out and end up saying things you don't mean and later regret? The next time you feel stressed, ask Jesus for the peace and calm he showed in stressful times.

During the first conversation between Pilate and Jesus, Pilate struggles to understand why the Jewish leaders are saying that Jesus claims to be a king. When Jesus explains that his role is to proclaim the truth, Pilate questions, "What is truth?" (John 18:38). It is ironic that Pilate asks this, as "the truth" (14:6) stands before him. Pilate then declares Jesus innocent and offers to free him. The crowd asks for Barabbas, the revolutionary, to be freed instead. Barabbas's name means "son of the father." The crowd does not see the irony as they seek freedom for the sinful "son of the father," while seeking the death of Jesus, the sinless "Son of the Father."

Pilate then has Jesus scourged and mocks him by dressing him in a royal purple cloak and a crown of thorns. Twice more he tells the crowd that he finds no guilt in Jesus. And twice more the crowd calls for Jesus' Crucifixion. Their reason is that they "have a law, and according to that law he ought to die, because he made himself the Son of God" (John 19:7). They want Jesus killed for **blasphemy**, which is the sin of claiming to be God; they do not realize that Jesus really is God. By providing all these ironic misunderstandings, the author of John is emphasizing the foolishness of those who deny that Jesus is the Messiah, the Son of God. The Gospel invites us to accept the truth and put our faith in Jesus Christ.

After his arrest, Jesus is brought before Pontius Pilate. Even though Pilate finds Jesus innocent, he still allows Jesus to be killed.

The Hour of Glory

As Jesus' moment of glorification arrives, he is still in control, even carrying his cross by himself (in the synoptic Gospels, Jesus has help from Simon the Cyrenian). As Jesus is lifted up, the soldiers affix a sign above his head, ironically declaring the truth: "Jesus the Nazorean, the King of the Jews" (John 19:19).

---

blasphemy ➤ Speaking, acting, or thinking about God in a way that is irreverent, mocking, or offensive. It is a sin against the Second Commandment.

UNIT 2

The sign is written in the three common languages of the Roman Empire: Hebrew, Latin, and Greek. Because everyone in the empire speaks one of these languages, this symbolically highlights that Jesus, as King, is drawing all people to himself, just as he said he would do.

We mentioned earlier that in the Gospel of John, the Last Supper was the day before Passover. This means that when Jesus is lifted up on the cross, it is the exact time that devout Jews are in the Temple area sacrificing their Passover lambs. Immediately after a lamb is killed for sacrifice, it is placed on a vertical stake. A horizontal stake is then used to spread its two forelegs so the blood can drain. The figure of the lamb on the stake looks remarkably like Jesus on the cross. The words of John the Baptist have come true: "Behold, the Lamb of God, who takes away the sin of the world" (John 1:29). Jesus becomes the new **Paschal** sacrifice for all.

Standing just below the cross are Jesus' mother, Mary, and the **Beloved Disciple**. Jesus directs the Beloved Disciple to take Mary as his own mother, and for Mary to see the Beloved Disciple as her own son. By creating this new relationship between Mary and the Beloved Disciple (who represents all believers), Jesus has established a new community. All of his disciples are to see Mary as their own mother. Mary is to see all of Jesus' disciples as her own children. This command includes us and helps to explain, in part, why we revere Mary so much and why Mary cares so deeply for each one of us.

Once Jesus knows he has finished what he was sent to do, he hands over his spirit. The Son of God dies. Like the lambs in the Temple area, Jesus' bones are not broken, and blood and water pour forth as his side is lanced. The author of John emphasizes that these details fulfill what the Jewish Scriptures had foretold (see 19:31–37). Jesus' body is taken down from the cross and prepared for burial. The arrest that took place hours earlier in a garden leads Jesus back to a garden. The chapter ends with hints of Jesus' glorification as he is buried in an expensive new tomb with fragrant spices in quantities typically used for royalty. ✳

HMMMMM...

What are some differences in the ways the Gospel of Mark and the Gospel of John portray Jesus during his Passion and death?

Beloved Disciple ➤ In the Gospel of John, an unnamed disciple who may have been the Apostle John.

Paschal (Mystery) ➤ The work of salvation accomplished by Jesus Christ mainly through his Passion, death, Resurrection, and Ascension.

Article 26
The Divine Son Returns

Losing someone you deeply love—a close friend, a sibling, your spouse—is perhaps the hardest thing most of us will ever have to face. A man who had lost his wife explained the weeks that followed like this: "After she died, it was like I had fallen into a pit with no way to get out. I had no energy for anything, even the things I used to love doing. I was just going through the motions of daily life. It was like all the color had drained from my life, and all I was left with was the grays."

We can only imagine that this is how Jesus' disciples felt immediately after his death. Their master and friend, the person who had inspired them with his hope and love, had been cruelly taken from them. Added to that was the fear that the Jewish and Roman leaders might be coming next for them. They hid in fear, not knowing what to do next. Little did they expect that the most amazing day of their life lay just around the corner.

UNIT 2

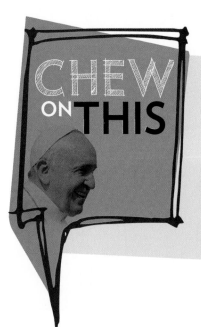

Be active members! Go on the offensive! Play down the field, build down the field, build a better world, a world of brothers and sisters, a world of justice, of love, of peace, of fraternity, of solidarity. ("Address of Pope Francis at the Prayer Vigil with the Young People on the Occasion of the XXVIII World Youth Day," July 27, 2013)

Mary Magdalene and the Disciples Meet the Risen Christ

As John, chapter 20, begins, Mary Magdalene approaches Jesus' tomb in the dark on Easter morning. She is about to discover that Jesus' hour of glorification has yet to be finished. Note once again the image of someone in darkness. Mary does not understand that Jesus is divine, and his dead body will not be in the tomb as she expects. The events of the next hour illustrate the disciples' confusion and lack of understanding.

When Mary Magdalene arrives at Jesus' tomb, she discovers the tomb is open and Jesus' body is missing. She runs to tell the disciples, and Peter and the Beloved Disciple then run to the tomb. They see the empty tomb and the abandoned burial clothes, and the Beloved Disciple believes while Peter remains confused. Is it possible that these two reactions illustrate how people still react to the Gospel today? Some people hear it and are immediately moved to believe in Jesus, while others hear it and need time to reflect and absorb everything before they come to belief?

Mary Magdalene is the first to encounter the Risen Christ. When he appears to her, she does not recognize him at first (see John 20:11–13). This is unlike his appearance to the disciples in the locked room, where they are shocked to see him, but he is immediately recognized. Once Mary recognizes Jesus (see verses 14–17), she accepts that he has risen. Imagine her pure joy, looking for a dead body and finding the Risen Lord! Jesus tells her his "hour" is not yet completed, but to go tell the others the Good News. This is why Mary Magdalene is sometimes called the Apostle to the Apostles (*apostle* means "one who is sent").

Mary Magdalene is the first to encounter the Risen Christ.

It appears that the disciples did not trust Mary's message, for they re-mained in hiding, behind locked doors, out of fear that they might suffer the same fate as their master, Jesus (see John 20:19). Yet not even locked doors can keep the Risen Lord away. Jesus appears to them and says, "Peace be with you" (verse 19). In the midst of paralyzing fear, the Son of God can break through and offer a peace that only God can give. The disciples' fear immediately turns to celebration. Jesus tells them that he is sending them out of this locked room and into the world to proclaim the Good News. Jesus fulfills his promise and gives them the Advocate, the Holy Spirit. Empowered by the Holy Spirit, they now have the responsibility to act on Christ's behalf, even forgiving sins. What an amazing gift and responsibility!

Thomas Needs Physical Proof

Unfortunately, Thomas was not in the room when Jesus appeared to the other disciples (see John 20:24–27). He wants physical proof. Even seeing Jesus is not enough; he wants to touch Christ's wounds. Imagine the others trying to convince Thomas over the course of a week, and him not believing their word. Then, once again, the Risen Lord appears in their midst. This time Jesus speaks straight to Thomas: "Put your finger here and see my hands, and bring your hand and put it into my side, and do not be unbelieving, but believe" (verse 27). The Gospel never mentions whether Thomas touches Jesus. But Thomas cries out what the entire Gospel has been pointing to regarding Jesus' true identity: "My Lord and my God!" (verse 28). Jesus then speaks directly to us, "Blessed are those who have not seen and have believed" (verse 29). We are the people Jesus is praising if we believe that Jesus is Lord and God based on the word of the witnesses through the centuries, the Church.

The final Resurrection appearance points us both back into the story and forward to the future. In this final appearance, the disciples have a bad night fishing, a stranger gives them fishing advice, and when they follow his advice, they have a miraculous catch of fish. At this point, we should not be surprised to discover that Jesus is the stranger on the shore. Jesus is demonstrating his authority over both people and nature. Many commentators see the bulging unbroken net full of fish as a symbol of the Church. When we follow Christ and spread the Good News, we help bring an abundance of people into the Church, the community of believers. The unbroken net symbolizes the unity that exists among all believers within the Church.

UNIT 2

When the disciples recognize Jesus, Peter is the one who jumps out of the boat and rushes to see him. Peter's actions reflect the enthusiasm and abandon all followers of Jesus should have when seeking the Lord. When the disciples arrive on the beach, Jesus graciously provides a cooked breakfast of loaves and fish.

What do you think the net full of fish represents in the final Resurrection appearance?

This meal calls to mind Jesus' multiplication of the loaves and fish during his ministry. His words "take and eat" point us toward the Sacrament of the Eucharist, where the community comes together in Christ's presence and shares a meal.

How fitting for Jesus to ask Peter three times about loving him, thus reversing and forgiving Peter's earlier three denials. Jesus then gives Peter an enormous responsibility. He is to tend Jesus' sheep, the Church, as the first pope. Peter is to follow in Jesus' footsteps by loving and caring for God's people. He will follow Jesus' footsteps all the way to his own death on a cross.

Encountering Jesus Christ Changes People

All these encounters with the resurrected Christ have something in common. Every disciple who meets the resurrected Christ is changed by it. Mary Magdalene is filled with grief over Jesus' missing body, but when she meets Jesus, her grief turns into joy. The disciples are locked in a room, paralyzed with fear. After Jesus appears to them, their fear is turned into courage as Jesus gives them the Holy Spirit and sends them out into the world. Thomas wants to believe but remains skeptical. Jesus appears, and Thomas's doubt is turned into faith. Finally, Peter is carrying the burden of guilt for having betrayed Jesus three times. After his conversation with Jesus, his guilt is removed and turned into confidence as he assumes leadership of the Church.

Encountering Jesus Christ still has this kind of impact on us today. Jesus is not going to physically appear in our classroom when we are stressed out about a test, but we encounter him in other ways. As the Divine Son of God, Jesus Christ is everywhere at all times, so it is up to us to seek him, just as the disciples did.

Maybe you have been in a situation like Rory; waiting for God to step in and fix things for you. Rory was stressed. His friends from middle school had somehow drifted apart, no longer the tight-knit group that always hung out on the weekends. Rory was uncomfortable without his group at school, but he hated lunch the most. Who was he going to sit with? His mom told him to go up to a table full of kids and ask if he could sit with them. Rory rolled his eyes at her. The seniors looked at him as if he were an insect, and the girls in his grade were only interested in upperclassmen. Rory desperately wished for a miracle. Couldn't God just make everything normal again?

How can you seek God's presence in your life rather than praying for God to fix things?

But faith isn't about God granting wishes. When we have faith that God is present in our lives, we need only to seek him to encounter his love and grace. If you have ever experienced stress like Rory, could you consider seeking God in any of these ways?

- Seek Jesus at Mass in the Eucharist. At Mass, when we receive the gift of **Real Presence**, we can "behold, the Lamb of God, who takes away the sin of the world" (John 1:29).
- Seek Jesus through prayer. When life seems overwhelming, we can center ourselves in prayer and ask Jesus for wisdom and peace.
- Seek Jesus by reaching out to your family and faith-filled friends. God has given us one another for support and care, especially when times are hard.

These are just some of the ways the Risen Christ is present to us, bringing us his peace and the strength needed to follow him. ✳

HMMMMM. . . How do the Resurrection appearances show us that Jesus is divine?

Real Presence ➤ The doctrine that Jesus is really or substantially present in the Eucharist, not merely symbolically or metaphorically.

UNIT 2

1. Instead of sharing the account of Jesus instituting the Eucharist at the Last Supper, what unique event does John relate instead?

2. How did Jesus pray for us at the end of the Last Supper?

3. Name three ways the Gospel of John shows that Jesus is in full control during his arrest, trial, and Crucifixion.

4. Identify several of the ironies present in Jesus' trial before Pilate.

5. How do the words of John the Baptist, "Behold, the Lamb of God" (John 1:29), come true during the Crucifixion?

6. Describe the reactions of Mary Magdalene and the disciples after seeing the empty tomb.

7. How is Thomas the Apostle's reaction to the Risen Christ a sign of Jesus Christ's divinity?

A MODERN REPRESENTATION OF THE RESURRECTION

In this painting called *Easter Morning*, the artist depicts an angel and three women at Christ's tomb on the morning of the Resurrection.

1. Who is the main figure in this piece of art?

2. If the piece is about the Resurrection, why is Jesus not pictured?

3. Why do you think the three women in the picture have their eyes closed or are looking downcast?

CHAPTER 7
The New Testament Letters Explore the Incarnation

WHY DOES IT MATTER THAT JESUS IS GOD?

SNAPSHOT

Article 27
Philippians: Christ Empties Himself

Mrs. Ruiz had been trying to explain the Trinity to her class for at least half of the period. Max raised his hand and said, "This doesn't really make any sense to me." Mrs. Ruiz was tempted to just reply: "It's a mystery we will never fully understand. We just need to accept it as part of our belief system." But she took a deep breath and tried yet another way to approach it.

Some dogmas of the Catholic Church are mysterious, but we can't just throw our hands up and not attempt to understand them. The mysteries of faith are not problems to be solved; rather, they are truths to be pondered. For example, it is ultimately a mystery how Jesus is both fully human and fully divine, but there is so much we can gain from exploring that mystery. We can use some of the letters in the New Testament as our guides, studying the early Christians' reflections on what Christ's Incarnation meant for them. Paul gives us insight into the Incarnation in his Letter to the Philippians.

Further exploration of dogmas, such as the Incarnation and the Trinity, can help us to better understand the mysteries of the Church.

UNIT 2

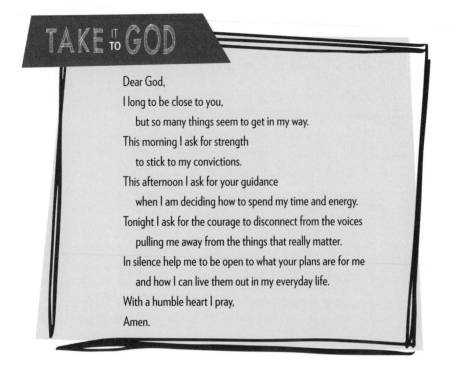

TAKE IT TO GOD

Dear God,

I long to be close to you,

but so many things seem to get in my way.

This morning I ask for strength

to stick to my convictions.

This afternoon I ask for your guidance

when I am deciding how to spend my time and energy.

Tonight I ask for the courage to disconnect from the voices

pulling me away from the things that really matter.

In silence help me to be open to what your plans are for me

and how I can live them out in my everyday life.

With a humble heart I pray,

Amen.

An Act of Humility

The Philippians were a predominately Gentile Christian community that Paul founded and deeply loved. Their mutual affection is evident in his letter. This community, centered in an agricultural area that specialized in wine and grain, was located on a major trade route. It was the home to many different religious cults. It is natural that the fledgling community at Philippi would encounter some challenges from these religious groups.

Although Paul is extremely pleased with the community at Philippi, he doesn't ignore the struggles they are facing. For one thing, the community is grappling with a lack of unity. They are also facing challenges from people outside their group, although we aren't certain who those outsiders are. Perhaps they are pagan members of the Philippian society or Roman authorities or Christians with strange ideas. Regardless, Paul urges the Philippians to remain steadfast and united in the face of frightening opposition (see Philippians 1:27–28). What should motivate them to maintain this unity? It is the example of Christ himself.

For Paul, disunity comes from selfishness and pride; unity is produced by humility and serving others. Paul lifts up Jesus as the model of humility and servanthood. He quotes a hymn (see Philippians 2:6–11) that begins by equating Christ with God the Father prior to the Incarnation. Yet Christ, in his human nature, does not seek equality with God. The hymn goes on to describe Jesus' willingness to humble himself:

> Rather, he emptied himself,
> taking the form of a slave,
> coming in human likeness;
> and found human in appearance,
> he humbled himself,
>> becoming obedient to death,
>> even death on a cross.
>
> (Verses 7–8)

The highest possible form of being, God, becomes the lowest form, a slave. A slave has no rights and is completely dependent on the will of another. This is Paul's challenge to the Philippians. If Jesus was humble and obedient, even to the point of death, can they follow his example and also humble themselves? Paul encourages them to model Jesus not only when Paul is with them but also in his absence. "Do everything without grumbling or questioning, that you may be blameless and innocent, children of God without blemish in the midst of a crooked and perverse generation, among whom you shine like lights to the world" (Philippians 2:14–15).

The hymn ends by raising Christ up once again (see Philippians 2:9–11). Because of his humility, Christ is **exalted**, so that all creation in Heaven and on Earth now kneels before him. Christ, the Divine Son became a slave and is now the King of all creation.

---

exalt ➤ To raise someone to a higher rank or character; to dignify or make someone noble.

A Great Example

Christ's amazing example of humility and eventual exaltation is the answer to the Philippians' problem. If they are humble about serving one another within the community, they will eventually unite as a community. Paul emphasizes the importance of putting the needs of their brothers and sisters in Christ ahead of their own wants and needs. And what does Paul say about the outsiders who are causing the Philippians to suffer? He calls them "enemies of the cross of Christ" (3:18). He tries to bolster the spirits of the Philippians by reminding them that the outsiders' "minds are occupied with earthly things. But our citizenship is in heaven, and from it we also await a savior, the Lord, Jesus Christ" (verses 19–20). If Christ was obedient to the will of the Father and endured suffering, then they too can endure their suffering with the sure hope of sharing in Jesus' reward in Heaven.

Philippians teaches us about the importance of humility. The Incarnation—that is, Christ taking on our human nature—is the perfect example of this. When we follow his example, we become the people we are meant to be, and together we become the Church God calls us to be. However, let's be clear about what humility means. Humility doesn't mean being weak or letting people use or abuse us. It does mean seeing every other person as equal to ourselves in dignity and worth. It means standing up for your rights and the rights of others. It means putting yourself at the service of others rather than seeking power and control. Most of all, it means seeking out God's will for your life rather than focusing on your own pleasure and privilege.

I DIDN'T KNOW THAT!

Would you rather die by crucifixion or beheading? Of course, the best answer is neither! But if you said beheading, you answered correctly, because it is a much less painful way to be killed. That is why Roman law dictated that Roman citizens receiving the death penalty were beheaded, not crucified. Jesus and Peter were not Roman citizens, so they were crucified. Paul was a Roman citizen, so tradition (lowercase *t*) says that he was beheaded when he was eventually put to death after his second imprisonment in Rome.

Here is how one teen is following Christ's example of humble service. Sarah is fifteen years old and volunteers at an event called "Sleepless San Diego."

She is part of a team serving the homeless free lunch and handing out clothing and hygiene packs in cooperation with the San Diego Rescue Mission. This event provides an opportunity for human connection between the teen volunteers and those in need. Sarah has learned that the homeless are people just like herself and her friends—they have just fallen on hard times. They have interesting stories and lives. Whether Sarah knows it or not, she is changing lives by respecting these people's dignity, putting a smile on their faces, and making their lives a little easier for the day. By following Christ's humble example, Sarah and the other volunteers are discovering that emptying themselves to serve God brings happiness and fulfillment. ✳

By treating others with respect and dignity, we are following Christ's example.

OVERVIEW of the Letter to the Philippians

- **Intended audience:** A beloved community founded by Paul consisting of Gentile Christians living in Philippi.

- **Theme:** By taking on a human nature, Jesus Christ showed humility and obedience, and as a result, he was greatly exalted by God the Father. His humility and obedience is a model for all Christians.

- **Reason for writing:** Paul wishes to praise and encourage the Philippians. He also seeks to address an internal issue of disunity and external threats causing suffering within the community.

HMMMMM. . . How is the Incarnation a model of humility for all Christians? In what ways is God calling you to humble yourself?

UNIT 2

Article 28

Colossians: Beware of False Teachings

When Gail moved to a new city, she was trying to make connections with people and find new friends. She quickly became close with Tina from her social studies class. Tina doodled pictures of astrological signs on her notebooks and wore jewelry that she said was made of healing crystals associated with her astrological chart. Gail was fascinated by this. Tina was more than happy to print out Gail's daily horoscope, and she also brought Gail some books to learn more about her sign. Soon Gail's conversations at home were all about horoscopes without a mention of her classes or her old friends. Her parents expressed their concerns at dinner one night. They explained that the Catholic Church teaches against the use of horoscopes and other fortune-telling practices such as astrology, palm reading, and Ouija boards because they attempt to take the place of God.

When we are feeling alone or unsure of ourselves, it is easy to get swept up in in popular fads. They can give us a sense of belonging and connection with other people. The danger is that we can lose sight of what is really true and important: the truths revealed by God. The people in Colossae are having a similar problem, but theirs is even bigger! They are being distracted by teachings that take their focus off Jesus Christ as the sole source of their salvation. As we examine how Paul addresses this young community, it becomes clear that we can learn a lot from both his words and the way he addresses the issue.

What are some fads or practices that can distract you from your relationship with God?

MAKE IT SO

In today's world, many distractions can cause us to lose our focus on Christ. What keeps us on track? It seems too simplistic and broad to say "go to church," "read the Bible," or "pray." This is why spiritual disciplines are important. Spiritual disciplines are practices, exercises, and habits that create space for an encounter between God and us. Which of the following spiritual disciplines are you willing to try?

- doing an examination of conscience
- fasting
- spending time in Eucharistic Adoration
- spending time in solitude
- simplifying your life
- engaging in a meditative reading
- keeping a gratitude journal
- going to the Sacrament of Penance and Reconciliation
- listening to uplifting music
- spending time in silence

UNIT 2

Looking for the Next Best Thing

Known for their fabric production and fine purple dyes, the Colossians, who live along a major trade route, are influenced by various traders' materials and religious beliefs, including some fascination with magic and spiritual beings. Given how new the Colossians' Christian faith is, it isn't too surprising that they are influenced by these outside ideas. Just like many people today, they are looking for the next big thing.

Oftentimes, Paul outright attacks his opponents in his letters. He does this in his Letter to the Galatians. However, in the Letter to the Colossians, he takes a different approach. He does reference his opponents, or false teachers, but focuses more on educating the young community. Paul tells the Colossians that he wants them to have "all the richness of fully assured understanding, for the knowledge of the mystery of God" (Colossians 2:2). By reminding them of the importance of Jesus Christ, he is giving them the tools they need to defend themselves against exposure to false beliefs. This approach can be useful today when others challenge our faith. Before we engage them in dialogue, we should have a deep understanding and grounding in our own faith. If necessary, we should focus on studying our own beliefs. Studying our faith keeps us spiritually grounded.

The teachers of these conflicting beliefs seem to be very persuasive as Paul calls their teachings "seductive philosophy" (Colossians 2:8). However, Paul points out the major problem with their teaching. These teachers claim, or at least imply, that faith in Jesus Christ is not enough for salvation. They promote other religious practices and worship "elemental powers of the world" (verse 8). These other practices appear wise but are not authentic because they are not based on Jesus Christ.

To help the Colossians defend themselves against these false teachings, Paul uses a hymn in Colossians 1:15–20 to reinforce the heart of his argument. The hymn makes the following claims about Christ:

Line from Hymn	Claim about Christ
"He is the image of the invisible God" (1:15)	Christ is God.
"all things were created through him and for him" (1:16)	Christ shared in the creation of the universe.
"He is the beginning, the firstborn from the dead" (1:18)	Christ is the source of our resurrection.
"And through him to reconcile all things, making peace by the blood of his cross" (1:20)	Christ is the source of our salvation.

Preeminence Still Matters Today

What does this teach us about the Incarnation? One answer lies in what the letter calls the **preeminence** of Christ. This means that as the Savior, as the image of the invisible God, Christ comes before all other things. Because Jesus Christ is true God, if we want to know about God, we must look to Jesus, who he is and how he lived. Because Jesus is true man, if we are looking for a model to live by, we must look to Jesus and what he taught and how he lived.

Have you ever idolized a musician, a sports hero, or some other celebrity? There is nothing wrong with wanting to have the songwriting ability of a famous musician or the throwing arm of a hall of fame quarterback. We only need to scroll through Instagram to find thousands of pictures of actors, models, and athletes to admire and compare ourselves to. However, these people are sinful human beings just like us. Eventually, these idols are revealed as human beings with weaknesses, whose "perfect" bodies have been photoshopped, and who sometimes make bad decisions. If we focus on these idols, we will be disappointed.

Paul's teaching about Christ's preeminence in Colossians reminds us that Christ should be the one we look up to. We need to remember that Jesus, as the Word Made Flesh, is the only one who is perfect and worthy of our praise and adoration. ✳

© LUke138 / iStockphoto.com

Christ the Redeemer, statue in Rio de Janeiro, Brazil, is 98 feet tall and has been named one of the New Seven Wonders of the World. It is for many a symbol of the preeminence of Christ.

UNIT 2

preeminence ➤ Surpassing all others.

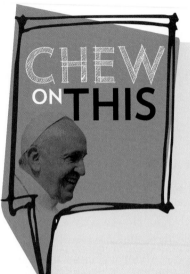

CHEW ON THIS

All believers must be particularly vigilant so that in living out with conviction our religious and ethical code, we may always express the mystery we intend to honor. This means that all those forms which present a distorted use of religion, must be firmly refuted as false since they are unworthy of God or humanity. ("Address of Pope Francis at the Meeting with the Leaders of Other Religions and Other Christian Denominations," September 21, 2014)

OVERVIEW of the Letter to the Colossians

- **Intended audience:** The young Christian community in Colossae.
- **Theme:** The letter emphasizes the preeminence of Christ. It calls the Colossians to make Christ the focus of their lives.
- **Reason for writing:** The community was being influenced by false teachers who argued that faith in Jesus Christ was not enough for salvation.

HMMMMM...

How can reflecting on the preeminence of Christ help you to keep your life in proper perspective?

Article 29

Hebrews: Our Divine High Priest

"What's the deal with you Catholics and priests? Why do you even have them?" Ryan asked his friend Zach. "The Bible says that Jesus is the last High Priest, that there's no longer any need for them," Ryan continued. "Really?" "Where does it say that?" asked Zach. "Somewhere in the New Testament," replied Ryan. "I can look it up for you if you want."

Imagine yourself in this conversation. Would you have an answer for Ryan about why we have priests in the Catholic Church? Ryan is probably referring to the Letter to the Hebrews. This letter discusses how Jesus Christ, the Divine Son of God, is the fulfillment of what was foreshadowed through **salvation history** in the Old Testament. It does this primarily by examining Christ's role as our Divine **High Priest**.

We do not know much about the author or the intended community of the Letter to the Hebrews. What we do know has been constructed from the letter itself. It appears that the author is a Jewish Christian who knows a lot about both Judaism and Greek culture. The audience seems to be Jewish Christians who have suffered some persecution and are in danger of giving up their Christian faith. The letter seeks to reassure these Jewish Christians that Jesus' life and mission fit perfectly with their Jewish heritage.

How would you explain the role of Catholic priests to a curious friend?

---

salvation history ▶ The pattern of specific events in human history in which God clearly reveals his presence and saving actions. Salvation was accomplished once and for all through Jesus Christ, a truth foreshadowed and revealed throughout the Old Testament.

High Priest ▶ This person led the religious services and conducted animal sacrifices held at the Temple in Jerusalem. The High Priest was appointed by the Jewish king with the approval of the Roman governor.

The Divine High Priest

Let's be clear right away; the Letter to the Hebrews is not an easy letter to understand. The author makes his arguments like a first-century Jewish teacher, and the arguments these teachers use don't always make sense to us today. But this doesn't make them any less true. For example, the letter begins by making a case that Jesus is God the Father's Son. It does this by taking some Old Testament verses and applying them to Jesus. It does not matter that these verses were originally about other people. Inspired by the Holy Spirit, the author of Hebrews understands that the purpose of the Old Testament books is to point God's people to Jesus Christ, the fulfillment of God's saving plan. The whole letter points to this truth.

The author of Hebrews goes on to explain that the unique combination of Jesus' divine and human natures makes him the perfect High Priest before God. As Hebrews states, "We have a great high priest who has passed through the heavens" (4:14). The author makes many arguments by comparing the priesthood of Jesus with the priesthood of the **Levites**. The Levites are of the Israelite tribe of Levi. From this tribe came the priests who offered **sacrifices** in the Temple on behalf of the people. The author of Hebrews

© Archivist / Alamy Stock Photo

The priests who offered sacrifices in the Temple on behalf of the people were from the tribe of Levi.

Levites ➤ Members of the Hebrew tribe of Levi, from whom came the priests who performed the sacrifices and led the worship in the Jewish Temple.

sacrifice ➤ A ritual offering made to God by a priest on behalf of the people as a sign of adoration, gratitude, and communion. The perfect sacrifice was Christ's death on the cross.

makes his point by comparing the "lesser" priesthood of the Levites with the "greater" priesthood of Jesus. In other words, if the priesthood of the Levites worked pretty well, how much greater is the priesthood of Jesus who was God the Father's sinless Son! Here's how the author of Hebrews compares Jesus' priesthood to the Levites' priesthood:

Question	Levitical Priests	Jesus the High Priest
Who are the priests?	They are mere mortals from the tribe of Levi (see 5:1 and 7:5).	"We have a great high priest who has passed through the heavens, Jesus the Son of God" (4:14).
Can they relate to the people they serve?	Yes, they are human just like us (see 5:2).	Yes, he is fully human just like us, but he has never sinned (see 4:15).
Who appointed them as priests?	They have a calling from God (see 5:4).	He was sent by God the Father; therefore, he too was called by God (see 5:5-9).
How long do the priests serve?	They serve until they die (see 7:23).	He serves eternally, as he has been raised from the dead (see 7:24-25).
Where do they serve?	They serve at the Temple on Earth (see 8:5 and 9:24).	He serves at the altar in Heaven (see 9:24).
What is the purpose of the sacrifice they offer at the altar?	It is a sacrifice for the forgiveness of sins on behalf of the people and themselves, because they too are sinners (see 5:3).	It is a sacrifice for the forgiveness of sins on behalf of all people. He has no need to do it for himself since he is sinless (see 7:26–27).
What do they offer?	They offer the blood of an animal (see 9:25).	He offers the perfect sacrifice, his own blood he shed on the cross (see 9:11–12).
How often do the priests have to offer this sacrifice?	They offer it once every year, meaning they need to keep repeating it (see 9:25).	His sacrifice was once for all time and never needs to be repeated (see 7:27).

UNIT 2

UNIT 2

The Levites are serving the **Old Covenant**. However, like all human beings (except Mary and Jesus), they are weak and sinful, so they never perfectly fulfill the Old Covenant. Hebrews explains that by perfectly fulfilling the Old Covenant, Jesus establishes a **New Covenant** with God's people. The letter shows that this covenant is prophesied in Jeremiah: "This is the covenant I will establish with them after those days, says the Lord: / I will put my laws in their hearts, / and I will write them upon their minds" (Hebrews 10:16). Through Jesus Christ the High Priest, God's people have found true forgiveness of their sins. "For by one offering he has made perfect forever those who are being consecrated" (10:14).

CATHOLICS **MAKING** A **DIFFERENCE**

Saint John Baptist de La Salle was a priest who made it his mission to be in service to God's people. Born the son of wealthy parents living in France over three hundred years ago, he was ordained a priest on April 9, 1678. While he was studying for his doctorate in theology, he became involved with a group of rough and barely literate young men in order to establish schools for poor boys. To be most effective in this work, he abandoned his family home, moved in with the teachers, renounced his wealth, and formed the community that became known as the Brothers of the Christian Schools. De La Salle and his brothers created a network of quality schools, started programs for training lay teachers, provided Sunday programs for working young men, and wrote the first books on Christian education for young people.

Old Covenant ➤ The covenant between God and the ancient people of Israel established in the Sinai Covenant with Moses; also called the Old Testament.

New Covenant ➤ The covenant or law established by God in Jesus Christ to fulfill and perfect the Old Covenant or Mosaic Law. It is a perfection on Earth of the Divine Law. The law of the New Covenant is called a law of love, grace, and freedom. The New Covenant will never end or diminish, and nothing new will be revealed until Christ comes again in glory.

Jesus the High Priest and Us

Temples and animal sacrifices can seem so foreign to us today. In a way, we can thank the Incarnation for that. Because Jesus Christ is the Word Made Flesh, his sacrifice made animal sacrifice obsolete. He is the perfect priest who is always extending God's compassion and mercy to us. He is the priest who is always on call. We can reach out to him anytime, anywhere. His "office" is in Heaven, in the chair right next to God the Father. Most important, Jesus offered his sacrifice for you, so that you may one day be in Heaven with him forever.

Let's go back to Ryan's question about why Catholics have priests. The answer is that Catholic priests are not the same as Levitical priests. Catholic priests share in the priesthood of Jesus. They do not offer a new sacrifice over and over again; rather, they make Christ's eternal sacrifice present to us in the Sacrament of the Eucharist. They bring us Christ's love, mercy, and grace through the other sacraments. Priests model themselves after Jesus the High Priest, striving to be of service to all God's people. ✳

UNIT 2

OVERVIEW of the Letter to the Hebrews

- **Intended audience:** It appears to have been written for Jewish Christians who were familiar with Greek and may have been falling away from the faith.

- **Theme:** Jesus Christ is the fulfillment of the Old Testament promises and now serves as our eternal High Priest.

- **Reason for writing:** It was written to encourage Jewish Christians to hold onto their faith and teach them about Jesus Christ's superior role and sacrifice.

HMMMMM. . . What does it mean to say that Jesus is our Divine High Priest? Why is this important to our faith?

1. What does Paul mean in his Letter to the Philippians when he says that Christ "emptied himself"?

2. Why does Paul emphasize Christ's humility in the Letter to the Philippians?

3. How does Paul's approach to addressing false teachers differ in the Letter to the Colossians from what he did in the Letter to the Galatians?

4. What does Paul mean when he refers to the "preeminence" of Christ?

5. What does the "fullness" dwelling within Christ refer to in the Letter to the Colossians (see 1:19)?

6. According to the Letter to the Hebrews, what makes Jesus greater than the angels?

7. Who are the Levites?

8. How is the high priesthood of Jesus different from the high priesthood of the Levites?

UNIT 2

ART STUDY

INSIGHT INTO THE MYSTERY OF MARY, THE MOTHER OF GOD

This mosaic explores Mary's title of Theotokos, or God-bearer.

1. What is the mystery explored by the artist?

2. What symbols do you notice in the artwork?

3. Notice the postures, gestures, and stances reflected in body positioning. What do they tell us about the people depicted?

UNIT 2 HIGHLIGHTS

CHAPTER 5

The Gospel of John: The Book of Signs

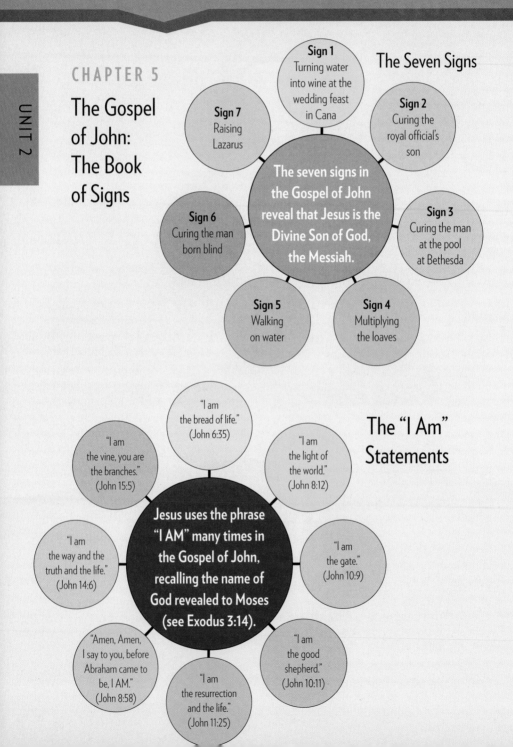

The Seven Signs

The seven signs in the Gospel of John reveal that Jesus is the Divine Son of God, the Messiah.

Sign 1 Turning water into wine at the wedding feast in Cana

Sign 2 Curing the royal official's son

Sign 3 Curing the man at the pool at Bethesda

Sign 4 Multiplying the loaves

Sign 5 Walking on water

Sign 6 Curing the man born blind

Sign 7 Raising Lazarus

The "I Am" Statements

Jesus uses the phrase "I AM" many times in the Gospel of John, recalling the name of God revealed to Moses (see Exodus 3:14).

"I am the bread of life." (John 6:35)

"I am the light of the world." (John 8:12)

"I am the vine, you are the branches." (John 15:5)

"I am the way and the truth and the life." (John 14:6)

"I am the gate." (John 10:9)

"Amen, Amen, I say to you, before Abraham came to be, I AM." (John 8:58)

"I am the resurrection and the life." (John 11:25)

"I am the good shepherd." (John 10:11)

CHAPTER 6 **The Gospel of John: The Book of Glory**

The Last Supper in the Synoptic Gospels
- Takes place on Passover
- Jesus shares bread and wine with the Apostles.

Events in All Four Gospels
- The chief priests plot the death of Jesus.
- Jesus is anointed.
- Jesus says he will be betrayed.
- Jesus says Peter will deny him.

The Last Supper in John
- Takes place the evening before Passover
- Jesus washes the feet of the disciples.
- Includes Last Supper Discourses

The Hour of Jesus, Glory

His Arrest and Trial Jesus Remains in Control	**His Death** Jesus Is Glorified	**His Resurrection** Jesus' Glory Is Made Known to All
Jesus sends Judas away rather than Judas leaving in secret.	Jesus gives directions to his disciples from the cross.	Mary Magdalene encounters the Risen Christ and shares the Good News with the other disciples.
Jesus directs the conversation with the soldiers.	Jesus purposely fulfills the Scriptures.	When the disciples encounter the Risen Christ, their fear turns to courage.
Jesus orders the soldiers to let his disciples go free.	Jesus decides the moment of his death and hands over his spirit.	Thomas wants to believe in the Risen Christ but is skeptical; when Jesus appears to Thomas, his doubt turns into faith.
Jesus lectures Pilate on the truth; Pilate cannot find fault in Jesus.	Jesus' death fulfills what has been foretold in the Jewish Scriptures.	

CHAPTER 7 The New Testament Letters Explore the Incarnation

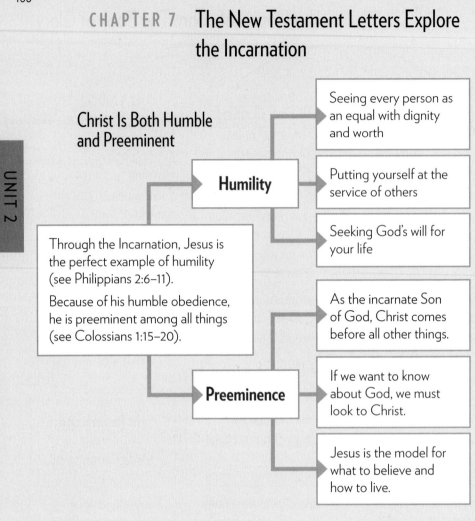

Christ Is Both Humble and Preeminent

Humility

- Seeing every person as an equal with dignity and worth
- Putting yourself at the service of others
- Seeking God's will for your life

Through the Incarnation, Jesus is the perfect example of humility (see Philippians 2:6–11).

Because of his humble obedience, he is preeminent among all things (see Colossians 1:15–20).

Preeminence

- As the incarnate Son of God, Christ comes before all other things.
- If we want to know about God, we must look to Christ.
- Jesus is the model for what to believe and how to live.

Jesus Christ, Our Perfect High Priest

Question	Levitical Priests	Jesus, the High Priest
Who are the priests?	They are mere mortals from the tribe of Levi (see Hebrews 5:1 and 7:5).	"We have a great high priest who has passed through the heavens, Jesus, the Son of God" (4:14).
Can they relate to the people they serve?	Yes, they are human just like us (see 5:2).	Yes, he is fully human just like us, but he has never sinned (see 4:15).
How long do the priests serve?	They serve until they die (see 7:23).	He serves eternally, as he has been raised from the dead (see 7:24–25).
Where do they serve?	They serve at the Temple on Earth (see 8:5 and 9:24).	He serves at the altar in Heaven (see 9:24).
What is the purpose of the sacrifice they offer at the altar?	It is a sacrifice for the forgiveness of sins on behalf of the people and themselves, because they too are sinners (see 5:3).	It is a sacrifice for the forgiveness of sins on behalf of all people. He has no need to do it for himself, as he is sinless (see 9:11–12).
What do they offer?	They offer the blood of an animal (see 5:3).	He offers the perfect sacrifice, his own blood he shed on the cross (see 9:11–12).
How often do the priests have to offer this sacrifice?	They offer it once every year, meaning they need to keep repeating it (see 9:25).	His sacrifice was once for all time and never needs to be repeated (see 7:27).

UNIT 2

UNIT 2
BRING IT HOME

WAS JESUS CHRIST REALLY DIVINE?

FOCUS QUESTIONS

CASEY
Mater Dei High School

Jesus is truly divine. It is important to look at it through the lens of the Gospels. The way I see it, the Gospels witness to Jesus' divinity. No one should just assume that Jesus is divine. Most people need proof of things to believe them. Jesus' divinity should not be taken any less. We can look to the Gospels for that proof.

REFLECT

Take some time to read and reflect on the unit and chapter focus questions listed on the facing page.

- What question or section did you identify most closely with?

- What did you find within the unit that was comforting or challenging?

UNIT 3
Jesus Reveals the True God

WHAT
ARE GOD'S
IMPORTANT
CHARACTERISTICS?

LOOKING AHEAD

UNIT 3

God can be characterized in many ways by many people. It is our calling to choose the important characteristics that most accurately represent him as he wanted us to. God is filled with love and forgiveness. He demonstrated this by delivering our savior, Jesus Christ. Through this action, I am assured that God cares for me and everyone else alike.

VINCENT
De La Salle Collegiate High School

CHAPTER 8
Jesus Reveals God's Mercy and Justice

DOES GOD JUDGE US OR FORGIVE US?

SNAPSHOT

Article 30

Luke: The Gospel of God's Mercy

To understand how unique the true God revealed in the Bible is, it is helpful to compare him to other gods worshipped at the time the Bible was written. Take Zeus, the king of the Greek gods and goddesses, for example. Prometheus (another Greek god) easily tricks Zeus into accepting sacrifices that consist merely of bones. This allows humans to keep the meat from the sacrifices for themselves. Once Zeus discovers his mistake, he punishes not Prometheus but humanity by hiding fire from them. In response, Prometheus steals Zeus's fire and shares it with humanity. Zeus then punishes Prometheus by chaining him to a rock for all eternity. Every day a bird eats his liver, and then the liver regrows at night so that his suffering can continue. In this story, Zeus is at times foolish, jealous, vengeful, and cruel. Who would want to worship such a god?

In stark contrast to Zeus and the other Greek and Roman gods is the one true God revealed by Jesus Christ in the Gospel of Luke. Because Luke's audience was primarily Gentile Christians, they would have known about the Greek and Roman gods. Jesus' teachings about a God of love, caring, wisdom, truth, mercy, healing, and justice would have been quite a contrast. Of the four Gospels, the Gospel of Luke most forcefully presents Jesus' teachings about God's mercy and justice.

© Barret12 / iStockphoto.com

UNIT 3

Besides Judaism and Christianity, worship of Greek and Roman gods and goddesses was a popular religious practice at the time the Bible was written.

Our Merciful God

The Gospel of Luke is sometimes called the Gospel of Mercy. In Luke, we frequently read about people crying out to Jesus, saying, "Have pity on us." The Greek word translated as *pity* can also mean "compassion" or "mercy" (see Luke 17:11–19, 18:35–43). In every case, Jesus Christ hears and answers the people's cries. The Gospel of Luke also contains several unique parables that focus on God's mercy and our call to be merciful. The Parables of the Lost Coin (see 15:8–10), the Lost Sheep (see 15:1–7), and the Good Samaritan (see 10:29–37) all reveal that God's mercy is available to all who seek it.

As you read the Gospel of Luke, you came across one of the Gospel's most famous parables, the Parable of the Lost Son (see 15:11–32). In this parable, we get a glimpse into God's amazing compassion and forgiveness. When the Pharisees and scribes question why Jesus hangs out with the tax collectors and sinners, Jesus tells this parable in response. Remember that although it is called the Parable of the Lost Son, the parable is really about the Forgiving Father.

The parable begins with the younger son asking for his inheritance. This is a dishonorable thing for the son to do since his father is not even dead yet! Surprisingly, the father, representing God, fulfills the request. The message? God will allow us to use our free will to reject him, just as the younger son does in the parable.

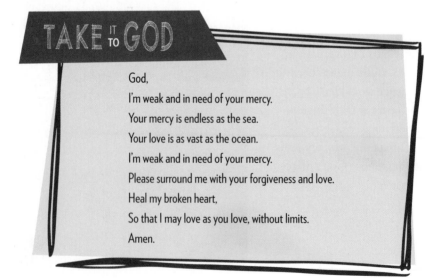

TAKE IT TO GOD

God,

I'm weak and in need of your mercy.

Your mercy is endless as the sea.

Your love is as vast as the ocean.

I'm weak and in need of your mercy.

Please surround me with your forgiveness and love.

Heal my broken heart,

So that I may love as you love, without limits.

Amen.

The Parable of the Lost Son is an amazing story of compassion and forgiveness in the Gospel of Luke.

UNIT 3

Everyone knows what happens next. The son blows through all his money. Hungry and desperate, he ends up taking care of pigs. For a Jew, this is about as bad a job as one can get. In Jewish Law, pigs are unclean, so working with them every day would be shameful. This shows us what can happen when we choose sin over God. Our sin puts us in embarrassing and shameful circumstances that we never imagined possible. Realizing this, the younger son decides to return home, not expecting to be treated as a son but hoping to be hired as a servant. He reasons that the servants in his father's house are living a better life than he is now. The son is ashamed for how he has behaved and what has become of his life, and he plans to ask his father for forgiveness.

Surprisingly, his father is watching for him and runs out to meet him while the son is still a distance away. The message? When we separate ourselves from God, he anxiously awaits for us to return to him. As soon as we admit sorrow for our sin, our compassionate God meets us the rest of the way. Before the son is able to make his full apology, the father reinstates him as a son. He does not humiliate his son, but restores his dignity. The father's joy over his son's return is overwhelming. It is so over the top that Jesus' listeners would have been embarrassed for him.

Meanwhile, the older brother refuses to share in the father's joy. Like the Pharisees, who do not understand why Jesus hangs out with sinners, the older brother cannot understand the father's mercy toward the younger brother. As before, we see the father go out, this time to meet the older brother. He reminds the older brother that they have always been together. The older brother has forgotten, or taken for granted, the importance of his relationship with his father. The parable ends before we hear the older brother's response. This ending presents the Pharisees with an unspoken question: Do they celebrate and welcome back the sinners as God does, or do they choose to stay outside the Father's house?

Good Thief on the Cross

In the Gospel of Luke, Jesus doesn't just talk about mercy, he shows us what true mercy and forgiveness look like. At no time is Jesus' forgiving heart more clear than when he hangs dying on the cross. Imagine that you were being tortured to death simply for telling the truth. What words would you have for your executioners? Jesus prays these words to his heavenly Father: "Father, forgive them, they know not what they do" (23:34). Wow! Even in a situation of unbearable pain and stress, Jesus extends his forgiveness to the very people who are executing him.

There's more to this story. The author of Luke tells us that two thieves were crucified on either side of Jesus (see 23:33). One criminal berates Jesus for not saving them. Then the second criminal, sometimes called the "good thief," speaks up. He acknowledges his guilt and he defends Jesus. Like the younger son deciding to return home, the good thief asks Jesus to remember him when he comes into his Kingdom. Jesus responds with these beautiful words: "Amen, I say to you, today you will be with me in Paradise" (23:43). This penitent thief is, by his own admission, a sinful man, yet Jesus shows him mercy simply because he asks for it. One of Jesus' final acts before he dies, this shows us that it's never too late to seek God's mercy.

This art is called Scene of the Passion: Christ on the Cross Between Two Thieves. How do the two thieves represent two ways of responding to Christ's offer of salvation?

Respond to God's Mercy by Being Merciful

Jeremy had a powerful experience of undeserved mercy on his Confirmation retreat. In elementary school, Jeremy and Alan had been best friends. In middle school, they became interested in different things and drifted apart. One day in gym class, Alan and Jeremy ended up playing basketball on the same team. When Alan was distracted, one of the other kids hit him hard in the face with the ball. Alan looked up to see a group of people laughing and making fun of him. Jeremy was right in the middle of the crowd. When Jeremy saw the hurt on Alan's face, he knew how wrong he was, but he didn't know how to apologize. So on their Confirmation retreat, Jeremy decided to take a chance and talk to Alan. He wasn't sure if Alan would respond with anger or forgiveness. Jeremy's apology was awkward, but after he was finished, Alan said he had already forgiven him. He told Jeremy that because God has shown us mercy, it is hard to justify not being merciful to others.

This is just one way of sharing God's mercy and love with others. The Church gives us a "playbook" of many other possibilities. They are called the **Corporal Works of Mercy** and the **Spiritual Works of Mercy**. They are fourteen concrete ways you can participate in showing God's mercy and love to others.

UNIT 3

Corporal Works of Mercy	Spiritual Works of Mercy
Feed the hungry.	Share knowledge.
Give drink to the thirsty.	Give advice to those who need it.
Shelter the homeless.	Comfort those who suffer.
Clothe the naked.	Be patient with others.
Care for the sick.	Forgive those who hurt you.
Help the imprisoned.	Give correction to those who need it.
Bury the dead.	Pray for the living and the dead.

Corporal Works of Mercy ➤ Charitable actions by which we help our neighbors in their bodily needs.

Spiritual Works of Mercy ➤ Actions that guide us to help our neighbors in their spiritual needs.

The Corporal Works of Mercy address the physical needs of our neighbors. The Spiritual Works of Mercy address spiritual and intellectual needs of our neighbors. The opportunities to practice the Corporal and Spiritual Works of Mercy are around us every day. When we perform these works, we do it simply out of our love for God, not seeking anything in return. ✳

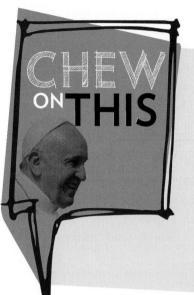

CHEW ON THIS

"It is my burning desire that . . . the Christian people may reflect on the *corporal and spiritual works of mercy.* It will be a way to reawaken our conscience, too often grown dull in the face of poverty. And let us enter more deeply into the heart of the Gospel where the poor have a special experience of God's mercy." (Pope Francis, *Bull of Indiction of the Extraordinary Jubilee of Mercy* [*Misericordiae Vultus,* 2015], number 15)

OVERVIEW of the Gospel of Luke

- **Intended audience:** The Gospel is addressed to Theophilus, which means "God-lover." Scholars are unsure if this is a specific individual or "God-lovers" in general. Either way, the intended audience appears to be primarily non-Jewish Christians.

- **Theme:** Jesus is the Savior of the world, who reaches out to the poor, women, non-Jews, and all those who are marginalized.

- **Reason for writing:** The Gospel is the first of two works by the author. The second is the Acts of the Apostles. The author says it was written so that Theophilus may have certainty about what he has been taught about Jesus Christ.

HMMMMM. . .

What motivates people to seek God's mercy? What are some reasons why someone would not seek God's mercy?

Article 31
Luke: The Gospel of God's Justice

Lucas Benitez came to the United States from Mexico when he was only sixteen years old. He first worked as a migrant farmworker picking tomatoes in Immokalee, Florida. Later he started the Coalition of Immokalee Workers in 1993, by getting together with other farmworkers to discuss the poor working conditions. For example, one farmworker was told he couldn't take a water break and was severely beaten when he stopped to take one anyway! Farmworkers were essentially enslaved by the growers. They were threatened with torture and death if they tried to leave. Little by little, the coalition began to take a stand against these injustices, staging protests and arranging for boycotts. They pushed for higher wages and appropriate working conditions.

Benitez and his colleagues are strategic, systemic thinkers who inspire farmworkers with the message that no matter the odds, they have choices. They can leverage their power within the corporate food system to fight against modern-day slavery and bring justice to the American food system. Using effective, nonviolent tactics, such as marches, boycotts, hunger strikes, and radio campaigns, they bring justice for those who once didn't have a voice. Benitez and the Coalition of Immokalee Workers live out Jesus' teaching on justice, which is highlighted in the Gospel of Luke.

UNIT 3

© Joseph Sohm / Shutterstock.com

The Coalition of Immokalee Workers banded together to take a stand against the unjust working conditions and treatment of migrant farmworkers.

I DIDN'T KNOW THAT!

The "social" in social media doesn't just mean staying in touch with your friends. Have you seen of any of these modern social justice issues on social media: the fight for racial equality, the immigration debate, the refugee crisis, fast-food strikes for fair wages, advocacy for affordable health care? Social media has become a forum for bringing attention to social justice issues. #icebucketchallenge raised record-breaking funds for research for Lou Gehrig's disease. #blacklivesmatter was among the top ten hashtags on Twitter in 2016. The media attention that comes from these social media plugs can bring about change!

God's Justice Turns Things Upside Down

The author of the Gospel of Luke places great emphasis on the social justice dimension of Christian living. This theme is established early on in the Gospel. In Mary's Magnificat, we read, "He has thrown down the rulers from their thrones / but lifted up the lowly. / The hungry he has filled with good things; / the rich he has sent away empty" (Luke 1:52–53). When people ask John the Baptist how they should change their lives, he tells them, "Whoever has two tunics should share with the person who has none. And whoever has food should do likewise" (3:11). A chapter later, Jesus begins his public ministry by proclaiming his mission to establish justice:

> The Spirit of the Lord is upon me,
> because he has anointed me
> to bring glad tidings to the poor.
> He has sent me to proclaim liberty to captives
> and recovery of sight to the blind,
> to let the oppressed go free,
> and to proclaim a year acceptable to the Lord.
>
> (4:18–19)

Luke also contains several unique parables not told in the other Gospels, which emphasize our call to practice justice. These include the Parable of the Good Samaritan and the Parable of the Rich Man and Lazarus.

The timeless Parable of the Rich Man and Lazarus begins by showing a great contrast between the two men (see Luke 16:19–31). The rich man has everything he could possibly want in life, from food to fine clothing. Lazarus is just the opposite. He has nothing as he lays outside the rich man's front door, starving to death. This scene, described in the first century, could easily take place today.

After both men die, things are reversed in the afterlife. Lazarus is in Heaven being comforted by Abraham, and the rich man is in **Hell** suffering torment. The rich man asks Abraham to send Lazarus to bring him some water, but Abraham says there is a great chasm between the two places so that no one can cross. The rich man begs someone to warn his family to repent, but Abraham offers little hope of them repenting.

What do we learn about God's justice from this parable of Jesus? One thing we can learn is that God's justice turns the world's values upside down. God's justice requires that we recognize the dignity of all people, especially those most in need. It is no accident that in the parable we know the name of the poor person but not the name of the rich person. Think of all the famous people whose names you know. Do you know the name of even one homeless person living in a park or under a highway overpass? Our culture focuses on wealth and getting ahead, but God calls us to turn our attention to those most in need.

The Parable of the Rich Man and Lazarus teaches that our eternal life depends on how well we practice charity and justice.

Hell ➤ Refers to the state of definitive separation from God and the saints, and so is a state of eternal punishment.

justice ➤ The Cardinal Virtue concerned with rights and duties within relationships; the commitment, as well as the actions and attitudes that flow from the commitment, that ensure we give to God and to our neighbor, particularly those who are poor and oppressed, what is properly due them.

UNIT 3

What's more, the parable teaches that our eternal life depends on how well we practice **charity** and justice. The rich man dies in torment not because he was wealthy, but because he ignored the poor person literally lying at his door. He still sees Lazarus as a servant when he tells Abraham, "Send Lazarus to dip the tip of his finger in water and cool my tongue" (Luke 16:24). Failing to recognize and protect other people's dignity, especially those most in need, is a danger to our spiritual life.

Justice and Judgment

One more theme in the Gospel of Luke shows how God's justice turns the world's values upside down. That theme is Jesus' teaching to leave judgment up to God. In Luke's Gospel, Jesus gives us a straightforward, but difficult teaching: "Stop judging and you will not be judged. . . . The measure with which you measure will in return be measured out to you" (Luke 6:37–38). How often do we judge people about the most trivial things? Disparaging comments about someone's clothing, hair, or facial features not only are hurtful but also go against God's call for justice.

However, Jesus' teaching goes well beyond refraining from negative comments about another person's appearance. It addresses our tendency to judge another person's heart. So often, someone hurts us and we are quick to judge that this person is bad. We have the ability to judge actions as good or bad. However, we have no right to judge the heart of a person as good or bad. That is to be left to God.

Rewriting the Rich Man's Story

In the story of the rich man, how could he have avoided ending up in torment? The rich man, either consciously or unconsciously, wrongly judged that Lazarus was not worth his time or effort. If the rich man had viewed Lazarus as his own brother suffering, the story would have been different. We are called to see everyone, especially the poor and marginalized, as our brothers and sisters who are of infinite value and deserving of our time and energy. When we begin to see all people as God's own children and treat them as our own brothers and sisters, meeting one another's spiritual and material needs, then we are fulfilling our calling to live in **solidarity** with one another.

---

charity ➤ The Theological Virtue by which we love God above all things and, out of that love of God, love our neighbor as ourselves.

solidarity ➤ Union of one's heart and mind with those who are poor or powerless or who face an injustice. It is an act of Christian charity.

Solidarity encourages cooperation at all levels—employees and employers, poor and rich, smaller nations with larger nations, and so on.

Living in solidarity means we can look beyond our differences and focus our common identity as children of God. How do we do this? By promoting charity, justice, and peace whenever we can. When someone forgets their lunch, offer to share some of yours. When you have the opportunity to participate in a service or mission trip, make it a priority. Educate yourself about people who have been denied their basic human rights—locally, nationally, and internationally. Create, sign, and circulate petitions for justice causes promoted by the Church. Become involved with your local community in assisting the hungry, the homeless, those who are sick, and those who need mentors or tutors. The opportunities to participate in God's plan to bring about a more just and peaceful world come before us on a daily basis. Part of the challenge is to train ourselves to look for those opportunities and to not get completely caught up in our own lives like the rich man did. ✳

HMMMMM. . . What motivates people to seek God's mercy? What are some reasons why someone would not seek God's mercy?

Article 32

Mary's Incredible Role in God's Plan

Laurie was confused when she spent the night at Eden's house. Before Eden went to bed, she prayed a Hail Mary for her sick grandmother and for her brother who is in the army. Laurie said to Eden: "God is all-powerful. Why are you praying to Mary?" Eden replied: "I do pray to God. But sometimes I pray to Mary to ask her to **intercede** for me. Mary is the mother of Jesus; if anyone understands my fears and need for comfort, it would be her! It's kind of like asking you to pray for me. Catholics don't think Mary is God. We just recognize her special role as the mother of Jesus."

Catholic beliefs about Mary are often misunderstood, but they are firmly rooted in the Bible. The Gospel of Luke tells us a great deal about Mary and her role in God's saving plan.

The Handmaid of the Lord

The Gospel of Luke begins with a situation that is a frequent theme in Scripture. A faithful husband and wife, Zechariah and Elizabeth, are entering old age without having had any children. Sound like anyone you know from the Old Testament? Just as God promised Abraham and Sarah a son in their old age, he promises Zechariah and Elizabeth a son (who will grow up to be John the Baptist). Zechariah has a hard time believing this could happen and is given an unusual punishment—you'll have to read it for yourself (see Luke 1:5–25). However, this is all a warm-up for the main event.

Catholics revere Mary for her special role as the Mother of Jesus.

---

intercede ➤ To intervene on behalf of another.

What comes next lays the foundation for the Incarnation and explains why Mary of Nazareth plays such an important role in God's plan and in the Catholic faith. As Luke tells it, the angel Gabriel comes to Mary, explaining that although she is and will remain a virgin, she will miraculously conceive and have a son through the power of the Holy Spirit (see 1:26–38). Keep in mind that Mary is a young woman when this occurs, probably just fourteen or fifteen years old. This pregnancy is a hardship and even dangerous. Joseph, her fiancé, might very well leave her (he doesn't). In her culture, as an unwed, pregnant woman, she would be shamed and very likely even stoned to death by her community. It is hard to imagine what she is thinking and feeling, but her response is a beautiful and powerful act of faith: "May it be done to me according to your word" (Luke 1:38).

Mary could say no, but she doesn't. Her openness to God's will leads to the Incarnation. At the moment she conceives, she becomes the Mother of God. The baby in her womb is the son of Mary and the Son of God, fully human and fully divine. As such an important moment in salvation history, it is no wonder we celebrate Mary's courageous yes to the angel Gabriel during the Feast of the **Annunciation**, on March 25 every year.

Can you imagine the all-powerful God allowing a key part of his plan for our salvation to depend on the actions of an uneducated teenager from a small, remote village? Yet this is what he does, and because of Mary's complete trust in God, she plays a crucial role in God's plan for our salvation. In Luke, she describes herself as the "**handmaid** of the Lord" (1:38). Mary is expressing her willingness to be God's servant, putting God's plan ahead of her own wants.

The feast of the Annunciation is March 25. How do you follow Mary's example of accepting God's invitation to have greater trust in him?

UNIT 3

© IOSIF CHEZAN / Shutterstock.com

Annunciation ➤ The biblical event that includes the angel Gabriel's visit to the Virgin Mary to announce that she is to be the Mother of the Savior, Mary's "yes" to God, and Christ's conception through the power of the Holy Spirit.

handmaid ➤ A term of humility and respectful self-deprecation in the presence of God; a woman who is in servitude to another.

"Full of Grace"

Our beliefs about Mary also show that even though God may ask a lot of us, he always provides for us and cares for us. When Mary says yes to the angel Gabriel, she does not know where this decision will take her. The author of Luke gives us a hint in chapter 2. Forty days after Jesus is born, Mary and Joseph go to the Temple in Jerusalem for Mary's purification (as required by the Mosaic Law) and to consecrate Jesus to God's service (see Luke 2:22–38). While they are there, a devout older Jew named Simeon recognizes that Mary's baby is the promised Messiah. Simeon blesses God for allowing him to see this and then makes a prediction. He tells Mary, "This child is destined for the fall and rise of many in Israel, and to be a sign that will be contradicted (and you yourself a sword will pierce)" (verses 34–35).

Simeon's prophecy must have been another shock to Mary. He is telling her that Jesus is going to change the world and that she herself will experience sorrow and pain. Her yes to the angel Gabriel will take her on a challenging journey. She will see her baby grow into a loving son. She will see him leave his family to complete his divine mission, following God the Father's will. The Jewish religious leaders' opposition to his mission will confuse her. And her heart will break when Jesus' mission seemingly ends as she witnesses his Crucifixion.

The presentation of Jesus in the Temple

Despite all these things, Mary's faith in God never wavers. She teaches us an important spiritual truth: God never asks us to do something without giving us the grace we need to handle it. God gave Mary unparalleled graces to prepare her to be the Mother of God. One of those graces was the gift of her **Immaculate Conception.** It's a popular misunderstanding that the Immaculate Conception is about Jesus' conception. It actually refers to Mary's conception. As the future mother of the Son of God, Mary is conceived without

---

Immaculate Conception ➤ The Catholic dogma that the Blessed Virgin Mary was free from sin from the first moment of her conception.

UNIT 3

Original Sin. Moreover, she remains free from sin throughout her whole life. Imagine that . . . living your entire life without once giving in to the temptation to commit a single sin!

God's grace guides Mary throughout her life. She remains a virgin her entire life, which is a sign of her total dedication to serving God as "the handmaid of the Lord" (Luke 1:38). This might seem confusing because some Scripture passages mention Jesus' "brothers" (see Luke 8:19–21). However, these are not Jesus' biological siblings. There are two possible explanations for this. The first is that Joseph may have been a widower when he married Mary, and these brothers are Joseph's children by his previous wife. The second explanation is that in the culture of that time, extended families were very close. You thought of your uncles and aunts as your second parents and your cousins as your brothers and sisters. So, people often referred to their cousins as their brothers and sisters.

God's grace also helps Mary in her role as the first disciple. A disciple is someone who follows an influential teacher. Mary is the most faithful follower of Jesus. She, along with Joseph, seeks the twelve-year-old Jesus when he is lost and find him in the Temple (see Luke 2:41–52). She is the first to believe in his power at the wedding in Cana (see John 2:5). She follows Jesus throughout his ministry, is at the foot of the cross (see Luke 23:49), and is in the upper room with the disciples awaiting the coming of the Holy Spirit (see Acts 1:14).

When Mary and the Beloved Disciple are at the foot of the cross, Jesus tells her, "Woman, behold, your son." He tells the Beloved Disciple, "Behold, your mother" (John 19:26–27). Jesus now shares his mother with the entire Church, represented by the Beloved Disciple. This is why we call Mary the Mother of the Church. As our mother, she wants the best for us, which is why we bring our needs and concerns to her in prayer, knowing that she will intercede for us with her Son, Jesus Christ.

There is one more unique way that God's grace is extended to Mary. Once Mary's time on Earth is completed, God takes Mary's body and soul into Heaven. We call this miraculous event the Assumption of Mary into Heaven or just the **Assumption**. Mary's body, the body that carried our Lord in its womb, is never to see decay. We celebrate the Feast of the Assumption on August 15.

UNIT 3

Assumption ➤ The dogma that recognizes that the body of the Blessed Virgin Mary was taken directly to Heaven after her life on Earth had ended.

UNIT 3

CATHOLICS **MAKING** A **DIFFERENCE**

Did you know that Saint Pope John Paul II was shot four times? He was nearly assassinated in St. Peter's Square by a man named Mehmet Ali Ağca. The Pope recovered and attributed his survival to the prayers of the Blessed Virgin Mary. As a true witness to mercy, he told the world that he had forgiven his attacker and called for everyone to pray for Ağca. Two years later, the Pope even went to the prison and met his attacker face-to-face to offer peace and forgiveness. One of the bullets removed from Saint Pope John Paul II's body is now encased in a crown on the head a statue of Mary.

God Works through His Creation

When Mary was a child, prior to meeting the angel Gabriel, do you think she ever dreamed what God would do with her life? It is amazing when you consider that after Mary accepts God's will for her, he then works through her, to bring about his saving plan. By respecting Mary's free will and then working through her to bring about the birth of Jesus Christ, God affirms the sacredness and dignity of our human nature. We are sinners in need of salvation, but we are also meant for eternal glory with God.

Just as he did with Mary, God continues to work through people to help sanctify, or make holy, the world. One way people work to sanctify the world is through the community of the Church. The Church shares the Good News with the whole world through the words and actions of her members. God uses other elements of creation as well in the sacraments—things such as water, bread, and wine—to make us holy and guide us on our journey to Heaven. Because God honors his creation in this way, we too are called to honor and respect all of God's creation. ✳

HMMMMMM. . .
What does Mary's life teach us about our own call to serve God?

sanctify ➤ To purify or make holy.

Article 33

God's Just and Merciful Plan

Our human tendency is to compare ourselves with others. Sometimes this takes the form of "I'm better looking than him" or "I'm smarter than her." Other times it involves a moral comparison, like "I'm a better person than her" or "At least I don't cheat" (or bully, act stuck-up, and so on). However, comparing our sins to other people's sins isn't helpful and here's why; any sin harms our relationship with God. We don't get a free pass just because someone else's sins might be more serious than our sins. And didn't Jesus have something to say about judging others?

We may not have dishonored our father by asking for our inheritance early like the Lost Son, or ignored a poor person dying outside our front door like the Rich Man. However, since we have all sinned, except Jesus and Mary, we really are in the same boat as the Lost Son and Rich Man. Saint Paul understood this and wrote about it in his Letter to the Romans. In this letter, we learn a great deal more about God's merciful and just plan for our salvation.

Sin Spread, but God Saved

At the heart of Paul's teachings about God's plan for our salvation is the justification of all who believe in Jesus Christ. In Romans, chapters 5–8, going back to Adam, Paul describes the dire situation all humans face and how Jesus Christ rescues us from it. God is a just God. This means that our offenses—whether against him or against other people—need to be made right. The problem is that on our own, we have no possible way to make up for having offended—that is sinned—against God.

Paul points out that it does not matter if someone is a Jew or Gentile; the problem is the same, "all are under the domination of sin" (Romans 3:9). All people have God's **natural law** to guide them. Natural law is the moral law that can be understood by all people through the use of our reason. It is based on our longing for God; it is a natural part of us and not imposed on us from outside of ourselves. Natural law is our God-given ability to understand what it means to be in right relationship with God, other people, the world, and ourselves. The Jews also had the Mosaic Law. Despite this, all people sin. Why is this?

---

natural law ➤ The moral law that can be understood by all people through the use of human reason. It is our God-given ability to understand what it means to be in right relationship with God, other people, the world, and ourselves. The basis for natural law is our participation in God's wisdom and goodness because we are created in the divine likeness.

Paul answers this in chapter 5 when he discusses the sin of Adam. Adam's sin in the garden set in motion a wave of sin throughout all of humanity. His Original Sin is something we all inherit. **Original Sin** wounds our relationship with God and gives us the inclination to sin, called **concupiscence**. Further, the entrance of sin into the world brought with it death, something none of us can escape (see Romans 5:12). Even when the Law was given to Moses and the Israelites on Mount Sinai, this did not stop the sinning. Paul shockingly argues that it did the opposite; it led to an increase in sinning (see verse 20)! Note his negative language when describing the human situation. He uses words like "helpless," "ungodly," "enemies", and "wrath" (see verses 6,9–10). Although we are created good and are meant for eternal glory with God, we still have sinned and therefore are in desperate need of salvation.

Original Sin ➤ The sin by which the first humans disobeyed God and thereby lost their original holiness and became subject to death. Original Sin is transmitted to every person born into the world, except Jesus and Mary.

concupiscence ➤ The tendency of all human beings toward sin, as a result of Original Sin.

Now all this sounds rather hopeless, but Paul isn't saying it to make us depressed, just the opposite. He's saying this to help us appreciate the source of our hope and salvation: God's infinite mercy. He writes, "But God proves his love for us in that while we were still sinners Christ died for us" (Romans 5:8). Jesus' life, Passion, death, and Resurrection have restored our broken relationship with God. Paul wants to show how God's justice and his mercy complement each other. *In accord with God's justice*, Christ became the ultimate and eternal sacrifice for the forgiveness of our sins. *In accord with God's mercy*, we have been reinstated as sons and daughters of God through Christ's Incarnation. Paul compares the impact of Adam's sin and the impact of Jesus' sacrifice in these powerful verses:

> In conclusion, just as through one transgression condemnation came upon all, so through one righteous act acquittal and life came to all. For just as through the disobedience of one person the many were made sinners, so through the obedience of one the many will be made righteous. The law entered in so that transgression might increase but, where sin increased, grace overflowed all the more, so that, as sin reigned in death, grace also might reign through justification for eternal life through Jesus Christ our Lord. (Romans 5:18–21)

UNIT 3

Through Christ, God justified the entire human race. We must choose to accept that grace, and the way we do that is by being baptized into faith in Jesus Christ. Through Baptism we become adopted children of God the Father with Jesus as our brother. We then live out our faith as members of his Church. Paul explains in Romans 6:1–11 that through Baptism, we die with Christ. This means that we die to our old way of life. We then have the hope of rising again to eternal glory with him and with God the Father.

Sin Must Not Reign!

Having identified the saving grace we receive through Baptism, Paul continues the rest of Romans, chapters 6–8, by turning to the question of combatting sin after you have been baptized. In these chapters, Paul writes of being slaves to the Law and to the flesh before Baptism and becoming a slave of God after Baptism (see 6:15–23). He explains that even though Baptism has cleansed us from Original Sin, we still experience temptation.

Paul even admits to his own struggle to avoid sin when he writes, "For I do not do the good I want, but I do the evil I do not want" (Romans 7:19). In 8:1–13, Paul discusses this internal struggle as a battle between the flesh (sinful desires) and the spirit (goodness). Having found freedom in Christ and a life in the spirit, he urges us to "put to death the deeds of the body" (verse 13). Paul's language might lead us to think that he is saying that our bodies are bad, but this is not the case. Paul is describing the lingering effects of Original Sin, which distort our good and natural desires, leading to the internal struggle Paul describes. This can be challenging, so to encourage us, Paul reminds us of our special status as a child of God (see verses 14–17). If that is not encouraging enough, Paul puts it another way, "If God is for us, who can be against us?" (verse 31).

MAKE IT SO

Learning more about your own Baptism can help you appreciate God's mercy and our own dying and rising with Christ. Ask your parents or those who were present to tell you about the day. See if they still have any items from your Baptism, like the candle or white garment. Do they have photos or videos you can look at? Consider celebrating the anniversary of your Baptism day each year. After all, it is the day you were "born again" to become an adopted daughter or son of God.

© myku / Shutterstock.com

Accepting God's Offer of Salvation

Do you remember your own Baptism? If you were baptized as an infant, then you probably don't. On the day you were baptized, you died with Christ in the hope of rising again, just as Paul explained. The Rite of Baptism includes many beautiful elements that help us understand what dying and rising with Christ really means. At your Baptism, water was poured over your head three times, symbolizing the three persons of the Holy Trinity. You were also clothed in a white garment after you were baptized, as the priest or deacon said these words:

> You have become a new creation, and have clothed yourself in Christ. See in this white garment the outward sign of your Christian dignity. With our family and friends to help you by word and example, bring that dignity unstained into the everlasting life of heaven. (*Rite of Baptism for Children in The Rites of the Catholic Church,* volume one, number 179)

These words and signs are a reminder that through Christ, you are now adopted sons and daughters of God. Like the Lost Son, you have been reinstated to your full dignity as a beloved child of God. Your godparents received, on your behalf, a candle symbolizing the light of Christ. Now you share in Christ's mission to bring God's light to the world around you. ✻

UNIT 3

OVERVIEW of the Letter to the Romans

- **Intended audience:** The Christians living in Rome.
- **Theme:** Although all have sinned, salvation is available to both Jews and Greeks through faith in Jesus Christ.
- **Reason for writing:** Paul had not been to Rome prior to writing the Letter to the Romans. This letter was his way of introducing himself to the Christians in Rome and letting them begin to understand his teachings better.

HMMMMM. . .
How is God's plan for our salvation both merciful and just?

1. Give several examples of how the Gospel of Luke teaches us about God's mercy.

2. What is the difference between the Corporal Works of Mercy and the Spiritual Works of Mercy?

3. What can we learn about God's justice from the Parable of the Rich Man and Lazarus?

4. What does living in solidarity mean?

5. Why is Mary's "yes" to God so important to us?

6. What do we celebrate at the Feast of the Assumption?

7. How do we receive the justification that God has offered all of humanity?

8. When we die with Christ, what does Paul say we can then hope for?

Parables That Explore God's Mercy

Parables are short stories told by Jesus to illustrate a moral or spiritual lesson.

UNIT 3

"I TELL YOU, THERE WILL BE REJOICING AMONG THE ANGELS OF GOD OVER ONE SINNER WHO REPENTS."
LUKE 15:10

Parable of the Lost Son, Luke 15:11–32

Parable of Lost Sheep, Luke 15:1–7

Parable of the Lost Coin, Luke 15:8–10

1. Which of these parables to you identify with the most?

2. How does each parable show God's mercy rather than judgment or reprimand?

CHAPTER 9
Jesus Reveals God as Trinity

WHY IS THE TRINITY SO IMPORTANT?

SNAPSHOT

Article 34

God: The One and Only

Faye could never explain the mystery of her grandmother's third eye when she was a little girl. Whenever Faye ate the last cookie, or fibbed about brushing her teeth, her grandma would know. When she asked her how she discovered her secret, her grandma would respond, "My third eye sees everything!" Faye was sure her grandma didn't really have a third eye. Still, whenever her grandmother let down her long hair to brush it, Faye couldn't help but look to see if there was a secret eye peeking at her!

Faye's mystery isn't too hard to understand. She gave herself away by the chocolate around her mouth or her dry toothbrush sitting in the cup. But as a child, she could not comprehend her grandma's "third eye" because she lacked the experience and perspective of her grandma. You can think of the mysteries revealed by God—the Incarnation and the Trinity, for example—in a similar way , but not completely similar. Yes, with greater experience and perspective we can better understand and appreciate them, but we will never completely understand them. God and his mysteries will always be beyond our human understanding, in this life and the next. Remember, mysteries of faith are to be pondered, not solved.

Faye's grandmother had experience and perspective that Faye did not when she was a little girl. How can experience and perspective help you to explore the mysteries of the Church?

UNIT 3

UNIT 3

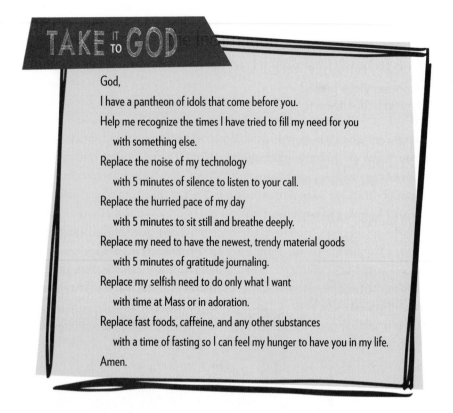

TAKE IT TO GOD

God,

I have a pantheon of idols that come before you.

Help me recognize the times I have tried to fill my need for you
   with something else.

Replace the noise of my technology
   with 5 minutes of silence to listen to your call.

Replace the hurried pace of my day
   with 5 minutes to sit still and breathe deeply.

Replace my need to have the newest, trendy material goods
   with 5 minutes of gratitude journaling.

Replace my selfish need to do only what I want
   with time at Mass or in adoration.

Replace fast foods, caffeine, and any other substances
   with a time of fasting so I can feel my hunger to have you in my life.

Amen.

There Is Only One God

Probably the most important truth that God has revealed about himself is
this: There is only one God. That may seem obvious to us now, but this belief
hasn't always been a given, especially during Old Testament times. Throughout much of human history, people practiced **polytheism**, which is the belief
in many gods. You may have studied some polytheistic cultures, like ancient
Egypt, Greece, and Rome. Each of these cultures had its own **pantheon**,
or group, of gods and goddesses. People in one city or region would have a
special devotion to a particular god or goddess who was their protector. They
would worship and offer sacrifices to this god or goddess in exchange for protection of their city or nation.

---

polytheism ➤ The belief in many gods.

pantheon ➤ All of the gods of a people or religion collectively.

When Abraham encounters God, this understanding begins to change for him and his descendants. Through God's covenant relationship with Abraham, God is revealing an essential truth: there is only one God, the Lord of all the Earth. Over time, Abraham and Sarah's descendants, who become known as the Hebrews, then later as the Israelites, and even later as the Jews, embrace **monotheism**, the belief in only one God.

As salvation history progresses, the importance of believing in only one God becomes clearer and clearer. For example, when Moses receives the Ten Commandments on Mount Sinai, the First Commandment states: "I am the Lord your God. . . . You shall not have other gods beside me" (Exodus 20:2–3). With this commandment, the belief and worship of gods other than Yahweh has become a serious sin. It will take many years, though, for the Israelites to completely stop worshipping other gods and goddesses.

As the Jewish people come to fully understand and embrace their monotheistic faith, they incorporate this belief into their prayer and worship. The Shema, the daily prayer of faithful Jews for many centuries, begins with these words, found in Deuteronomy 6:4: "Hear, O Israel! The Lord is our God, the Lord alone!"

UNIT 3

© Jorisvo / iStockphoto.com

Moses with the Ten Commandments on Mount Sinai

monotheism ➤ The belief in one God instead of many gods.

By the time we come to the New Testament, the belief in one God is taken for granted by Jesus and his Jewish disciples. Everything Christ says and does affirms this belief. For example, in the Gospel of Mark, a scribe asks Jesus which is the first of all the Commandments (see Mark 12:28). Jesus quotes the words of the Shema, replying: "The first is this: 'Hear, O Israel! The Lord our God is Lord alone! You shall love the Lord your God with all your heart, with all your soul, with all your mind, and with all your strength'" (Mark 12:29–30). Jesus himself tells us there is only one God.

When Abraham encounters God and responds to his call to embrace monotheism, he is going against the cultural norms of the time. Why is Abraham and his descendants' message of monotheism so important? What are people finding in monotheism that they are not experiencing in their pantheon of gods? The answer is fairly simple. Only the one, true God can fill the spiritual hole in our hearts—the God of mercy, justice, and unconditional love. Most of the Egyptian, Babylonian, Greek, and Roman gods were manipulative, jealous, vengeful, unfair, and violent. The monotheism of Jews and Christians presents a completely different vision of divinity. The one, true God is omnipotent, omniscient, and just. His love is faithful and eternal. He is not angry or jealous. Our hearts do not find their peace in worshipping a god for fertility and a god for good harvest. Our true peace is found in the one, true God's unconditional love.

I DIDN'T KNOW THAT!

What happened to the Greek and Roman gods and goddesses that were so popular during the time of Christ and the early Church? By the time Christianity was endorsed by the Roman Emperor Constantine in AD 313, it was major competition for the classical pagan religions. The idea of one eternal and all-powerful God was beginning to make more sense to many people. Eventually the classical religion we know as Greek and Roman mythology ended around the ninth century AD. The love and mercy of the Christian God and the universality of Christian beliefs and practice inspired conversions, and belief in the classical gods and goddesses eventually died out.

Don't Take Belief in One God Lightly

Aaron always feels like something is missing. When he sees a brand new truck at the dealership, he obsesses until he is able to buy one. The new truck only makes him happy for a little while (until he realizes how much it costs to fill it up!). When he went to watch a game at a friend's house, he started obsessing over his friend's newest, high definition, 74-inch television. Aaron can't stop thinking about how awesome it would be to have one of those. He opens a store credit card just to buy one. New clothes, season tickets, eating out— Aaron moves from needing to have one thing to needing another, never really being satisfied. He tries all of these things to make himself feel happy and important. And they do . . . but only for a little while.

© REDPIXEL.PL / Shutterstock.com

UNIT 3

Consumerism can be a form of idolatry.

What does this have to do with monotheism and **idolatry**? Think about the words you say at Mass during the Nicene Creed. A **creed** is a statement of beliefs. And the first line of the Nicene Creed is, "I believe in one God." It is our belief that we should not put anything else in our lives ahead of God. In our modern times, we aren't typically worshipping statues representing other gods or goddesses. Sadly, we can let things in our life take priority over God. This is what happened to Aaron. The things he purchased didn't give him lasting satisfaction because nothing can truly fill the "God-shaped hole" in our lives. Whenever we make another person, activity, or possession a priority over God, we have created an idol.

Putting our faith in the one, true God is more than just an idea. If you truly believe in the God revealed in Scripture and Tradition, then you must know that God wants to be in a relationship with you. This is not the same thing as having a relationship with another human being, as God is not visible or tangible to our physical senses. But just as building a friendship or relationship with another person requires time and effort, so too does building our spiritual relationship with God.

The Church provides us many opportunities to practice the spiritual disciplines needed to strengthen our relationship with God. For example, you can do this by participating in Mass and listening to his Word. God reveals himself to us in Scripture, and if you take just a few minutes every day to read and think about what those words are saying to you, you are drawing closer in relationship to God. Worshipping in community opens up so many more possibilities than praying alone. You can be inspired by the music and the families you see worshipping with you. Take that time to be thankful for all of the blessings in your life. The Church offers you the opportunity to seek forgiveness. Confessing your sins aloud and hearing the words of absolution is a powerful experience; one that you can only have through Reconciliation. By participating in these and other spiritual disciplines, your relationship with God will grow stronger. ❋

HMMMMM. . . In what ways does belief in one God shape our faith?

idolatry ➤ The worship of other beings, creatures, or material goods in a way that is fitting for God alone.

creed ➤ An official profession of faith, usually prepared and presented by a council of the Church and used in the Church's liturgy. Based on the Latin *credo*, meaning "I believe."

Article 35

Trinity: The Central Christian Mystery

Christianity is not the world's only monotheistic faith. Judaism and Islam are also monotheistic, as well as several lesser-known faiths such as Bahá'í, Rastafari, and Zoroastrianism. Christianity, however, makes a unique claim about the one God. We believe that God is three-in-one.

The teaching of Jesus Christ revealed the mystery of the Holy **Trinity**, the mystery that the one God exists in three Divine Persons—the Father, the Son, and the Holy Spirit. The Trinity is one of the Church's most important and fundamental teachings. It is the central mystery of our faith.

The Trinity Is Revealed in Scripture

It may surprise you that the word *Trinity* is not in the Bible. That is because the term was not used until the late second century, and the Church did not completely articulate the doctrine of the Trinity until the Ecumenical Councils of the fourth and fifth centuries. However, even though the word *Trinity* is not in the Bible, teaching about the Trinity is clearly found in Sacred Scripture, especially in the New Testament. We see several references to the concept of the Trinity in the Gospel of John. For example, several times in the Gospel, Christ equates himself with God the Father. Recall John's Prologue, which describes how the Son existed with the Father from before all time.

Stained glass depicting the Holy Trinity: Father, Son, and Holy Spirit

UNIT 3

© jorisvo / Shutterstock.com

Trinity ➤ Often referred to as the Blessed Trinity, the central Christian mystery and dogma that there is one God in three Persons: Father, Son, and Holy Spirit.

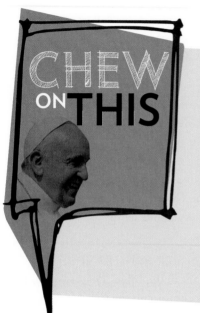

CHEW ON THIS

But the mystery of the Trinity also speaks to us of ourselves, of *our relationship with the Father, the Son and the Holy Spirit.* In fact, through Baptism, the Holy Spirit has placed us in the heart and the very life of God, who is a communion of love. . . . . Our being created in the image and likeness of God–Communion calls us to understand ourselves as beings-in-relationship and to live interpersonal relations in solidarity and mutual love. (Pope Francis, *Angelus,* May 22, 2016)

Later, Jesus states, "Whoever has seen me has seen the Father" (John 14:9). And Jesus, just hours before his death, prays to God the Father for his disciples, asking, "that they may be one just as we are" (17:11). These examples point to the two Divine Persons, God the Father and God the Son, existing as one in the Godhead.

The Gospel of John also introduces the Third Person of the Trinity, the Holy Spirit. We read how Jesus discusses the work of the Holy Spirit in the Last Supper discourses: "The Advocate, the holy Spirit that the Father will send in my name—he will teach you everything and remind you of all that I told you" (John 14:26). With these words, Jesus explains that the Holy Spirit is intimately connected to the Father and the Son, and that all three Divine Persons share in the same saving work of God.

The clearest naming of the Holy Trinity comes not in the Gospel of John, but at the end of the Gospel of Matthew. Just before Jesus is taken up into Heaven, he commissions the disciples to go out into the world to proclaim the Good News. In this event, called the Great Commission, Jesus tells the disciples to baptize "in the name of the Father, and of the Son, and of the Holy Spirit" (Matthew 28:19). This should sound familiar to you. These are the words of the Sign of the Cross, the short prayer evoking the Holy Trinity, which Catholics use at the beginning and end of our prayer times.

The Trinity: United, Yet Distinct

The three Divine Persons are inseparable both in what they are and what they do. They are inseparable in what they *are* because each Divine Person is fully God—complete, whole, and entire. The fullness of God is contained in God the Father. The fullness of God is contained in God the Son. The fullness of God is contained in God the Holy Spirit. All three share the same divine attributes. The Father, the Son, and the Holy Spirit is each all-powerful, all-knowing, all-loving, and eternal.

The three Divine Persons of the Trinity are inseparable in what they *do* because each Divine Person has the same job description, so to speak. Each of the three Persons is engaged in the work of our salvation. Each acts to create us in love, to redeem us, and to make us holy. The work and mission of Father, Son, and Holy Spirit are inseparable.

Even though they are inseparable, the three Persons of the Holy Trinity are truly distinct from one another. This distinction does not divide their divine unity. The Father, Son, and Spirit are always in perfect communion with one another.

If the Persons of the Trinity are united, how are they distinct? First, they are distinct in their relationship with one another. The Father loves the Son and loves the Spirit, as distinct Persons. Similarly, the Son loves the Father and the Spirit, and the Spirit loves the Father and the Son. This was true even before their work for our salvation. These relationships result from each Divine Person's origins. Even though all three Divine Persons are eternal, existing without beginning or end, they each have a distinct origin. God the Father is unbegotten, meaning that he "is the source and origin of all divinity" (Council of Toledo VI [638]). [SL 23] God the Son is eternally begotten of God the Father. In the words of the Nicene Creed, Jesus is "the Only Begotten Son of God, born of the Father before all ages." [SL 30] The Nicene Creed also proclaims that the Holy Spirit "proceeds from the Father and the Son." [SL 35]

UNIT 3

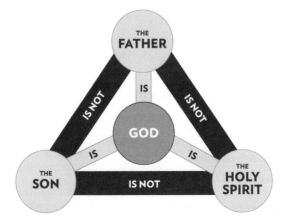

Second, each Divine Person carries out the work of our salvation in the way that is most proper to him. For example, God the Father draws us to follow Christ, God the Son became incarnate, and God the Holy Spirit gives us the gifts of the Spirit. In the next article, we will explore further the distinctiveness of each Person of the Trinity—the Father, the Son, and the Holy Spirit.

The Trinity and You

Our belief in the Trinity permeates our prayer, both when we pray alone and when we gather as a Church. We refer to it every time we make the Sign of the Cross. We mention the Trinity frequently throughout the prayers at Mass. For example, you will often hear: "Through our Lord Jesus Christ, your Son, who lives and reigns with you in the unity of the Holy Spirit, one God, forever and ever" (*Roman Missal*, page 139). Even the structure of the Nicene Creed we pray at Mass is based on the Trinity: "I believe in one God, the Father, the Almighty. . . . I believe in one Lord, Jesus Christ, the only Son of God. . . . I believe in the Holy Spirit, the Lord, the giver of life."

Each time you make the Sign of the Cross, you are invoking the Trinity in prayer.

Why all this emphasis on the Trinity in our prayer? What does the Trinity have to teach us? Pope Francis teaches us that the Trinity has the features of a family. Imagine that every human family reflected the love and unity that the three Divine Persons of the Trinity have for one another. Better yet, imagine that every relationship you have reflects the love among God the Father, Christ the Son, and the Holy Spirit. We would have Heaven on Earth! Which is precisely God's saving plan—that saved from sin and death by Christ and empowered by the Gifts of the Holy Spirit, each of us will be a seed of God's Kingdom, reflecting the love of the Holy Trinity in all our relationships. Each time you make the Sign of the Cross and invoke the Holy Trinity, let it be a reminder to you to love other people with the love of the Father, Son, and Holy Spirit. ✳

HMMMMM. . . How would you explain to someone that our belief in the Trinity does not goes against our belief in one God?

UNIT 3

Article 36

The Distinctness of the Father, Son, and Holy Spirit

Everett's youth minister always started prayer by saying, "Father, God, we come before you today . . . " Everett thought about it, and the next day in religion class, he asked his teacher, "Why only pray to God the Father, if the Son and the Holy Spirit are also equal persons in the Trinity?" She explained there are different situations in which people may feel more comfortable praying to the Son or to the Holy Spirit. She confided that she was often nervous speaking in front of colleagues. "I just take a deep breath and ask the Holy Spirit to guide me and provide me with the right words to say. I trust that the Holy Spirit will work through me to bring the right message. If it were me alone, I might be too nervous to speak at all!"

"When would you pray to Jesus?" Everett asked. "Remember all that Jesus suffered in his Passion?" his teacher asked. "When you are suffering, or struggling, or feel like an outsider, pray to Jesus. He knows exactly how you feel. God hears all of your prayers. Just pray in the way that is most comfortable for you."

UNIT 3

© Godong / Alamy Stock Photo

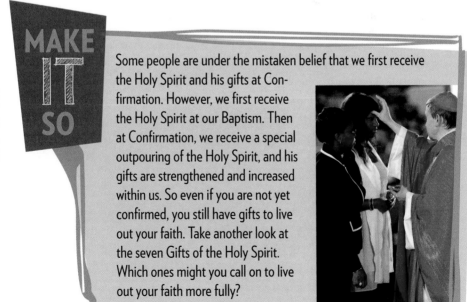

MAKE IT SO

Some people are under the mistaken belief that we first receive the Holy Spirit and his gifts at Confirmation. However, we first receive the Holy Spirit at our Baptism. Then at Confirmation, we receive a special outpouring of the Holy Spirit, and his gifts are strengthened and increased within us. So even if you are not yet confirmed, you still have gifts to live out your faith. Take another look at the seven Gifts of the Holy Spirit. Which ones might you call on to live out your faith more fully?

God the Father

When we profess that God is our Father, we acknowledge that he is the Eternal Source of all life; that all creation, visible and invisible, exists because of him. We also acknowledge that God is all-powerful and desires to be in an intimate, loving relationship with his creation. He loves us, cares for us, provides for us, heals us, forgives us, and is just and faithful. Even if the love of an earthly father—or mother, or friend, or any other person—disappoints us, God's love will never fail us.

In the Gospel of Matthew, we learn that Jesus came to teach us more about our Heavenly Father: "No one knows the son except the Father, and no one knows the Father except the Son and anyone to whom the Son wishes to reveal him" (11:27). So, what did Jesus reveal to us about the Father? In the Gospels, Jesus calls God *Abba*, which, in his native language of Aramaic, means "Father" and has the loving sense of intimacy. This reveals two things about Jesus' relationship with God the Father. First, it reveals that Jesus' relationship with God is filial—that is, a father-son relationship that is from all eternity. As a result, we began to understand God as Father in terms of his being the First Person of the Trinity, the Eternal Father of the Eternal Son. Second, the loving sense of the word *Abba* shows us the intimate nature of the relationship between the Father and Son. Not all father-son relationships are ideal, so Jesus' relationship with his Father is the perfect example for all of us. It shows us how children should love their parents and how parents should love their children.

Jesus calls God Abba, meaning Father.

---

filial ➤ Having to do with the relationship between a child and his or her parent.

Jesus does more than teach us about his loving Father and give us an example of right relationships. He actually invites us to call God "Father" ourselves. We see this most clearly when he teaches his disciples to pray the Our Father (see Matthew 6:9–15). Jesus invites us into the intimate relationship he has with his Divine Father—into the communion of the Holy Trinity. What an honor that Jesus is inviting us to share in the loving community of the Trinity. We can do so because through Baptism we become God the Father's adopted daughters and sons. Saint Paul writes:

> For you did not receive a spirit of slavery to fall back into fear, but you received a spirit of adoption, through which we cry, "Abba, Father!" The Spirit itself bears witness with our spirit that we are children of God, and if children, then heirs, heirs of God and joint heirs with Christ, if only we suffer with him so that we may also be glorified with him. (Romans 8:15–17)

This does not mean that God cares for us only if we are baptized. On the one hand, the Church affirms the necessity of Baptism for salvation. On the other hand, we believe that God's infinite love and tender mercy extend to all people, even in ways we cannot fully understand.

UNIT 3

CATHOLICS MAKING A DIFFERENCE

Saint Elizabeth of the Trinity wasn't always so saintly. In fact, she was described as a holy terror as a toddler. She once shouted: "Bad priest! Bad priest! That's my doll!" at a priest who had borrowed her doll to be used in a Nativity scene. Elizabeth was deeply touched at her First Communion and Confirmation, and she made the bold decision at that young age to take a vow of chastity and become a Carmelite nun. Elizabeth's mother sent her to parties and arranged for boys to pursue her, in hopes that she would marry instead. Elizabeth eventually entered a Carmelite convent in 1901. Her greatest desire was to be enveloped by the Trinity and to surrender to God's love. She died only five years later, at the age of twenty-six, from Addison's disease. Before her death, Elizabeth wrote that it would increase her joy in Heaven if people would ask for her help. Pope Francis declared her a saint in 2016.

God the Son

The Second Person of the Trinity is God the Son, Jesus Christ, who assumed a human nature for our salvation. Recall that when we studied the Gospel of John we learned that Jesus Christ is eternally begotten, meaning he has existed with the Father since before time began. Just as the Father is God, Jesus Christ is God too. He is also the Incarnate Son of God, born of the Virgin Mary, both fully God and fully human. The Incarnate Son of God is the perfection of what it means to be human, which makes him the ideal person for us to imitate. The work that is proper to Christ, the Second Person of the Blessed Trinity, is redemption or salvation. Jesus Christ is our **Savior**. Even Jesus' name in Hebrew points to his role as our Savior because it means, "God saves." What does it mean to call Christ our Savior? First, it means he came to reconcile us to himself because sin had separated humanity from God. Second, it means that he came to reveal God's divine love to us and show us how to be holy. Third, it means he came into the world so that we might share in the divine life as adopted sons and daughters of God.

Couldn't Christ have entered the world as an adult, fully ready to begin his ministry? Why was it necessary for him to enter the world as an infant?

Savior ➤ One who brings salvation; specifically, Jesus Christ.

We also call Jesus Christ our **Redeemer**. *Redeemer* is not a word frequently used today outside of Church discussions, so we need to look back at the ancient Roman world to understand its true meaning. In the first century, a "ransom" was the price paid to buy the freedom of a slave. The person who paid the ransom was known as a *redeemer*. Guided by the Holy Spirit, the early Christians began to reflect on the meaning of the death of Jesus, and borrowed this concept from the Roman world (remember, they were living in the Roman Empire). They were also aware of Old Testament prophecies promising that God would save the people from their sin. Therefore, the early Christians taught that Jesus had "paid the price" to "ransom" us from our slavery to sin; therefore, Jesus, the Second Person of the Trinity, is truly our Redeemer.

God the Holy Spirit

The Third Person of the Trinity is the Holy Spirit. In the words of the Nicene Creed, the Holy Spirit is "the Lord, the giver of life who proceeds from the Father and Son." The Holy Spirit had been active in salvation history, but in a humble way. The Holy Spirit never points to himself; instead, he directs us to, and reveals, the Father and Christ, his Word.

In fact, the second verse of the Bible already alludes to the Holy Spirit! This verse says there was "a mighty wind sweeping over the waters" (Genesis 1:2). The Hebrew word for *wind* is the same word used for *breath*. The Holy Spirit is often equated with breath or wind. So it is the Holy Spirit, as God's breath, that brings order out of the waters of chaos. It is the Holy Spirit who speaks to God's people through the ancient prophets and who anoints Jesus for his special mission to redeem and save us. However, the Holy Spirit is not fully revealed until after Jesus' death and Resurrection.

Recall reading in John's Gospel that when Jesus knows that the hour of his death is near, he promises his disciples that he will ask God to send them an **Advocate** (in Greek, *Paraclete*; see John 14:16–17). An advocate is someone who is on our side to help us, strengthen us, and empower us for holiness. This Advocate that Jesus promised is the Third Person of the Holy Trinity, the Holy Spirit. Jesus told the disciples that the Spirit would teach them everything they need to know (see verse 26).

UNIT 3

Redeemer One who frees others from distress, harm, captivity, or the consequences of sin; specifically, Jesus Christ.

Advocate ➤ Another name for the Holy Spirit. The Third Divine Person of the Blessed Trinity, the personal love of Father and Son for each other. Also called the Paraclete and the Spirit of Truth.

After Jesus dies and rises from the dead, he makes good on his promise. The Risen Lord appears to the disciples, breathes on them, and says, "Receive the holy Spirit" (John 20:22). When we study the Acts of the Apostles, we will learn that at **Pentecost** Jesus sends the Holy Spirit, now fully revealed, to be with his disciples forever—both those who were his earliest followers and for us today.

The Holy Spirit sanctifies the People of God by offering us seven gifts to help us as we strive to live as Christians. Receiving the **Gifts of the Holy Spirit** means that the mission of Jesus becomes the mission of the Church. In fact, it becomes *our* mission. Through the Gifts of the Holy Spirit, we are empowered to be true followers of Christ. When we seek to use the Gifts of the Holy Spirit, we allow the Holy Spirit to form in us the **fruits of the Holy Spirit**. They are called fruits, because they are the firstfruits of our eternal glory, the signs of what is to come in Heaven.

❋

© sedmak / iStockphoto.com

Notice the use of light and color in this painting of Pentecost. What is the artist highlighting with these effects?

UNIT 3

Pentecost ➤ The fiftieth day following Easter, which commemorates the descent of the Holy Spirit on the Apostles and Mary.

Gifts of the Holy Spirit ➤ At Baptism, we receive seven Gifts of the Holy Spirit. These gifts are freely given to us to help us live as followers of Jesus and to build up the Body of Christ, the Church. The seven gifts are wisdom, understanding, right judgment or counsel, fortitude or courage, knowledge, piety or reverence, and fear of the Lord or wonder and awe.

fruits of the Holy Spirit ➤ When we cooperate with the graces and gifts we receive from the Holy Spirit, we see the effect of the Holy Spirit's presence in our lives in special qualities and attitudes that we develop as we grow in faith. The twelve fruits of the Holy Spirit are love, joy, peace, patience, kindness, goodness, generosity, gentleness, faithfulness, modesty, self-control, and chastity.

GIFTS OF THE HOLY SPIRIT	
Wisdom	Opens our eyes to see God's plan for the world and helps us follow his plan until our ultimate union with him in Heaven.
Understanding	Makes it possible for us to follow the correct course of action in difficult or confusing situations.
Counsel	Also called Right Judgment; helps us to know right from wrong and to choose the good consistently.
Fortitude	Also called Courage; enables us to do the right things, even when we are afraid.
Knowledge	Empowers us to use our intellect to learn more about our faith.
Piety	Also called Reverence; reminds us that God is God, and enables us to recognize that all we are, all we do, and all we have comes from God.
Fear of the Lord	Also called Wonder and Awe; fills us with a spirit of profound respect as we marvel at God's power and goodness.

UNIT 3

HMMMMMM. . . How might you pray in a slightly different way to each Person of the Holy Trinity?

1. What is monotheism, and why is it important?

2. What is idolatry, and how is it manifested today?

3. What does Jesus quote in response to a question about the Greatest Commandment?

4. What is the central mystery of the Christian faith?

5. Explain how the three Divine Persons are inseparable and distinct.

6. What does Jesus reveal to us about God the Father?

7. We call Jesus Christ our Redeemer. What was a redeemer in ancient Rome, and how does that concept apply to the saving work of Christ?

8. What is the proper work of the Holy Spirit?

9. What is formed in us when we use the Gifts of the Holy Spirit?

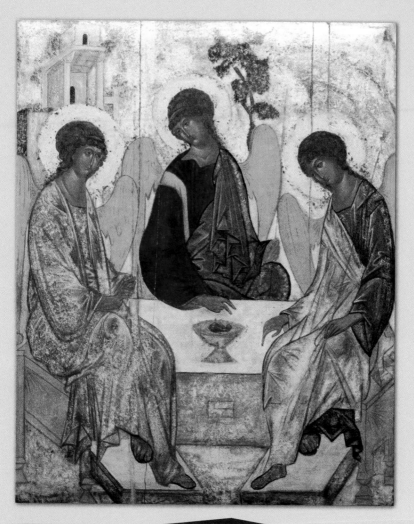

ART STUDY

REPRESENTATION OF THE TRINITY

The unique relationship between the three Divine Persons of the Trinity is explored in this icon.

1. What feature of this painting indicates an invitation to the viewer to enter into the mystery, story, or relationship depicted here?

2. Look closely at the facial features of each figure. Why do you think they are virtually the same?

3. What symbols do you notice in the artwork?

UNIT 3

CHAPTER 10
The Church Teaches and Safeguards the Truth

HOW DO PEOPLE MISUNDERSTAND THE TRINITY?

SNAPSHOT

Article 37

The Early Church Faces Challenges to Apostolic Faith

With their knowledge of Jesus' life and teaching, and under the guidance of the Holy Spirit, the Apostles worked to help people correctly understand their faith in Jesus Christ. But this was not always easy. Other people came forward to promote their personal theories about Jesus' identity. We call these false teachings **heresies**. Some heresies can cause a lot of confusion among the faithful because they may sound reasonable even if they are not true. The early Church defended the true teachings, passed on by the Apostles, against these heresies.

UNIT 3

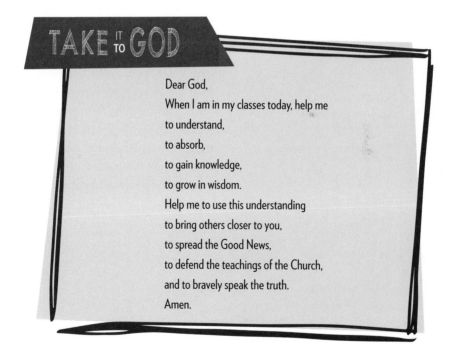

TAKE IT TO GOD

Dear God,
When I am in my classes today, help me
to understand,
to absorb,
to gain knowledge,
to grow in wisdom.
Help me to use this understanding
to bring others closer to you,
to spread the Good News,
to defend the teachings of the Church,
and to bravely speak the truth.
Amen.

heresy ➤ The conscious and deliberate rejection by a baptized person of a truth of faith that must be believed.

The New Testament letters testify to the early Church's struggles against heresies. The author of the First Letter of John warns against "antichrists" who are pushing false teachings (see 4:3). These people are teaching that Jesus is not human, that he did not suffer in the flesh. They have just enough truth in their theory for it to sound plausible, but it is still not correct. The letter makes clear that true faith in Jesus means believing that Jesus came in the flesh, that he is true God and true man.

In the Second Letter to Peter, we read about another Church struggle to protect God's revealed truth. In this letter, the author condemns another group of false teachers, calling them "irrational animals" who teach others to live a life full of sin (2:12). These letters represent the beginning efforts of the Church to help the faithful understand their faith and defend it against false teachings.

Church Fathers used the language of Greek philosophers to help the people of their time understand Church doctrine.

UNIT 3

© stefanel / Shutterstock.com

Finding the Right Words

After the deaths of the Apostles, their successors take up the responsibility of guiding the faithful and defending the apostolic teaching. As the Church's doctrine develops, the bishops and **Church Fathers** turn to the language of Greek **philosophy** to express the doctrine in a way that makes sense to the people of their time. This language, though often difficult for us to understand today, was in common use at the time.

Church Fathers ➤ Church teachers and writers of the early centuries whose teachings are a witness to the Tradition of the Church.

philosophy ➤ In Greek, this word literally means "love of wisdom." It refers to the study of human existence using logical reasoning.

Paragraph 252 of the *CCC* explains some of the words the Church Fathers use, which are still used today, to describe Trinitarian doctrine:

- The word *substance* is used to name "the divine being in its unity."
- The word *person* (in Greek, *hypostasis*) is used to refer to the Father, Son, and Holy Spirit, each fully God, yet each distinct.
- The word *relation* is used to indicate that the distinction among the three Persons lies in the relationship of each to the others.

Developing this standard vocabulary when discussing the Trinity enables the Church Fathers to more easily express the faith to the early Christian community in words they can understand. It also enables them to defend their faith to those who challenge it.

Learning the Language of Our Faith

Why is knowing the language of our faith important anyway? Because words matter. Because the truth matters. Let's consider the language used to describe the reality of the Trinity. It is important that we call each member of the Trinity a Divine *Person*. If we called them a "force" or "power," we would take away from the truth that God is loving and relational. It is important that in the **Nicene Creed** we describe Jesus Christ as being "*consubstantial* [of the same substance] with the Father." If this were not true, the three Persons of the Trinity would not be one God but three different gods. By being precise in our language, we hold onto the truth that God has revealed and preserve it for future generations. ✳

UNIT 3

HMMMMMM. . . Why are the words we use so important when we talk about our faith?

Nicene Creed ➤ The formal statement or profession of faith commonly recited during the Eucharist.

Article 38
Early Heresies about Jesus

How can 100 percent man and 100 percent God equal 100 percent Jesus? That just doesn't seem to add up! The mystery of Jesus' being fully man and fully God doesn't make sense as math or science. During the first centuries of the Church, some heresies, or incorrect beliefs about Jesus, developed. The early bishops and Church Fathers struggled to articulate and defend the mystery of Christ's human and divine natures against these **Christological** heresies.

Trying to find the right balance when speaking about Jesus Christ as true God and true man requires an ongoing effort. We must fully affirm Jesus' human and divine natures without diminishing either his divinity or his humanity. During the first several centuries of Christianity, many teachers failed to keep that balance. As a result, their teachings led to some bizarre conclusions. The early bishops and Church Fathers had to work hard against these Christological heresies to acknowledge and promote a correct understanding of Jesus' true nature.

The early bishops and Church Fathers battled against the "fake news" of heresies in order to help Christians understand Jesus' true nature.

© shockfactor.de / Shutterstock.com

Christological ➤ Having to do with the branch of theology called Christology. Christology is the study of the divinity of Jesus Christ, the Son of God and the Second Divine Person of the Trinity, and his earthly ministry and eternal mission.

CATHOLICS **MAKING** A DIFFERENCE

"Bishop Exiled from Own Diocese Five Times!" This could have been a headline in the fourth century. The supporters of Arianism were powerful in the early Church. They frequently combined forces with the political elites to promote their teachings. Saint Athanasius, the Bishop of Alexandria, fought back against these false teachings. He was just twenty years old at the beginning of the Council of Nicaea. Though not a bishop, Athanasius made a name for himself by disputing the Arian teaching. He continued to assert his anti-Arian position by defying the emperor Constantine in refusing to restore Arius to communion with the Church. As a result of sticking to his principles, he was exiled five times!

UNIT 3

Getting It Wrong about Jesus' Divinity

Some Christological heresies downplayed or denied the divinity of Jesus, falsely presenting Jesus as merely human, or something like an angel. For example, Arianism claimed that Jesus was a creature begotten by God before he created the rest of the world. Arius, its proponent, believed that if Jesus was begotten, he could not be God and he did not have the same substance as the God the Father. In other words, Arius did not deny that Jesus was the Word of God, but he denied that Jesus was divine. The Ecumenical Council of Nicaea condemned Arius and Arianism in AD 325, proclaiming that Christ was the Son of God, begotten by the God the Father, and consubstantial with (having the same substance as) the Father. The Nicene Creed that we say in Mass today was initially developed at the Council of Nicaea and modified and extended at the Council of Constantinople to refute the teachings of Arianism.

Nestorianism put forward that in Jesus Christ there were actually two persons. One was divine and one was human. Nestorius argued that it was wrong to say things like "God suffered and died for us" or "God was born of

---

Arianism ➤ A heretical movement that claimed that Jesus was a creature who, although begotten by God the Father, lacked a divine nature. Arius denied that Christ was consubstantial with God the Father.

Nestorianism ➤ A heretical movement that claimed there were actually two persons joined together in Christ, one divine and the other human.

the Virgin Mary." These statements would apply to the human person Jesus but not to the Divine Person. Nestorius was concerned about stressing the humanity of Jesus. He would not even allow the Virgin Mary to be referred to as the Mother of God. By dividing Jesus' two natures, Nestorianism breaks the unity within Christ, wrongly implying that there are two different persons within Christ.

Getting It Wrong about Jesus' Humanity

Other heresies downplayed the humanity of Jesus. **Docetism** alleged that Jesus' humanity was a sort of disguise—he looked like a human and acted like a human, but inside he was really God. For example, Docetists claimed that Jesus didn't really suffer on the cross. They said he *appeared* to be suffering, but he couldn't *really* suffer a human death because he was God. If this were true, it implies Jesus was just faking it on the cross and therefore Jesus could not have been our Redeemer. **Monophysitism** is similar to Docetism. Monophysitism proposed that Jesus' divinity fully absorbed his humanity. In essence, Monophysitism claimed that Jesus was only divine and not human. This approach undercuts Jesus' role as our Redeemer. Without Jesus taking on a human nature in the Incarnation, he could not suffer as we do, or experience death.

The Gnostics were yet another heretical group that embraced views that were quite different than the others. **Gnosticism** claims that Jesus was not a man at all, but a semidivine being. The name comes from *gnosis*, the Greek word for "knowledge." Gnostics believed that salvation could be reached only by getting special, secret knowledge from God or God's agent. They believed that God sent Jesus to share this special knowledge with a select, elite group of people he wanted to save. The Gnostics had their own writings and gospels, which were not accepted as part of the Canon of the New Testament. Their "proof" for Jesus acting as God's agent to dispense this secret knowledge cannot be found in any of the accepted writings of the New Testament. Their idea that God would only provide salvation for a select few creates division and strife.

Docetism ➤ A heretical movement that claimed Jesus' humanity was a sort of disguise—he looked like a human and acted like a human, but he was only divine, lacking a human nature.

Monophysitism ➤ A heretical movement that claimed Jesus' divinity fully absorbed his humanity, so that, in the end, he was only divine and not human.

Gnosticism ➤ A heretical movement that claimed that only a select, elite group could attain salvation by acquiring special, secret knowledge from God.

UNIT 3

Early Christological Heresies

HERESIES DOWNPLAYING JESUS' DIVINITY	
Heresy	**Beliefs**
Arianism	Jesus was a creature without a divine nature, who was not consubstantial with God the Father.
Nestorianism	In Jesus there were actually two persons, one divine and one human. It was improper to speak of them as one.
HERESIES DOWNPLAYING JESUS' HUMANITY	
Heresy	**Beliefs**
Docetism	Jesus' humanity was a sort of disguise—he looked like a human and acted like a human, but inside he was really God.
Monophysitism	Jesus' divinity fully absorbed his humanity so that, in the end, he was only divine and not human.
Gnosticism	Only a select, elite group can attain salvation by acquiring special, secret knowledge from God.

UNIT 3

The Effect of False Teachings

The Church's battle against Christological and Trinitarian heresies teaches us the danger in denying or changing God's revealed truth. The danger is this: The fabric of our faith is so interconnected that if a false belief, or the rejection of one truth, does not remain isolated, it can ultimately affect our acceptance of other revealed truths too.

Consider for a moment this important truth revealed by God: All human beings have an inherent dignity and right to life, from conception to natural death. The Church teaches us to respect and protect every person's life, from the unborn, to the sick and aged, to those on death row. Some people reject this truth, deciding that it is morally okay for someone who is terminally ill to take their own life. From there it is only a small step to believing abortion is probably okay if a child is going to have severe birth defects. When we choose which revealed truths to believe and which ones to reject, we put ourselves on a dangerous **slippery slope** that can lead us far away from the true teachings of Jesus Christ.

When there is a part of your Catholic faith that you do not understand or that you struggle to accept, that is where God is calling you to dig deeper. How can you dig deeper? Pray about it and try to learn more about the teaching and why the Church teaches it. You can research it, or ask your parents, a priest, teacher, or other knowledgeable friends to help you understand why this is part of our faith. You will find a lot of collective wisdom you can rely on. ✳

© Marijus Auruskevicius / Shutterstock.com

What is part of your faith that you struggle to understand or accept?

HMMMMMM. . .

How do the Christological heresies fail to keep a balanced view of Jesus Christ?

---

slippery slope ➤ A course of action that seems to lead inevitably from one action or result to another, with unintended consequences.

Article 39

The Ecumenical Councils of the Early Church

As the world's politics change, our cultural beliefs and practices change, and new developments in science and technology emerge. Because of these changes, the bishops see new challenges among the people they shepherd. If the bishops agree that there is a need to address a particular issue or set of issues, they meet to discuss it and make decisions.

When all the bishops of the world meet to address pressing issues, the gathering is called an Ecumenical Council. There have been twenty-one Ecumenical Councils over the past two thousand years. A particular focus of the Ecumenical Councils in the early centuries of the Church was the heresies that challenged the Christological and Trinitarian doctrines. Seven Ecumenical Councils were held between AD 325 and AD 787. Of these seven, the two that specifically addressed the heresies of Arianism and Gnosticism, and thereby cemented our creed, were the Councils of Nicaea and Chalcedon.

UNIT 3

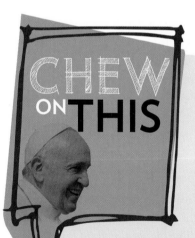

CHEW ON THIS

When discussing the Second Vatican Council, Pope Francis reminds us that the Ecumenical Councils go well beyond simply ensuring that teachings are correct. They get at the heart of our missionary calling as followers of Jesus Christ, to go spread the Good News:

Before all else, the Council was an encounter. A genuine encounter between the Church and the men and women of our time. An encounter marked by the power of the Spirit, who impelled the Church to emerge from the shoals which for years had kept her self-enclosed so as to set out once again, with enthusiasm, on her missionary journey. ("Homily for the Inauguration of the Jubilee," December 8, 2015)

The Council of Nicaea

By AD 325, Arius's false teaching that Jesus was more than an ordinary human but less than God, was cause for the bishops to come together. This gathering of bishops is called the Council of Nicaea. At Nicaea, they declared that God the Son is "of the same substance" as God the Father. In other words, Jesus is truly God. By stating and defending this belief, the bishops directly countered heretical claims of Arianism.

The Council of Nicaea was held in AD 325 to address Arianism.

The Council of Nicaea also produced the first formulation of what is now known as the Nicene Creed. This Creed was modified and expanded at the Council of Constantinople to become the creed we usually pray at Mass. When you pray the creed, notice how much focus we put on Jesus Christ's identity as the fully Divine Son of God. We proclaim that Jesus was "born of the Father before all ages, God from God, Light from Light, true God from true God." Clearly, the council wanted to leave no doubt, or room for misunderstanding, that Jesus is fully divine. Next time you are at Mass, pay close attention to the words you are professing. They were written nearly seventeen hundred years ago, yet continue to express, with both beauty and clarity, Jesus' identity as the Second Person of the Trinity.

The Council of Chalcedon

Just as Arianism needed to be addressed at Nicaea, Nestorianism was the focus of the Council of Chalcedon. Nestorius taught that in Jesus there are actually two Persons—one divine and one human. The bishops realized that they needed to clarify the relationship between Jesus' humanity and divinity. In the year 451, the 350 bishops attending the Council of Chalcedon declared that Jesus' two natures (his human nature and his divine nature) are undivided and inseparable. Jesus is fully man and fully God. He is not half man and half God; nor is he two Persons somehow pushed into one. Jesus, the Son of God, is *one* Divine Person with *two* natures. The Council of Chalcedon concluded that Jesus is of the same substance as God the Father when it comes to his divinity, and that he is of the same substance as us when it comes to his humanity.

Do Our Catholic Beliefs Change?

Rose was recently learning about the Ecumenical Councils in her religion class. When her teacher was explaining the shifts in teachings and practice that happened with Vatican Council II, Rose was confused. She asked, "If so many things changed in the Church after Vatican Council II, did the Pope and the bishops change what we believe?" Her teacher responded, "No, but there were definitely changes to the way we practice our faith."

"Think about it this way, Rose. When you were little, did you hug and kiss your parents often to show them how much you loved them? Maybe you held your mom's hand in the store or always wanted one more hug goodnight?" Rose nodded her head in agreement. "You still love your parents just as much as when you were little, but the way you show it might have changed. Maybe now the way you say I love you is a high five after a good practice or a kiss on the cheek in the car or a heart emoji in a text message." Rose nodded and smiled. Her teacher concluded, "Over all those years, even though the way you are expressing your love has changed, the truth that you love them has not."

In one respect, the decisions by the Ecumenical Councils of the Church can be viewed the same way. When the early Church councils made statements about Jesus Christ, they were not changing what we believe. They were merely clarifying what we have believed since "we were young," during the time of the Apostles. It is the same for Vatican Council II. At the opening of the Second Vatican Council, on October 11, 1962, Pope John XXIII said the following:

"The substance of the ancient doctrine of the Deposit of Faith is one thing, and the formulation in which it is clothed is another." In other words, who God is and the divine truths revealed by God do not change, but the way we express them can change over time. We believe that under the guidance of the Holy Spirit, the bishops speaking as one at an Ecumenical Council will guard the faith from error and help us to grow in expressing our faith. ✴

How has the way you express love and care for your parents changed over the years?

UNIT 3

HMMMMM. . . If the revealed truths of our faith never change, why do we need Ecumenical Councils?

Article 40

The Nicene Creed

Have you ever used an online encyclopedia where you can look up virtually any topic you want? Let's say you want to read about the Declaration of Independence, so you go to that page. There you can read the actual words of the Declaration, but some of the words, like *liberty* or *government*, are also hyperlinks that you can click. These hyperlinks lead you to another related page so you can learn even more. The links are virtually endless, and they help reveal the depth of meaning captured by the words of the Declaration. In a way, you can think of the Nicene Creed as the Church's main web page, like in an online encyclopedia. The creed is a summary statement of our Catholic faith into which we can delve much deeper into the essential topics it professes.

The Nicene Creed is a summary statement of our Catholic faith and a good starting place to more deeply explore what we believe.

Proclaiming Shared Beliefs

You've probably studied the Declaration of Independence in one or more of your classes so far. Part of it sums up what people in the British colonies of North America believed in 1776 about their rights. In a similar way, a creed is a summary statement of the beliefs of an individual or community. The creed

Catholics pray most frequently is the Nicene Creed. The formal name for this creed is the Niceno-Constantinopolitan Creed. It is the product of two Ecumenical Councils, the Council of Nicaea held in AD 325 and the Council of Constantinople in AD 381.

Even if you are familiar with the Nicene Creed, take the opportunity to read it carefully now and find where it expresses these key doctrines of our faith:

- A Trinitarian faith in God the Father, God the Son, and God the Holy Spirit.
- Jesus' birth, death, Resurrection, and Ascension as key events in our salvation.
- The four "Marks" or characteristics of the Church: the Church is One, Holy, Catholic, and Apostolic.
- Belief in the resurrection of the dead and in the **Last Judgment**.

UNIT 3

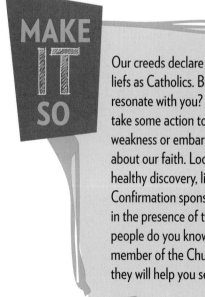

MAKE IT SO

Our creeds declare a simple and clear statement of our core beliefs as Catholics. But how does this universal statement of beliefs resonate with you? If the Nicene Creed seems abstract or lifeless, take some action to explore its meaning. Ask questions! It isn't a weakness or embarrassment to not know the answers to questions about our faith. Look to those you know who will guide you in healthy discovery, like your parents, teachers, youth ministers, Confirmation sponsor, or the priest at your parish. Put yourself in the presence of those who can witness their faith to you. What people do you know who are doing their best to follow Christ as a member of the Church? Surround yourself with these people, and they will help you see the creed come alive!

Last Judgment ➤ The judgment of the human race by Jesus Christ at his second coming. It is also called the Final Judgment.

The Nicene Creed

I believe in one God,
the Father almighty,
maker of heaven and earth,
of all things visible and invisible.

I believe in one Lord Jesus Christ,
the Only Begotten Son of God,
born of the Father before all ages.
God from God, Light from Light,
true God from true God,
begotten, not made, consubstantial with the Father;
through him all things were made.

For us men and for our salvation
he came down from heaven,
and by the Holy Spirit was incarnate of the Virgin Mary,
and became man.

For our sake he was crucified under Pontius Pilate,
he suffered death and was buried,
and rose again on the third day
in accordance with the Scriptures.
He ascended into heaven
and is seated at the right hand of the Father.
He will come again in glory
to judge the living and the dead
and his kingdom will have no end.

I believe in the Holy Spirit, the Lord, the giver of life,
who proceeds from the Father and the Son,
who with the Father and the Son is adored and glorified,
who has spoken through the prophets.

I believe in one, holy, catholic and apostolic Church.
I confess one Baptism for the forgiveness of sins
and I look forward to the resurrection of the dead
and the life of the world to come. Amen.

Think of the key words in the Nicene Creed as hyperlinks, and ask your-self what you'd be linked to if you clicked on one. If you clicked on *Father*, you could learn about monotheism and how Jesus revealed our God as a loving Father. If you clicked on *Baptism*, you could discover more how we celebrate the sacrament, and what it means for our salvation. The depth and breadth of our faith is unbelievable, and the creed can be the door to exploring it.

Catholics Pray the Nicene Creed at Mass

Harper complained loudly to her friends that going to Mass was boring: "Stand, sit, kneel. Stand, sit, kneel. It's the same thing over and over. We even say the same prayers. I already have the creed memorized. Why do we need to say it every single time?" There are many ways to respond to Harper's complaints. The most important thing to focus on is why we say the creed. It is similar to singing the national anthem at the beginning of a sporting event. We sing the anthem because it is a sign of unity and tells a story of our early founding. Likewise, the creed helps bring us together and express the core of our beliefs.

UNIT 3

Proclaiming the creed together at Mass is a communal expression of our beliefs that binds us to one another in faith.

This recitation of the Nicene or Apostle's Creed during a liturgy is called the Profession of Faith. Praying the creed together in this way allows the gathered assembly to "respond to the word of God proclaimed in the readings taken from Sacred Scripture and explained in the homily and that they may also call to mind and confess the great mysteries of the faith" (*Roman Missal*, page 34, number 67). If you have ever heard an inspiring homily or if you have ever personally identified with a reading or song during Mass, you know that it can inspire you to believe. The word *creed* comes from the Latin for "I believe." So, when we recite the creed, we are saying, "I believe!" The creed highlights our unity as one community of faith. We can help and support one another in our efforts to be faithful to the truths we profess together. Moreover, because we belong to a global Church, we are united in faith, through the creed, with Catholics throughout the world. ✳

UNIT 3

HMMMMM. . .

How does the creed help to define and defend our faith?

Article 41

The Trinity: Model for Human Relationships

We have explored how the Early Church defined and guarded our faith in the Trinity. But that was a long time ago. You may be wondering, "What does the Trinity have to do with me?" For many Catholics, the Trinity can seem like an incomprehensible mystery, a distant reality, or an abstract theory. In fact, the Trinity isn't unrelated to our human experience. There are similarities between the unity of the Persons of the Trinity and the kind of relationships we should have with one another.

A Relationship of Perfect Love

Do you remember reading what happened in the Gospel of Luke after Jesus was baptized by John the Baptist? Luke writes:

> After all the people had been baptized and Jesus had been baptized and was praying, heaven was opened and the holy Spirit descended upon him in bodily form like a dove. A voice came from heaven, "You are my beloved Son; with you I am well pleased." (3:21–22)

In this brief passage, we get a glimpse into the relational aspect of the Trinity. Notice how Jesus is in communication with the Father through the Holy Spirit as he is praying. Observe how the Holy Spirit descends upon him. What a loving image of the Holy Spirit's care, support, and presence for Jesus. Don't overlook the Father; offering his support to Jesus in words every child wants to hear from their parent, "I am well pleased with you."

John the Baptist baptizes Jesus.

UNIT 3

© Alan_Lagadu / iStockphoto.com

In this passage, we see three distinct Persons—Father, Son, and Holy Spirit—reaching out to one another in love and support. Our Triune God is not distant from us, unconcerned with our joys and struggles; rather, this is a perfect example of our God involved in human history.

Guided by the Life of the Trinity

This is the God in whose image we are created. This is the God—Father, Son, and Holy Spirit—in whose name we are baptized, and with whom we are destined to live forever in Heaven. While we live on Earth, we are to live like our God—in relationship with others, not in isolation. How can you do that? Dialogue with others about their beliefs and yours. Be of service to others. Put down your phone and engage in personal, one-on-one interaction with others. Look in their eyes when you talk to them. Share your gifts of art, music, drama, dance, compassion, public speaking, empathy, and love. In this way, the Trinity, as a communion of Divine Persons, gives us a foundation for relationships built on unity, truth, and love.

How often do you make it a point to put down your phone and interact with others face-to-face, with no interruption of technology?

O most Holy Trinity,
Undivided Unity,
Holy God, Mighty God,
God immortal be adored!

Is this an excerpt from the *Catechism?* No, it's a verse from the hymn "Oh God, Almighty Father." There are many hymns about the Holy Trinity in our Church hymnals. Often these hymns are centuries old, dating back to a time when most people couldn't read. So how did the Church teach people the truths of the faith? Through art and music! Singing these hymns not only helped people worship God but also taught people about God. So the next time you are singing in Church, think about what the words are teaching, as well as enjoying the tune!

UNIT 3

How can you use the Trinity as a model for your own relationships?

- You can be involved in the lives of your family members. Listen, support, and be present.
- You can reach out to a new student at your school.
- You can enlarge your circle of friends and acquaintances to include people that others may have overlooked or excluded.
- You can take on a new role or ministry in your parish community.

Can you think of other ways?

When we live out our call to community in these and other ways, we are truly following God's plan for humanity. That plan is revealed for us in the mystery of the Holy Trinity: three Divine Persons living forever in unity and love as one. ✳

HMMMMM. . . In what ways is the life of the Trinity reflected in my life?

1. What problems can heresies cause among the faithful?

2. What are the benefits of developing a standard vocabulary for describing the Trinity?

3. What were the two main types of heresies about Jesus in the early Church?

4. What was wrong with Arius's heresy?

5. Explain what Ecumenical Councils are and what their purpose is.

6. What did the Council of Nicaea declare about Jesus? What belief were they defending?

7. What are some of the key doctrines of the Catholic faith stated in the Nicene Creed?

8. Describe how the three Divine Persons of the Trinity appear at Jesus' Baptism as described in the Gospel of Luke. What do we learn about their relationship from this biblical account?

UNIT 3

PETER AND PAUL

This icon focuses on the bond between Peter and Paul and the end of the Council of Jerusa-lem.

1. Based on what you read in this chapter about heresies and Church councils, why do you think Peter and Paul might be embracing?

2. What do you think happened before this scene?

3. Why do you think the artist chose this topic for his artwork?

UNIT 3 HIGHLIGHTS

CHAPTER 8 Jesus Reveals God's Mercy and Justice

Unique Stories of Mercy

- The Parable of the Lost Coin (Luke 15:8–10)
- The Parable of the Lost Sheep (Luke 15:1–7)
- The Parable of the Good Samaritan (Luke 10:29–37)
- The Parable of the Lost Son (Luke 15:11–32)
- The Story of the Good Thief on the Cross (Luke 23:39–43)

Unique Stories of Justice

- The *Magnificat* (Luke 1:46–55)
- Instruction by John the Baptist (Luke 3:11)
- Jesus proclaims his mission to establish justice (Luke 4:18–19)
- The Parable of the Good Samaritan (Luke 10:29–37)
- The Parable of the Rich Man and Lazarus (Luke 16:19–31)

God's Merciful Plan

- The heart of Paul's teaching about God's saving plan is the justification of all who believe in Jesus Christ.
- Though we all sin, God's infinite mercy is the source of our hope and salvation.
- Jesus' life, Passion, death, and Resurrection have restored our broken relationship with God.
- Through Baptism, we die with Christ, to our old way of life.
- Having died with Christ, we have the hope of rising again to eternal glory with him and God the Father.

Mary's Unique Role

- Mary courageously answers "Yes!" to God's invitation (celebrated on the Feast of the Annunciation).
- Mary describes herself as the "handmaid of the Lord" (Luke 1:38).
- Mary is the first disciple, the most faithful follower of Jesus.
- By respecting Mary's free will, God affirms the sacredness and dignity of our human nature.

CHAPTER 9 Jesus Reveals God as Trinity

The Relational Nature of the Trinity

Christianity makes the unique claim that the One God is three Divine Persons, the Holy Trinity.

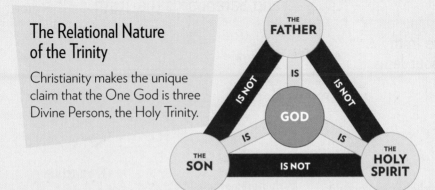

UNIT 3

The Distinctiveness of Father, Son, and Holy Spirit

God the Father

- We acknowledge that God is the Eternal Source of all life.

- Jesus calls God *Abba,* which means "father."

- Jesus invites us to call God father ourselves.

God the Son

- Jesus Christ assumed a human nature for our salvation.

- The Incarnate Son of God is the perfection of what it means to be human.

Even though the three Divine Persons are unique in their relationship to one another, they all share the same saving work.

God the Holy Spirit

- The Holy Spirit is the Lord, the giver of life who proceeds from the Father and Son.

- The Holy Spirit is the Advocate that Jesus promised his disciples he would send.

- The Holy Spirit is not fully revealed until after Jesus' death and Resurrection.

CHAPTER 10 The Church Teaches and Safeguards the Truth

Fishing for the Truth about Jesus

UNIT 3

Arianism

Early heresy focusing on Jesus' humanity

Belief: Jesus was created, just as we were, and was not consubstantial with the Father.

Belief: Jesus was a higher creature than humans but less than God.

Nestorianism

Early heresy focusing on Jesus' humanity

Belief: In Jesus, there were actually two Persons, one divine and one human.

Belief: It was improper to speak of them as one Person.

Docetism

Early heresy focusing on Jesus' divinity

Belief: Jesus' humanity was a sort of disguise—he looked like a human and acted like a human, but he was really just divine, lacking a human nature.

Gnosticism

Early heresy focusing on Jesus' divinity

Belief: Only a select, elite group can attain salvation, by acquiring special, secret knowledge from God.

Monophysitism

Early heresy focusing on Jesus' divinity

Belief: Jesus' divinity fully absorbed his humanity, so that in the end, he was only divine and not human.

Jesus is consubstantial, or of the same substance, as the Father.

Jesus is both truly human and truly divine.

Jesus suffered, died, and rose for all people, not just a select few.

Two Early Ecumenical Councils

When all the bishops of the world meet to address pressing issues, the gathering is called an Ecumenical Council. There have been twenty-one Ecumenical Councils over the past two thousand years. Two of the early Church councils addressed heresies and cemented our creed.

Council of Nicaea	Council of Chalcedon
• Called in AD 325	• Called in AD 451
• Called to address Arius's false teaching that Jesus was more than human, but less than God	• Called to address Nestorius's claim that in Jesus there are two separate people, one human and one divine
• Outcome = declared that Jesus is "of the same substance" as God the Father	• Outcome = declared that Jesus' two natures are undivided and inseparable
• Outcome = produced the first draft of what is now known as the Nicene Creed	• Outcome = declared that Jesus is fully man and fully God, not half man and half God, not two Persons somehow pushed into one

UNIT 3

UNIT 3
BRING IT HOME

WHAT ARE GOD'S IMPORTANT CHARACTERISTICS?

FOCUS QUESTIONS

CHAPTER 8   Does God judge us
             or forgive us?

CHAPTER 9   Why is the Trinity
             so important?

CHAPTER 10   How do people misunderstand
             the Trinity?

VINCENT
De La Salle Collegiate High School

UNIT 3

One of God's many characteristics is forgiveness/mercy. I have learned about specific cases in which Jesus shows mercy when most of us would be too flooded with emotion to forgive. I learned that if I am patient enough, I can forgive and help those in need as Jesus did. I also learned that when I sin, and put myself in a position away from God, he is always waiting for me to return. In all, God is a being of love, care, wisdom, truth, mercy, healing, and justice.

REFLECT

Take some time to read and reflect on the unit and chapter focus questions listed on the facing page.

- What question or section did you identify most closely with?

- What did you find within the unit that was comforting or challenging?

UNIT 4
Jesus and the Early Church

WERE
THE FIRST
CHRISTIANS
THAT
DIFFERENT
FROM US?

LOOKING AHEAD

UNIT 4

The first Christians were like us in many ways. Although they did not have a hierarchy, and the Church was scattered, the main ideas and beliefs of Christianity were present and part of their everyday lives. We face many of the challenges and hardships they did but in different ways.

MATT
Providence Catholic High School

CHAPTER 11

Acts of the Apostles: The Church Spread throughout the World

HOW DID THE CHURCH START?

SNAPSHOT

Article 42

Pentecost: The Church's Public Beginning

How many people did the Church start with? There were thirteen for sure, the Twelve Apostles and Mary, who were all present at Pentecost. Or let's be generous and include the five hundred that Saint Paul says the Risen Christ appeared to (see 1 Corinthians 15:6). Now, nearly two thousand years later, there are an estimated 2.2 billion Christians in the world, 1.1 billion of whom are Catholic. How the Church grew so tremendously, often in the face of strong opposition, is an amazing story. The first part of the story is told in the Acts of the Apostles, the sequel to the Gospel of Luke. Acts tells us about the missionary journeys of the Apostles and the new Christian communities they established. As you read Acts, you will see how the first Christian missionaries, guided by the Holy Spirit, continued Jesus' mission through the growth and development of his Church.

Luke, Part Two

The opening scene to a sequel is often a short recap to remind everyone what happened in the first book or movie. Acts starts out the same way. The opening verses address Theophilus, as does the Gospel of Luke. This means that the author's primary audience is the same for both books. They are predominately Gentile Christians, who want to know how they, as Gentiles, fit into God's plan. The first chapter of Acts briefly summarizes the Gospel and retells the story of Jesus' **Ascension** into Heaven.

UNIT 4

In this retelling, Acts gives us new information about where the book will lead us. Jesus says, "But you will receive power when the holy Spirit comes upon you, and you will be my witnesses in Jerusalem throughout Judea and Samaria, and to the ends of the earth" (Acts 1:8). The Holy Spirit will have a dominant role in Acts, guiding and empowering the Apostles and early Christian missionaries. The three geographic regions mentioned (Judea, Samaria, and the ends of the Earth) provide a rough outline for where the action is to take place. With his groundwork set, Luke begins to tell us the next incredible steps in God's plan for our salvation.

Ascension ➤ The "going up" into Heaven of the Risen Christ forty days after his Resurrection.

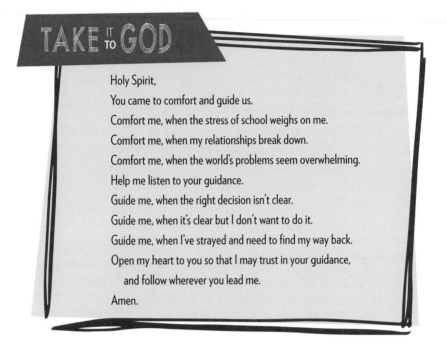

TAKE IT TO GOD

Holy Spirit,

You came to comfort and guide us.

Comfort me, when the stress of school weighs on me.

Comfort me, when my relationships break down.

Comfort me, when the world's problems seem overwhelming.

Help me listen to your guidance.

Guide me, when the right decision isn't clear.

Guide me, when it's clear but I don't want to do it.

Guide me, when I've strayed and need to find my way back.

Open my heart to you so that I may trust in your guidance,

and follow wherever you lead me.

Amen.

The Church Made Manifest

The first thing the disciples do after Jesus' Ascension is select another Apostle as the successor to Judas. Note these important points about their actions:

- It is symbolically important to have twelve Apostles lead the community. This called to mind the Twelve Tribes of Israel, assuring both Jewish and Gentile Christians that the newly forming Christian Church is a fulfillment of the promises God had made to Israel.
- The Apostles set criteria for an acceptable candidate to fill their ranks. They set a precedent of having clear criteria for qualifications of candidates to the **episcopacy**.

At the beginning of chapter 2, the disciples are gathered on the Jewish Feast of Pentecost. In the Jewish religion, Pentecost celebrates the Israelites' entering into their covenant with God at Mount Sinai, fifty days after they had left Egypt. Consider these similarities between the two events:

- The image of fire representing God's presence is found in both the Exodus account at Mount Sinai (see 19:18) and in the room with the Apostles (see Acts 2:3).
- Moses baptizes the Israelites with blood (see Exodus 24:8), and the Apostles baptize the people with water (see Acts 2:41).

---

episcopacy ➤ The position or office of a bishop.

These similarities are meant to indicate that the Old Covenant God made with the Israelites at Mount Sinai is fulfilled by the New Covenant God is making with people from every race and nation. Just as the people of Israel became God's people that day at Mount Sinai, now people of all nations become God's people in the new Pentecost.

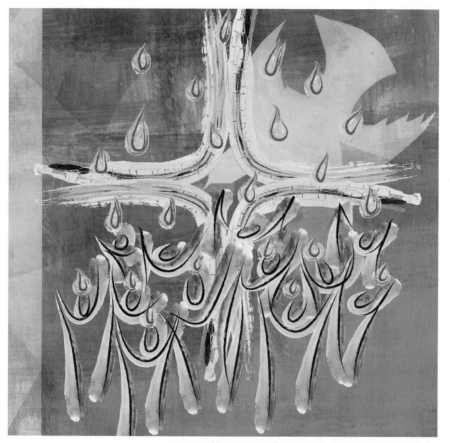

© Thoom / Shutterstock.com

How many different symbolic images and symbolic colors can you identify in this image of Pentecost?

The arrival of the Holy Spirit, represented as tongues of fire resting upon the Twelve Apostles and Mary, the mother of Jesus, is so much more than a grand entrance. This moment marks a turning point in all of human history. We have entered into the age of the Church. This age includes us, since it will last until the end of time when the Reign of God is brought to completion at the **Parousia**.

Parousia ➤ The second coming of Christ as judge of all the living and the dead, at the end of time, when the Kingdom of God will be fulfilled.

As the Twelve Apostles receive the Holy Spirit, they are transformed into courageous **evangelizers**. Miraculously, they are able to speak so that people of other languages can understand. We quickly realize there is no barrier, not even language, that will keep the Holy Spirit from doing his work. Even Peter, the one who denied Jesus three times in fear, now boldly stands up and proclaims the Good News to everyone present. Peter stirs up faith in Jesus Christ among the crowds of people, and many are baptized as the Church begins to grow.

After the inspiration of the Holy Spirit at Pentecost, the Apostles boldly proclaim the Good News, and many are baptized that day.

UNIT 4

evangelizers ➤ Those who proclaim the Gospel of Jesus Christ through word and witness.

The author of Acts ends chapter 2 by giving us a glimpse into what life was like in the early Church (verses 42–47). He describes how the early Christians, led by the Holy Spirit, focused on four areas:

1. **Teachings of the Apostles:** They wanted to continue learning more about the faith.
2. **Communal Life:** They made sure that they cared for the basic needs of all of their members.
3. **Breaking of the Bread:** They gathered to celebrate the Lord's Supper.
4. **Prayer:** They took time to give thanks to God and ask for continued strength and guidance from the Holy Spirit.

The author of Acts tells us that these early Christians were greatly admired. Their life together was marked by unity, sharing, and service. This was different from the competitiveness and self-centeredness that marked much of the rest of their society. Acts reminds us that when Christians follow the guidance of the Holy Spirit and truly live the values of Jesus, they will naturally draw others to want to learn more. ✳

OVERVIEW of the Book of Acts of the Apostles

- **Intended audience:** Like the Gospel of Luke, the Acts of the Apostles is addressed to someone named Theophilus, a name that means "God-lover." Scholars are unsure if this is a specific individual or God-lovers in general. Either way, the intended audience appears to be predominately Gentile Christians.

- **Theme:** The Church spreads throughout the Roman Empire as the Holy Spirit guides and protects the Apostles and the first Christian missionaries.

- **Reason for writing:** To show how the mission of Christ continues through the growth of the early Church.

UNIT 4

HMMMMMM. . . How did life for the Apostles change after the descent of the Holy Spirit?

Article 43

The First Christians

When Jesus sends out his followers to preach and heal in his name, he never asks them to fulfill this mission alone. Instead, Jesus encourages his disciples to work together to help fulfill his mission. Jesus wants his followers to live and work as a dedicated community, together demonstrating Christian unity and service to all people. After Jesus' death and Resurrection, Jesus' disciples continue to follow his example and his instruction by creating communities of faith. The Acts of the Apostles describes how the early Christians draw strength from their life in community:

> They devoted themselves to the teaching of the apostles and to the
> communal life, to the breaking of the bread and to the prayers. . . . Every
> day they devoted themselves to meeting together in the temple area and
> to breaking bread in their homes. They ate their meals with exultation
> and sincerity of heart, praising God and enjoying favor with all the people
> (2:42,46–47).

Although these early Christians were not walking an easy road—they would be ridiculed, misunderstood, and persecuted—their shared life of faith enabled them to persevere in holiness.

MAKE IT SO

When Michael was new to youth group, he had never volunteered at the homeless shelter before. On his first trip there, he was nervous about the people he would meet. "What do I say to them?" he wondered. After packing the toothpaste and toothbrushes into personal hygiene kit bags, he handed them out to the residents. As he did, he began to relax and really enjoy briefly chatting with them. He realized that the people he was serving weren't all that different from him and other people he already knew.

The Holy Spirit often calls us into new and uncomfortable situations. When we learn to trust the Spirit's guidance, we find real joy and fulfillment. Where is the Holy Spirit calling you to step out of your comfort zone and help others?

Growing Pains

The pattern of preaching the Good News, followed by people's conversion, followed with support from the community, then followed by persecution, can be seen clearly in Acts, chapter 3. Peter and John encounter a man, crippled from birth, begging for alms at the gate to Jerusalem. "He paid attention to them, expecting to receive something from them. Peter said, 'I have neither silver nor gold, but what I do have I give you: in the name of Jesus Christ the Nazorean, [rise and] walk'" (verses 5–6). Peter heals the crippled

Peter heals the crippled man at the gate to Jerusalem.

man, and people are astonished and amazed. In fact, people rush toward them, giving Peter a curious audience to which to preach the Gospel. His speech is an early example of *kerygma*, or proclaiming the Gospel in a way meant to introduce a person to Jesus and to appeal for their conversion. Peter makes it clear that the crippled man was not healed by Peter's power. Faith in the name of Jesus Christ is what healed him (see verse 16). This miraculous healing brought five thousand people to believe in Christ, and they praised God for what had happened (see 4:4).

Word quickly gets back to the Sanhedrin, who arrest Peter and John. Echoing Jesus' troubles with the Jewish leadership, Peter and John are brought before a group of the priestly class, including Annas, Caiaphas, John, and Alexander. Peter boldly says that the priests, and all the people of Israel, should know that they healed the man in the name of Jesus the Nazorean (see Acts 4:5–10). The Sanhedrin is now in the uncomfortable position that Pontius Pilate had been in during the trial of Jesus. Just as Pontius Pilate told the Sanhedrin that Jesus had done no evil (see Matthew 27:23), the priests can't convict Peter and John of any crime. However, they don't want them to continue to preach and teach, so they forbid them from teaching in the name of Jesus (see Acts 4:17).

Peter, emboldened by the Holy Spirit, refuses to back down. He replies, "Whether it is right in the sight of God for us to obey you rather than God, you be the judges. It is impossible for us not to speak about what we have seen

---

kerygma ➤ This refers to the initial Gospel proclamation designed to introduce a person to Christ and to appeal for conversion.

UNIT 4

and heard" (Acts 4:19–20). This is a far cry from Peter's behavior after Jesus' arrest. Back then he denied even knowing Jesus, not to powerful authority figures but to a random woman in the crowd who said she'd seen Peter with Jesus (see 26:69–74). Peter's retort to the priests is a powerful witness to the gift of Courage, or Fortitude, he received from the Holy Spirit.

In Acts, chapters 5–9, we learn more about the Holy Spirit's miracles in the early Church. Peter is again thrown in jail for teaching the crowds about Jesus Christ (see verses 17–18). An angel miraculously frees him from jail at night and sends him back to the Temple area to continue preaching (see verses 19–20). As Peter continues preaching, we see the Apostles growing more confident and bolder in proclaiming the Good News. Even when the Sanhedrin orders them to stop, they preach all the more (see verses 28–32). This is how our faith can grow. The more we practice it, the more confident in it we become.

This image depicts the martyrdom of Saint Stephen. Are there places in the world today where people are being persecuted and even killed because of their faith or religious beliefs?

Even when there are awful setbacks, like when Saint Stephen becomes the first martyr (see Acts 6:8–8:1), we see how the Holy Spirit uses it for good. Recall how everyone but the Apostles scatters because of Stephen's death. When they scatter, they take the message of Jesus Christ with them and share it farther than ever before. Even the man who officially witnesses Steven's death, Saul, is converted. He becomes one of Christianity's greatest Apostles, Saint Paul. When evil happens and things look hopeless, the lessons of the early Church remind us that the Holy Spirit can step in and make good come out of even the worst situations.

What We Can Learn

These accounts of the first evangelizers' courage and absolute faith in Christ are inspiring. There are still Christians around the world who risk arrest and even death for practicing their faith. Even though we hope and pray that we will not be put to this test, we can learn many things from the first evangelizers:

- Although the beggar wants alms (a donation), Peter gives him something far greater—his health and faith. We are called not only to help those in need with charity but also to offer them hope and dignity. The next time you give money to a homeless person on the street, do something more. Try looking them in the eye and speaking to them as a friend.

- The healed beggar became a source of inspiration for others. When we reach out and empower others because of our faith in Jesus Christ, they then have the potential to become witnesses of Christ's love as well.

- Peter used the opportunity of having everyone's attention to proclaim the Good News because of the healed beggar. As Christians, we too should seek those moments to share the Good News with others. It can be as simple as answering, "Why are you so happy today?" You can explain something God has done for you recently.

- Peter's refusal to back down before the Sanhedrin is a courageous example for speaking the truth to power. Just because someone holds a position of power doesn't mean they always do the right thing. We too need to be unafraid in respectfully pointing out to powerful people the ways their words and actions go against God's Law of Love.

- Paul being thrown in jail is a reminder that living your faith with integrity will not always be well received. In Second Timothy, Paul is clear that we should not be ashamed of our faith: "So do not be ashamed of your testimony to our Lord, nor of me, a prisoner for his sake; but bear your share of hardship for the gospel with the strength that comes from God" (1:8). Others may see our faith in Jesus as a threat to what they believe or how they live.

- Peter tells the community about his release from prison, and the community rejoices. As Christians, we are called to share and celebrate one another's success. If God does something amazing during your day, it is your responsibility to share that story with someone else. ✳

HMMMMM. . . What are some things we can learn about sharing our faith with others from the first Christian evangelizers?

Article 44

Welcoming the Gentiles

Have you ever been to a concert or major sporting event where everyone is gathered outside the stadium waiting to enter? Sometimes just a few doors are opened and people trickle through as you anxiously wait to get in. Then the remaining doors are opened, and the crowd floods into the stadium. The early Church experiences similar growth in Acts, chapters 10–15, as the Holy Spirit leads the Apostles to open wide the doors of Christianity to the Gentiles.

Just as a crowd surges through the gates to a concert or event, the Holy Spirit opens wide the door of Christianity.

Opening the Doors to the Gentiles

At the beginning of Acts, chapter 10, the author describes two interesting visions that take place. The first is Cornelius's encounter with an angel who tells him to send for Peter, a person he has never met. Cornelius is a God-fearing Gentile who lives in Caesarea working as a centurion. Peter's vision occurs a day later. In Peter's vision, God is apparently declaring all food clean, meaning that it's okay to eat food that was previously forbidden under the Jewish Law. However, Peter does not fully understand the meaning of this vision.

Peter follows the direction of the Holy Spirit and accepts Cornelius's invitation to come to his house. When Peter experiences Cornelius's faith and hears about his vision, he finally understands the meaning of his own vision. He declares, "In truth, I see that God shows no partiality" (Acts 10:34). Peter realizes his vision was about people, not just food. The Gentiles should no longer be viewed as "unclean" but should be lovingly accepted into God's family through Baptism. Peter shares this event with the other Apostles. As a result, Gentiles in other regions begin to be baptized as well. This is a huge turning point for the Church. Christianity is now more than a Jewish **cult**—it is now a faith open to all the people in the world.

---

cult ➤ A small religious group that is not part of a larger and more accepted religion and that has beliefs regarded by many as extreme or dangerous.

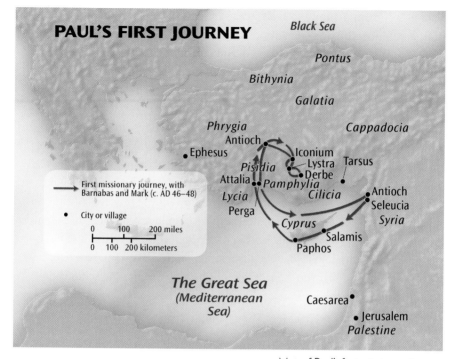

Map of Paul's first missionary journey

Acts then turns to Paul and his missionary work. Chapters 13 and 14 describe the first of Paul's three missionary journeys that take place over a ten-year period. (We will examine his other two journeys in the next article.) Paul and Barnabas are led the by the Holy Spirit to a synagogue in Pisidia (see Acts 13:14). The official at the synagogue says to the worshippers gathered, "My brothers, if one of you has a word of exhortation for the people, please speak" (verse 15). Notice how Paul takes the opportunity to preach when he is given the chance! The crowd loves what they hear from Paul, but things change a week later when Paul returns. The leaders of the synagogue argue with Paul and Barnabas, and eventually run them out of town (see verses 44–52). The Gentiles in the city, on the other hand, welcome Paul's message and become Christians. In Acts 14:10–17, we learn that a similar thing happens in the next city, Iconium, where Paul has mixed success. Some of the people even seek to kill Paul and Barnabas, so they flee.

When Paul and Barnabas visit Lystra, they are treated like rock stars (see Acts 14:8–20). Actually, better than rock stars—they are treated like gods, namely Zeus and Hermes. These people believe that Paul and Barnabas are actually gods in human form, because Paul had miraculously healed a lame man.

Paul uses the opportunity to convince the Gentiles to stop worshipping their idols and follow the one true God. Unfortunately, people arrive from the previous cities Paul and Barnabas visited, and convince the crowds to stone Paul. Fortunately, Paul survives and is able to continue his missionary work. Clearly, Paul and Barnabas's preaching has a powerful effect on people, who are either attracted to the Gospel message or threatened by it.

When Paul and Barnabas return from their journey, a question arises about how to let Gentiles into the community. Paul is thrilled that many of the Gentiles he met want to become followers of Christ and receive Baptism. Yet, some of the Pharisees who have converted to Christianity insist that the Gentile believers must be circumcised and follow all the precepts of the Mosaic (Old) Law (see Acts 15:5). Basically, these people are arguing that Gentiles would also have to become full Jews in order to become Christians. The Apostles gather in Jerusalem to decide this matter (see verses 6–29). Led by Peter, the Apostles agree that the Gentiles do not have to be circumcised nor do they need to follow all the precepts of the Old Law to become Christian.

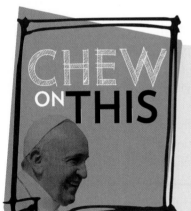

CHEW ON THIS

Pope Francis speaks of a new evangelization by which our faith makes a difference in this world as well as the next:

Faith is truly a good for everyone; it is a common good. Its light does not simply brighten the interior of the Church, nor does it serve solely to build an eternal city in the hereafter; it helps us build our societies in such a way that they can journey towards a future of hope. . . . The hands of faith are raised up to heaven, even as they go about building in charity a city based on relationships in which the love of God is laid as a foundation. (*On Faith* [*Lumen Fidei*, 2013], number 51)

One of the Apostles, James, suggests that the Gentile Christians agree to the following code of conduct (see Acts 15:13–21):

1. Avoid idols.
2. Avoid unlawful marriage.
3. Avoid meat from strangled animals.
4. Avoid blood.

Everyone approves James's decree, and a letter describing the Council's decision is written and sent with Paul, Barnabas, and two other witnesses to be shared with the Church in Antioch. The decision is accepted with joy in Antioch, as the doors are now wide open for the Gentiles who wish to become followers of Jesus Christ.

Lessons from Early Christians

Saint James presides over the Council of Jerusalem. James wisely suggests a compromise that provides a path for Gentiles to become Christian.

UNIT 4

I DIDN'T KNOW THAT!

Did you know that any two people on Earth have over 99.9 percent of the same DNA? We all have 100 percent of the same genes; they just have slight variations that cause our differences in appearance, like height or hair color. When you look at the numbers, we are far more alike than we are different. Science verifies the spiritual truth revealed by God through Peter: "I see that God shows no partiality" (Acts 10:34). If God does not show partiality, should we?

What can we learn from this pivotal time in the Church's history? Perhaps the clearest thing is the importance of following the guidance of the Holy Spirit. We see this come up three times in these chapters. The first time is with Peter and Cornelius's visions, where we learn that the Holy Spirit speaks to us through others, even people we do not know. Peter does not know Cornelius, but God uses him to help show Peter the true meaning of his vision. For us, it means we need to be open to the Holy Spirit speaking to us in surprising ways. Sure, the Holy Spirit will speak to us through our family, friends, and leaders of the Church. But the Holy Spirit can also speak to us through the students at school with whom we get along the least.

From Paul and Barnabas's first missionary journey, we learn that even when the Holy Spirit is guiding us, some people will accept us and others will not. Paul and Barnabas show perseverance when faced with opposition, but they also have the wisdom to know when it is time to move on. This is a challenging skill to master—knowing when to stand up and argue our beliefs and when to walk quietly away.

From the Council of Jerusalem, we learn how the Church works when faced with difficult questions. First, Church leaders come together to pray and ask the Holy Spirit to guide them. They dialogue about the issues affecting their communities. After hearing arguments regarding the issues, they make a communal decision clarifying the official Church teaching on these matters. The same steps can be used when we face challenges with our family or friends. Face-to-face gatherings, prayer asking the Holy Spirit to guide us, and respectful discussion can lead us in the right direction. ✳

HMMMMM. . . In what ways does the Holy Spirit lead the early Church to open the doors to the Gentiles?

Article 45

The Church Spreads throughout the World

Stephanie is a kindhearted teenager who truly tries to do the right thing and be helpful to others. She was having one of those days where everything she tried seemed to go all wrong. She studied the night before for her test only to find out she studied the wrong chapter. She went to help a friend whose locker was stuck, only to have a teacher tell her to hurry up and get to class. At home, she decided to clean the dirty plates on the counter to help out her mom. Right after she rinsed them, her brother told her those plates were part of his science experiment that was due tomorrow. If you've ever had one of these days, you've probably wondered why sometimes even our good intentions are thwarted. It can make life feel out of control. But is it?

Can you think of a time when all of your good intentions seemed to go wrong?

UNIT 4

The Holy Spirit Has the Master Plan

As Acts continues to describe how the Church spreads throughout the world, it focuses on the mission work of Saint Paul. Paul, like Stephanie, ran into difficulties despite his good intentions. As you read Acts, chapters 16–28, you likely noticed who is really in control of the early Church's expansion: the Holy Spirit. Paul's work is the central focus, but the Holy Spirit guides Paul the entire time. This is a core theme in the Acts of the Apostles.

God, the Holy Spirit, knows how the Church should grow and can share that wisdom with us if we are open to receiving it. This means that sometimes the Holy Spirit stops Paul from well-intentioned actions. For example, in Acts 16:6–10, we read about the Holy Spirit preventing Paul from preaching in Asia. Paul has good intentions and his own ideas about where he should go, but he wisely follows the Holy Spirit's guidance.

At other times, the Spirit miraculously removes barriers that are in Paul's way. One example is the earthquake opening the doors to the jail in Acts 16:25–26. The Holy Spirit literally removes physical barriers to the work he wants Paul to complete. When we give ourselves over to the will of the Holy Spirit as Paul did, we can begin to trust that there's a purpose behind the challenges we face. That is not to say that there was a greater purpose in Stephanie's bad luck day. However, if Stephanie can trust that she was just having a bad day, rather than a bad life, she can pick herself up and keep going. Trusting that God is ultimately in control gives us the strength to begin again when things are difficult. That is a powerful witness to the Holy Spirit working in our lives.

CATHOLICS MAKING A DIFFERENCE

Would you still cling to your faith if your spouse died? What if your family and friends rejected and persecuted you? Saint Elizabeth Ann Seton (1774–1821) never lost her faith, even in the face of these horrible tragedies. Born two years before the American Revolution, Elizabeth grew up in the upper class of New York society. She married William Seton, but soon her husband's business and health failed. He eventually died of tuberculosis. Elizabeth's only comfort was her faith. She converted from the Anglican faith to Catholicism. This alienated her from many of her friends and family. Yet Elizabeth would not be deterred. She, along with two other women, began plans for a religious community that would come to be known as the Sisters

of Charity. The Sisters of Charity established the first free Catholic school in America. Elizabeth Ann Seton was the first native-born citizen of the United States declared an official saint of the Church. Today, six separate religious congregations trace their roots to the beginnings of the Sisters of Charity. Schools and universities are named after her. Elizabeth is the patron saint of Catholic schools.

UNIT 4

Missionary Journeys and Heading to Rome

As Acts continues, the Holy Spirit proceeds to guide Paul and his companions' travels. We often speak about Paul's missionary journeys as if he were traveling by himself, but the reality is that he never traveled alone. Other evangelizers accompanied him, people like Barnabas, Timothy, Apollos, and Priscilla and Aquila, to name a few.

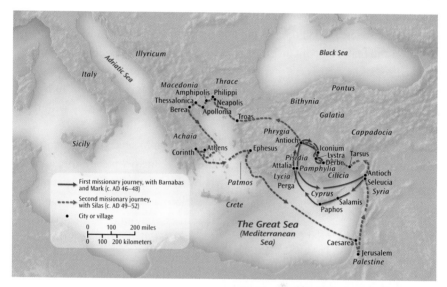

Paul's missionary journeys in the first century

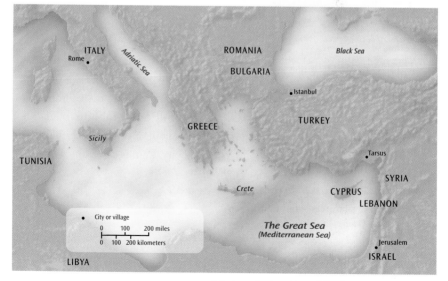

Modern-day locations of Paul's missionary journeys

In the previous article, we examined elements of Paul's first missionary journey. During his second and third missionary journeys, Paul and his companions visit new cities, and they stop to check on churches Paul founded on previous journeys. As you read these chapters in Acts, you will see that Paul follows a similar pattern in each city he visits. If there is a Jewish **synagogue** in the city, he first preaches the Good News in the synagogue. If he doesn't get a friendly reception at the synagogue, he then preaches in a public square. The Jews and Gentiles who accept the Good News form Christian communities—the first churches. Paul and his companions teach them a new way of life, a life based on the teachings of Christ. As they get to know the people, they appoint **presbyters** and overseers to guide the community. These presbyters and overseers are the first priests and bishops. Then Paul and his companions move on to another city—although sometimes one or two of them might stay with the young community to continue providing guidance and support.

Paul and his companions experience many joys and successes in their missionary travels. But they also experience dangers. Some people are threatened

by their message. These people seek to have Paul and his companions driven out of town, arrested, or even killed. However, the Holy Spirit always protects them, giving them the courage to continue (see Acts 6:16–40).

As Paul ends his third journey, he heads for Jerusalem despite death threats and the pleading of friends to stay away from the city (see Acts 21:12). Paul bravely trusts and follows the calling of the Holy Spirit for him to head to Jerusalem. Not long after being in the city, Paul is seized by a crowd

Paul composed several of his letters from prison which may have been a kind of house arrest.

UNIT 4

---

synagogue ▶ The building where a Jewish assembly or congregation meets for religious worship and instruction.

presbyter ▶ A synonym for *elder* in the Acts of the Apostles and an alternative word for *priest* today.

and is about to be killed (see verses 27–31). A Roman guard saves Paul from the crowds and allows Paul to address them (see verses 31–40). How does Paul defend himself? He shares his own faith journey with the crowd (see 22:1–21). Paul teaches us the power of sharing our own stories of our encounters with God. Our stories are probably not as dramatic as Paul's, but they can often inspire others to begin seeing God in their lives as well, and perhaps to become followers of Jesus Christ. Paul's trip to Jerusalem does not end in his death; the Holy Spirit is in control and promises that he will make it all the way to Rome (see Acts 23:11). The remainder of Acts tells of Paul's imprisonment and his journey to Rome to see the emperor. As he arrives in Rome, he continues preaching the Good News (see 28:11–20). The Gospel has made it to the center of the Roman Empire that extends to the ends of the known world at that time.

The Story Continues

When you were reading, did you notice the major difference between the structure of Luke's Gospel and the structure of the Acts of the Apostles? In the Gospel, Jesus comes down from Heaven, walks the earth and then returns to Heaven. In Acts, the Holy Spirit comes down from Heaven, moves across the world, but does not return to Heaven. In a way, the story of the work of the Holy Spirit is still being written. We are part of that story, which will not end until our Lord returns in glory. Each generation in the Church adds its mark to the story. What do you hope to add to the story with your life? If future generations look back upon you and your classmates, how might they know that you too were following the guidance of the Holy Spirit? ✳

UNIT 4

HMMMMM. . .

How does the author of the Acts of the Apostles portray the work of the Holy Spirit in the early Church?

1. The Holy Spirit is manifested on Pentecost. Why is this significant?

2. What are four characteristics of the early Church that Luke describes shortly after Pentecost?

3. Name three things we can learn from Peter's encounter with the beggar.

4. How does the Holy Spirit use Saint Stephen's martyrdom as a means to spread the Gospel?

5. Explain how the visions of Peter and Cornelius are related.

6. How do the people of Lystra react to Paul and Barnabas's miracle and preaching?

7. Where was the first Ecumenical Council, and what did it decide?

8. Explain Paul and his companion's typical process upon arriving in a new city.

9. Jesus promises that his message will be preached to the ends of the Earth. How does the author of the Acts of the Apostles show that this happened?

UNIT 4

Paul Is Led by the Holy Spirit

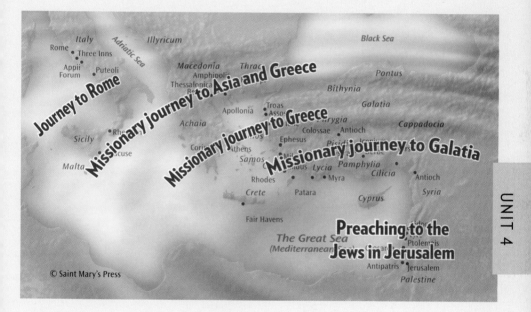

1. What does this graphic tell us about the importance of Paul's missionary journeys for the growth of the Church?

2. In what way do you think the Holy Spirit impacted Paul while he was on his missionary journeys?

CHAPTER 12
The Early Church Responds to Challenges

HOW DOES THE CHURCH PRACTICE WHAT IT PREACHES?

SNAPSHOT

Article 46

The Pastoral Letters: Responsibilities of the Church Leaders

© fbxx / iStockphoto.com

If you were shipwrecked on a deserted island, how would you prepare for long-term survival? The disciples had to accept that they had to prepare for a future without Jesus' imminent return.

UNIT 4

Imagine that you and your friends are shipwrecked on a deserted island. When you first find yourself stuck there, what is one of your main concerns? Most likely, it is getting rescued. You may set fires, hoping a plane overhead notices the light or smoke. But what if the rescuers don't come for a few days? What is your focus now? You still keep the fire going, hoping to get off the island, but now you also focus on your long-term survival. You may work on building better shelters and establishing a food supply. You get ready for the long haul, but always keep your eyes on the horizon for that rescue.

The early Church also seems to have gone through several phases in anticipating Jesus Christ's return. After Jesus ascends into Heaven, the Apostles believe that he will soon return to take all of his followers home with him to Heaven (see John 14:1–3, 1 Thessalonians 4:15). They believe they just have a short time left to continue Jesus' mission, so they put an emphasis on preaching the Good News and baptizing as many people as possible, as quickly as possible.

As the years pass, the early Church recognizes that Christ's **second coming** may be later than they expected. They continue to focus on preaching and baptizing, but they also begin to focus on establishing structures that will enable the Church to thrive and grow over the long term. We can see these structures developing in the **Pastoral Letters**, the Letters to Timothy and Titus. These letters are addressed to pastors, and they offer guidance on issues affecting fledgling Christian communities. They reflect the Church's early efforts to lay a foundation for its future, as it continues to spread the Good News in joyful hope of Jesus' return.

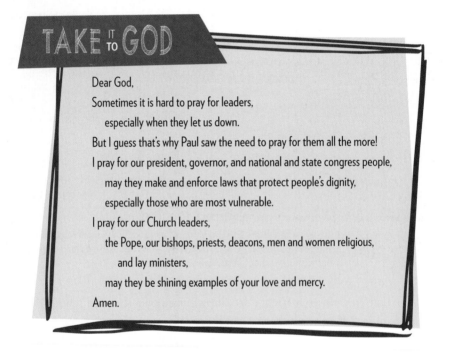

TAKE IT TO GOD

Dear God,

Sometimes it is hard to pray for leaders,

  especially when they let us down.

But I guess that's why Paul saw the need to pray for them all the more!

I pray for our president, governor, and national and state congress people,

  may they make and enforce laws that protect people's dignity,

  especially those who are most vulnerable.

I pray for our Church leaders,

  the Pope, our bishops, priests, deacons, men and women religious,

    and lay ministers,

  may they be shining examples of your love and mercy.

Amen.

UNIT 4

---

second coming ➤ The second coming of Christ as judge of all the living and the dead, when the Kingdom of God will be fulfilled. Also called the Parousia.

Pastoral Letters ➤ The Pastoral Letters are three books of the New Testament: First Timothy, Second Timothy, and Titus. They are addressed to the pastors in the early Church, and they offer advice for dealing with false teachers and the roles of Church leaders.

First Timothy

The First Letter to Timothy is written from Saint Paul to Timothy, a younger evangelizer converted by Paul, who traveled with Paul on his second and third missionary journeys. (Whether Paul himself wrote these letters, or a secretary or later disciple wrote them in his name, is the topic of scholarly debate.) In the letter, Paul reminds Timothy to focus on the authentic Gospel message (see 1:3–7). Timothy can help with this by protecting the Church against those who promote false teachings. Because of his close association with Paul, Timothy is well versed in the Gospel message. Now, as the leader of a community, he is called to protect the purity of that message (see 1:18–20, 6:20).

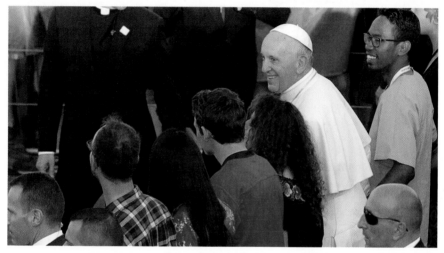

Just as the early disciples were called to protect the purity of Christ's message, the Pope today has that same responsibility.

Like the shipwrecked group stuck on an island, Timothy is challenged to focus on the long-term survival of the community. In 1 Timothy 3:1–7, Paul explains the qualifications for those who are to be bishops over the community. These bishops will guide the community into the future. The focus is more on the character of the individual than on the duties of the bishop: "Therefore, a bishop must be irreproachable, married only once, temperate, self-controlled, decent, hospitable, able to teach" (3:2). Paul emphasizes that it is essential for bishops—the successors to the Apostles, the ones who teach and guard the Gospel message—to be above reproach in their personal conduct.

UNIT 4

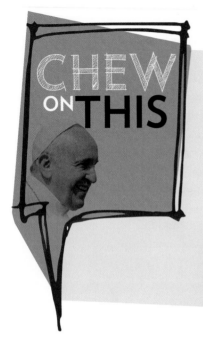

CHEW ON THIS

Remain steadfast [young people] in the journey of faith, with firm hope in the Lord. This is the secret of our journey! He gives us the courage to swim against the tide. Pay attention, my young friends: to go against the current; this is good for the heart, but we need courage to swim against the tide. Jesus gives us this courage! (Pope Francis, "Homily of Pope Francis at the Holy Mass and Conferral of the Sacrament of Confirmation," Saint Peter's Square, April 28, 2013)

UNIT 4

The letter gives similar criteria for deacons. It is interesting to compare Paul's requirements with the current requirements for deacons according to the Church's **Code of Canon Law.**

1 Timothy 3:8–9	Canon Law 1029: Requirement for Deacons
"Similarly, deacons must be dignified, not deceitful, not addicted to drink, not greedy for sordid gain, holding fast to the mystery of the faith with a clear conscience."	They must "have integral faith, are moved by right intention, have the requisite knowledge, possess a good reputation, and are endowed with integral morals and proven virtues."

You can see how the First Letter to Timothy lays the groundwork for the qualifications of Church leaders that has lasted for two thousand years.

Code of Canon Law ➤ The collected body of rules and regulations used to govern the Church in its mission toward the salvation of souls.

Second Timothy

Like the First Letter to Timothy, the Second Letter to Timothy also provides the Church with guidance that spans the centuries. In Second Timothy, Paul encourages Timothy to keep the faith over the long run. The Church is beginning to understand that the second coming of Christ may not occur for some time, which means that Christian leaders must develop the endurance to lead and serve the faithful over a lifetime. The letter provides a beautiful image for keeping up one's energies: "Stir into flame the gift of God that you have through the imposition of my hands" (2 Timothy 1:6). Just as red-hot timbers in a fire pit flame up when we stir them with a stick, the spiritual "fire" of Church leaders needs to be nourished in order to remain bright.

The letter also reminds Timothy not to be complacent about preaching the Word: "Proclaim the word; be persistent whether it is convenient or inconvenient" (2 Timothy 4:2). This puts proclaiming the Good News on the top of the priority list. Preaching the Word of God remains an essential role for bishops, priests, and deacons today.

Finally, the letter encourages Timothy to "put up with hardship; perform the work of an evangelist; fulfill your ministry" (2 Timothy 4:5). The letter acknowledges that this will not be easy. There will be hardships along the way. Jesus calls his followers to embrace suffering and sacrifice for the sake of the Gospel. Like Timothy, we are called to fulfill our own ministry. Imagine that Paul is speaking to you as a young disciple. What radical challenge might you take on to bring God's love and mercy to others?

How do you stir up the flames of your "spiritual fire" in order to remain a bright example for others?

UNIT 4

Titus

Our final Pastoral Letter is addressed to Titus, a former companion of Paul who leads a community in Crete. This letter too lists important qualities necessary for Church leaders. Like the Letters to Timothy, Titus also gives advice on how people should treat one another at home.

Some of the advice, particularly about the role of women, can be confusing because of differences in cultural expectations. The underlying principle is that whatever role you have in life, you are called to live it in a way consistent with the Gospel. The letter extends this principle to our actions in the public arena as well when it says, "Remind them to be under control of magistrates and authorities" (Titus 3:1). As believers here for the long run, we are called to be good citizens wherever we live. Paul stresses the importance of not living in a way that would discredit the faith by appearing to be a cult or removed from the world. ✳

OVERVIEW of the First and Second Letters to Timothy

- **Intended audience:** The letters are written to Timothy, who is a Church leader, or pastor.
- **Theme:** Church leaders must fight against false teachings and encourage people. They also provide guidelines for who should assume various roles in the community.
- **Reason for writing:** The letters give guidance and support for Timothy as he seeks to lead his community faithfully.

OVERVIEW of the Letter to Titus

- **Intended audience:** An early Church leader in Crete named Titus.
- **Theme:** The various members of a community need guidance on how to live as Christians. This letter advises the leader, Titus, on how to teach those members.
- **Reason for writing:** To give advice to Titus on how to lead his community.

HMMMMM. . .

How did the delay in Jesus Christ's return affect the early Church?

Article 47

Letter of James: Living the Values of Jesus

When Daniel was a young boy, he used to dread going to his grandparents' house to visit. Daniel was a talkative eight-year-old, and his Grandpa would always say things like, "Son, there's a reason why God gave you two ears and one mouth." Daniel didn't understand what his grandfather meant, but he knew he didn't like it. Years later, when Daniel was in high school, his grandpa passed away. Daniel thought a lot about him and began to smile when he thought about Grandpa's funny sayings, like the one about the ears and mouth. Being older now, Daniel understood the sayings and began to admire the wisdom behind them. Daniel would even find himself saying the same things to his eight-year-old brother.

What is one piece of timeless wisdom you have received from a relative, mentor, teacher, or religious leader?

Like Grandpa's sayings, some wisdom is timeless. As you read the Letter of James, what timeless wisdom did you recognize? It can feel as if the letter were written only yesterday. As James addresses the challenges facing the early Church, he sounds like a grandpa with wise advice about living the values of Jesus. We do not know much about James or his audience, other than what the first verse tells us. It simply indicates that James is a "slave of God" and is writing to the "twelve tribes in the dispersion" (James 1:1). However, what follows is five chapters of sound advice on Christian living. Let's explore three of James's wise sayings and how they apply to us today.

UNIT 4

MAKE IT SO

Thankfully James wrote down his wisdom for us. Consider how many people have heard his wisdom over the last two thousand years. Wise people are all around us, and if we fail to ask them about their experiences when we have the chance, we are missing out! Do you have older relatives that you can talk to? Take time to listen to the wisdom of people who have years of life experience. Ask them about their teenage years. What did they learn about life as a teen, and what advice would they give teens today? You may find out that although some things were very different back then, the emotional and faith-oriented challenges have not changed that much over time.

Timeless Wisdom from James

"But if any of you lacks wisdom, he should ask God who gives to all generously and ungrudgingly, and he will be given it" (James 1:5).

When you are young, the difference between right and wrong seems pretty black and white. Now that you are older, things may not always seem so clear. There can be some gray areas as decisions and choices become more complicated. For example, let's say you are driving around with your friends on a Friday night, and they suggest going to a party at another friend's house. When you arrive, you can see that people are drinking. Your friends want to stay. You want to leave, but you are their ride home. It seems wrong to leave them to find another ride with someone who could be under the influence. On the other hand, you don't want to make it look like you approve of teens using alcohol. What do you do?

When faced with decisions without an easy answer, James reminds us that the first thing to do is pray for wisdom! He reminds us that if we ask, we will receive. When we ask God for something important, we align ourselves with his will. We remind ourselves to rely on God for what we need, rather than just relying on ourselves. This opens us up to receiving what God has to give! After praying, you may even feel like you can handle the situation with more confidence.

"Everyone should be quick to hear, slow to speak, slow to wrath" (James 1:19).

Being in the presence of a angry person makes for a tense situation. It makes you fear for your safety, both physically and emotionally. James might not have used the term *anger issues*, but his writing shows his familiarity with emotional situations. To respond, James turns things upside down. Rather than being quick to take offense, he tells us to be quick to hear. He's talking about hearing the Gospel, of course. When we think first about the values taught by Jesus Christ, and apply those values thoughtfully and lovingly, many highly emotional situations will become less tense.

Imagine if we really followed this advice. People would think before they flew off the handle at each other. Parents and their kids would not lash out at each other when frustrated. Classrooms would be more productive as teacher-student relationships improved. Even though James had no idea about texting and social media, his wisdom could certainly help those conversations as well.

"Be doers of the word and not hearers only" (James 1:22). "So also faith of itself, if it does not have works, is dead" (James 2:17).

To listen to the Gospel message, but not practice it, is a failure to improve oneself. James is making the crucial point that we cannot separate our faith in Christ from good works. It has been said that James contradicts what Paul says in Romans: "But when one does not work, yet believes in the one who justifies the ungodly, his faith is credited as righteousness" (4:5). Paul's teaching is that salvation is "by grace" and "through faith" (see Ephesians 2:8–9). Just doing good works is not the source of our salvation. In other words, we cannot save ourselves from sin and death simply by our own efforts—we need God's help. Paul's teaching that salvation "by grace through faith" highlights the comforting truth that salvation is God's work, not ours.

Yet James clearly says that "faith of itself, if it does not have works, is dead" (James 2:17). James does not deny that faith saves. He is teaching that faith that does not produce works is not a saving faith. In other words, a person who claims to put their faith in Christ and then keeps on living a life of sin and selfishness—without any efforts to do better—does not have true faith. True faith that brings salvation shows itself in a changed life. This kind of saving faith produces good works. Paul essentially says the same thing in Galatians when he teaches what ultimately matters is "faith working through love" (Galatians 5:6).

So why do Paul and James sound so different? Why does it appear that their teachings are contradictory? We need to remember that their letters were written to specific churches, each facing their own individual challenges. Paul wrote to a community where the people were tempted to trust in their works for salvation. James wrote to a community who thought their claims of faith alone would save them. This is the importance of interpreting Scripture as a whole, rather than focusing only on pieces of it. Paul and James's teachings though worded differently, are actually complimentary.

UNIT 4

James's Healing

The Letter of James also reveals the healing ministry of the Church. Jesus showed tremendous concern for the sick and instructed his followers to do the same. The Sacrament of Anointing of the Sick, one of the Seven Sacraments of the Catholic Church, has its roots in the Letter of James:

Anointing of the Sick is one of the Seven Sacraments of the Catholic Church.

Is anyone among you sick? He should summon the presbyters of the church, and they should pray over him and anoint [him] with oil in the name of the Lord, and the prayer of faith will save the sick person, and the Lord will raise him up. If he has committed any sins, he will be forgiven. (5:14-15)

The Sacrament of Anointing of the Sick offers the grace one needs to endure suffering and not lose faith. It helps nourish a person both spiritually and physically by uniting their suffering with the suffering Christ endured for us. Through the grace of the sacrament, the sick can become a witness to the rest of the faith community.

The Anointing of the Sick "is not a sacrament for those only who are at the point of death. Hence, as soon as anyone of the faithful begins to be in danger of death from sickness or old age, the fitting time for him to receive this sacrament has certainly already arrived"[1] (*CCC*, number 1514). Only bishops and priests are ministers of the Anointing of Sick. The bishop or priest anoints the patient's forehead with blessed oil. The following are the effects of the special grace of the Anointing of the Sick (see numbers 1499–1532):

- the uniting of the sick person to the Passion of Christ, for his good and that of the whole Church
- the strengthening, peace, and courage to endure in a Christian manner the sufferings of illness or old age
- the forgiveness of sins, if the sick person was not able to obtain it through the Sacrament of Reconciliation
- the restoration of health, if it is conducive to the salvation of his soul
- the preparation for passing over to eternal life ✷

I DIDN'T KNOW THAT!

The Sacrament of Anointing of the Sick used to be called Extreme Unction, which means "last anointing." People assumed it was called this because it was the last sacrament a person received before dying, but it was really because it is the last of the sacraments in which a person is anointed with oil. Catholics are anointed with holy oil or chrism first at Baptism and then at Confirmation, and hopefully receive the Anointing of the Sick much later in life (and not necessarily only before they die).

OVERVIEW of the Letter to James

- **Intended audience:** From the letter itself, it is difficult to determine much about the intended audience. Biblical scholars generally agree that it was written for Christians in Palestine, Syria, or Rome.
- **Theme:** The letter addresses the importance of enduring trials, gives practical advice on life issues, and promotes the power of prayer.
- **Reason for writing:** The letter was written to encourage believers to consistently live the values of Christ. James wants his readers to grow in the practice of their faith.

UNIT 4

HMMMMM. . .

What are some ways the Letter of James can help you live Christian values?

Article 48

Letter to Philemon: A Case Study in Confronting Social Injustice

Arianna was so excited as she hung up the phone and ran downstairs yelling: "Mom! Cheryl just invited me to go to the concert this Friday. It's my favorite band and she has front-row tickets!" Mom looked concerned as she reminded Arianna that her grandmother was going to be in town this weekend. Her grandmother was turning ninety, and they were throwing a huge party for her on Friday night. Her mom explained that she would not force Arianna to attend the party, but thinks it would be best. Her mom then said the famous parenting words, "It is up to you, but I know you will do the right thing."

Parents have a unique ability to help steer their children in the right direction, but they did not invent the "I know you will do the right thing" technique. Saint Paul had it mastered over two thousand years ago. As you read his short Letter to Philemon, you can see his persuasive techniques at their best. Paul needs to convince Philemon to make the right decision about something far greater than the weekend's concert. This challenge is about a man's life and freedom.

When have you had to make a choice between a family or school commitment and spending time with friends?

He's My Brother in Christ!

In the Roman Empire, slavery was a complicated and vital part of the economic structure. Slavery was not based on race, but it was still an abusive and degrading practice. Some slaves were people captured during wars and forced into slavery; other slaves were poor people who sold themselves into slavery, but most slaves were born into slavery. Some slaves were well educated and served as doctors or accountants. Some slaves were treated well and others very poorly. However, all slaves were the property of their owners, who could sell or rent them out at any time.

People who found runaway slaves were legally obligated to return them. Slave owners had the legal right to severely punish a returned runaway slave. Onesimus, whose name means "useful," is a runaway slave whom Paul has befriended. Onesimus has become a Christian and helper of Paul, who is currently in prison. Paul, following Roman law, is sending Onesimus back to his owner, Philemon. However, Paul uses his power of persuasion to ask Philemon for something radically different than society would expect.

Paul praises Philemon's faith, talks about how much he has grown to love Onesimus, reminds Philemon that he is an old man and in prison, and then asks Philemon a personal favor based on their friendship. Paul asks Philemon to not only forgive Onesimus but also to welcome him back as a free man and a brother in Christ. Paul even offers to pay Philemon for anything that Onesimus owes him. Wow! From the letter, we do not know what Philemon decides, but it is hard to imagine that he could turn down such a powerful and emotional request from his friend Paul.

CATHOLICS MAKING A DIFFERENCE

The U.S. Conference of Catholic Bishop's Anti-Trafficking Program was established to educate the faithful on the scourge of human trafficking as an offense against the fundamental dignity of the human person, to advocate for an end to modern-day slavery, and to provide training and technical assistance on this issue. Each year, an estimated seventeen thousand vulnerable men, women, and children are trafficked across our borders and forced into slavery. For over a decade, the United States Conference of Catholic Bishops has been a national leader in advocacy and education to eradicate sex and labor trafficking. Migration and Refugee Services leads efforts to combat trafficking in human persons, carrying out the commitment of the U.S. Bishop's Committee on Migration to protect the life and dignity of the most vulnerable. Their initiatives include advocacy, awareness, training and technical assistance, and integration services.

Should Paul Have Done More?

Like many people, you may be wondering why Paul didn't just come out and say, "Slavery is wrong." One way to understand it is to go back to the analogy at the beginning of the chapter, being stranded on an island for a long time. Philemon was most likely written during the time when the Church was focused on getting the Gospel message out as quickly as possible. If you think Jesus is coming back soon, do you have the time to change deeply ingrained unjust social structures? At that time, slavery was such an important part of the Roman Empire's economic structure, to dismantle it would have taken considerable effort. Given the pressure Paul felt to bring others to faith in Christ, he put his available time into preaching the Good News.

What does Paul have influence over? Onesimus's fate. We must not overlook the important fact that Paul seeks the release of Onesimus, a slave. Paul even goes beyond Onesimus's slave status when he clearly explains that in a Christian community there are no slaves and masters: all are equal. Paul may not have outright said, "Stop all slavery." However, when we consider what he did for Onesimus, and consider his words about all Christians living as brothers and sisters in Christ, in his own way, he did say it.

What Can We Learn from This Letter?

Scripture and Tradition reveal that all people have equal dignity and fundamental human rights that must be respected. Philemon has the right in Roman law to walk all over Onesimus's dignity, but Paul calls him to a higher standard. Human law does not surpass God's Law. Even if we have the legal right to deny someone their dignity, God's Law calls us to a higher standard. Just because we can do something, does not mean that we should. The Letter to Philemon reminds us that we are called to respect and protect every person's dignity.

When there is injustice, we are called to stand in solidarity with those who are marginalized.

UNIT 4

When there is an injustice, we need to do all we can to help within reason. Paul uses every means of persuasion he can think of to convince Philemon to do the right thing. Paul mentions that he could simply demand Philemon do it, but chooses against that approach. Paul wants the goodness to come freely from Philemon. By doing this, Paul is respecting the dignity of Philemon as well.

Sometimes when we confront an injustice, we do so with such force that we create another injustice in the process. For example, on the sports field when one team commits a terrible foul against one of our players, a teammate may retaliate against another player or scream in the referee's face about it. We are right to be upset about an injustice, but this does not give us the right to commit another injustice. Like Paul, we must be wise about how we stand up against injustice and use the means we have with love.

However, our responsibility does not end there. Did you notice the line toward the end of the letter where Paul mentions his plan to visit Philemon soon? Paul plans to check in to make sure Onesimus is being treated justly. We too are called not only to act against injustice but also to take an ongoing interest in assuring that it does not return. ✳

OVERVIEW of the Letter to Philemon

- **Intended audience:** A Christian named Philemon whose church community meets at his house. He is the owner of a runaway slave named Onesimus.

- **Theme:** Within the Christian community, there is no distinction between slave and slave owner. All are brothers and sisters of equal dignity.

- **Reason for writing:** Paul is asking Philemon to welcome back his runaway slave as a free man and brother in Christ.

HMMMMM. . .

What is the benefit of using persuasive techniques to achieve change, rather than just condemning an injustice?

1. Why do we refer to the Letters to Timothy and Titus as the Pastoral Letters? How are they different from the other letters we've studied so far?

2. What are the main themes in the Letters to Timothy?

3. What are the main themes in the Letter to Titus?

4. What does James tell us to do if we lack wisdom?

5. How does James help clarify a misunderstanding about Paul's teaching regarding faith and works?

6. How does the Letter of James help lay the foundation for the Sacrament of Anointing of the Sick?

7. Who does Paul want to welcome Onesimus back as a brother in Christ?

8. What persuasive techniques does Paul use to argue for Onesimus's freedom?

THE EARLY CHURCH:
Building a Church to Last

Each of these figures from the New Testament contributed to the solid foundation of the Church today.

1. What does this graphic mean to you?

2. What other "stones" would you add to the building?

CHAPTER 13
Revelation: Christ's Ultimate Triumph

DOES REVELATION PREDICT THE END OF THE WORLD?

SNAPSHOT

Article 49
Letters to the Seven Churches

Dan's friend Michael loves to watch shows about a zombie apocalypse and doomsday preparedness. Dan usually laughs off Michael's talk, until one day when Michael started talking about the end of the world and the Book of Revelation. Watching shows about zombies is one thing; finding evidence for the end of times in the Bible seems much more serious to Dan. Michael said: "The end is almost here, look at all the wars and natural disasters that have been on the news. Haven't you read the Book of Revelation? It tells us exactly what will happen. And it is happening now!" Dan felt anxious. He had always heard that the Book of Revelation was scary and hard to understand. Was Michael right? What does the Book of Revelation really tell us?

What images come to your mind when you think about the Book of Revelation?

Apocalypse or Apocalyptic?

To understand the Book of Revelation, the final book in the New Testament, we must first realize what it is not. Despite Michael's words of certainty, the book is not a checklist for the events leading up to the final apocalypse, the end of the world. Throughout the centuries, people have tried to use it as such, and all have failed. The book is ultimately a message about God's **providence**, his divine care and protection. It is a message that remains true for Christians throughout the ages.

As with every other book in the New Testament we have studied, information about the human author and the original context of the situation are critical to understanding the Book of Revelation. The opening tells us that a man named John wrote it. He is a Christian who was been sent into exile on the island of Patmos by the Roman authorities. Like many Christians at that time, John tells us that he too is being punished for proclaiming the Good News. But perhaps the most important key for understanding the Book of Revelation is its literary genre.

providence ➤ God's divine care and protection.

UNIT 4

© Bluberries / iStockphoto.com

Revelation is what we call **apocalyptic literature.** This type of writing is very symbolic, usually involving visions of other worlds, in this case Heaven. It is a literary genre typically written during a time of persecution. What sets the Book of Revelation apart from other apocalyptic writings is its focus on Jesus. The visions come from Jesus and are about Jesus.

The writing in the Book of Revelation is highly symbolic and focuses on Jesus.

Learning from the Seven Churches' Struggles

In the first three chapters of Revelation, Jesus appears to John and instructs him to share a message, or letter, with the churches in seven different cities. Each letter has the same general structure:

- an opening address
- a description of the Risen Christ
- a discussion of the church's strengths or weaknesses
- a stern warning with the threat of terrible consequences
- an encouragement to listen and a promised reward for those who do

Although each church has its own unique strengths and weaknesses, they all have three problems in common: (1) persecution, (2) false teachings, and (3) complacency. Let us explore each of these problems and consider how they might also be issues today.

apocalyptic literature ➤ A literary form that uses dramatic events and highly symbolic language to offer hope to a people in crisis.

UNIT 4

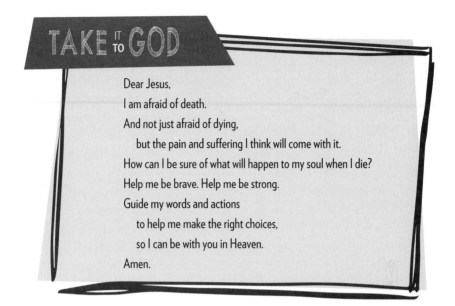

TAKE IT TO GOD

Dear Jesus,

I am afraid of death.

And not just afraid of dying,

but the pain and suffering I think will come with it.

How can I be sure of what will happen to my soul when I die?

Help me be brave. Help me be strong.

Guide my words and actions

to help me make the right choices,

so I can be with you in Heaven.

Amen.

Persecution

The first issue is the **persecution** that the Christians in these churches are suffering under the Roman Empire. Christians are being imprisoned and even killed for remaining true to their faith. It is not difficult to imagine these Christians wondering if remaining Christian—at least publicly—is worth the suffering. They may have even witnessed others denying their faith to avoid the persecution.

Catholics still suffer from persecution. In some countries, it is dangerous to practice the Christian faith. Anti-Christian groups have forced Christians out of their homes and countries. Their homes, businesses, and churches have been vandalized and burned, and religious leaders have been threatened or even martyred. Some studies show that Christians are the targets of nearly 80 percent of religious persecution across the world.

Just as the early Christians were tempted to deny their faith, Christians experiencing persecution today are also tempted. It is in these unsure times that we can look to the Book of Revelation for hope. The book isn't written to scare us about the end of the world, but rather to comfort us by describing Jesus Christ's ultimate victory over evil and Satan.

UNIT 4

---

persecution ➤ The act or practice of harassing or abusing those who differ in origin, religion, or social outlook.

False Teachings

The second area of concern for these churches is the issue of false teachings. Three of the seven churches face this issue. In Ephesus, they "tested those who call themselves apostles but are not, and discovered that they are impostors" (Revelation 2:2). This is a good lesson for all of us. Don't believe everything you hear or read. Many people are ill-informed about matters regarding faith, and then they pass their opinions along as fact. Like the church in Ephesus, we need to test what we learn. We need to look to trusted sources, like our parents, teachers, church leaders, and the Magisterium for guidance.

The problem at the church in Pergamum is people holding onto teachings that go back to the pagan prophet Balaam (Numbers, chapter 22). This is a good reminder that when we discover something we once believed was wrong, we need to let it go. For example, Sarah's dad was Jewish and her mom was Catholic. When her dad got sick and died, an acquaintance at school approached her at her locker. She said, "I'm sorry about your dad." Sarah replied: "Thanks. I'm sad, but I appreciate you saying that." The girl then said: "I meant I'm sorry about your dad because he was Jewish. Because he didn't accept Jesus Christ, he isn't in Heaven. I'll pray for him."

Sarah was so stunned she didn't know what to say. She knew her classmate couldn't be right. Fortunately, her Mom helped her find a Vatican document called "The Gifts and Calling of God Are Irrevocable" (2015). This document made it clear that even though there is only "one path to salvation" (36), the Jewish People are also part of God's saving plan. The document states: "That the Jews are participants in God's salvation is theologically unquestionable, but how that can be possible without confessing Christ explicitly, is and remains an unfathomable divine mystery" (36). Though it might be difficult for Sarah to convince her acquaintance at school of this, Sarah was glad that she had searched for the real truth.

How would you handle a situation if someone shared with you ill-informed and even hurtful ideas about your faith?

For the Church in Thyatira, the problem is even greater. They have a false teacher among them, and they tolerate this teacher leading people astray. In our culture today, we often do not want to offend others. It is important to be polite and respectful, but at the same time we must not let falsehoods and injustices go unchallenged. We must live up to our calling to speak the truth and help others grow in the faith.

Complacency

The third challenge confronting these churches is the issue of **complacency**. From the letters, we learn that the people of Ephesus have let their love for God diminish and do not even realize how far they have fallen away from him. In Sardis, the church has this great reputation for being alive in their faith, but in reality, their faith is dead. The church in Laodicea is neither hot nor cold. It is as if they are just going through the motions, but their heart is not in it.

Like the seven churches, each of us may have struggles with our faith. Sometimes we may feel persecuted and want to quit, while other times we may find ourselves holding onto beliefs that we know are convenient but not true. We may have grown complacent in living out our faith and find ourselves drifting farther and farther away from God and the Church. Like the seven churches, the Book of Revelation has a message for us. There is time to make changes. The time is now. We need to hold onto our faith with all our might, knowing that we can count on God and his promise of eternal life with him in Heaven. ✳

UNIT 4

OVERVIEW of the Book of Revelation

- **Intended audience:** The seven churches in Asia Minor that are being persecuted.
- **Theme:** Although it appears that evil is winning, God is ultimately in charge and Christians are to endure the suffering with the sure hope of God's victory.
- **Reason for writing:** Rome was persecuting the churches, and Christians needed encouragement to hold onto the faith.

HMMMM. . . Of the three issues that the seven churches were facing—persecution, false teaching, and complacency—which do you see as the greatest challenge for teens today? Why?

complacency ➤ A state of self-satisfaction, especially when accompanied by unawareness of actual dangers or deficiencies; unaware or uninformed self-satisfaction.

Article 50
Signs and Symbols

Have you ever seen the fish symbol on the back of someone's car? Evidence shows that it is an ancient symbol Christians used to secretly identify themselves to other Christians during times of persecution. The Greek word for fish is *ichthys*, which is an acronym for "Jesus Christ, Son of God, Savior." Christians would put the *ichthys* symbol outside of meeting places so other Christians would know it was safe to gather there. Non-Christians would see it and think, "What an interesting fish drawing." Christians would see it, and know that they had found other brothers and sisters in Christ.

Just as the fish symbol signified a gathering place for Christians, the Book of Revelation contains symbolic language and images that were a kind of code for early Christians.

Much of the Book of Revelation is written in this type of code. The signs and symbols used in the book mean something to John and the people in the seven churches. But if the Romans intercept the book, they will have little idea what it is about. When we read the Book of Revelation, we should not read it literally, or we will be confused like the Romans. Let's examine some of the symbols used to describe the events that take place in chapters 4–16.

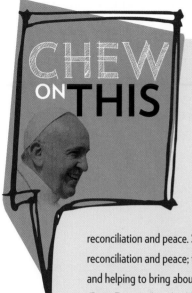

In fact, the Kingdom of Heaven is for those who do not place their security in material things, but in love for God; for those who have a simple, humble heart that does not presume to be just and does not judge others; for those who know how to suffer with those who suffer and how to rejoice when others rejoice. They are not violent but merciful and strive to be instruments for reconciliation and peace. Saints, whether men or women, are instruments for reconciliation and peace; they are always helping people to become reconciled and helping to bring about peace. Thus holiness is beautiful, it is a beautiful path! (Pope Francis, *Angelus*, November 1, 2013)

Decoding the Message

Have you ever seen a lamb with seven horns and seven eyes as described in Revelation 5:6? Probably not, unless it was a drawing or computer-generated image on the internet. John doesn't have those options, so it must mean something special. In fact, it does.

The number 7 represents the idea of something being perfect or universal. The horns symbolize power, and the eyes represent knowledge. A living lamb that seems to have been slain is of course Jesus Christ. Putting it all together, we have Jesus Christ, the Lamb of God, who has universal power and knowledge. Only God has universal power and knowledge, so this vision is telling us that Jesus Christ is God.

You may notice that there are many numbers mentioned in the Book of Revelation. Remember, the number 7 symbolizes perfection or universality, like the seven seals or seven trumpet blasts (see Revelation 4:4–5, 8:6). The number 4 represents completeness, as in the four directions or the four seasons (see 7:1–4). Thus, the four horsemen who appear when the first four seals are broken represent all the evils that human empires bring into the world: conquest, war, famine, and death (see 6:1–17).

The number 12 is a reference to the Twelve Tribes of Israel or the Twelve Apostles. The number 1,000 symbolizes a number so large you cannot count it. It's like when your mom says exasperatedly, "Haven't I told you to pick up your dishes a thousand times?" So, when you read that 144,000 Israelites will be saved (see Revelation 7:1–4), it is not a literal number. It represents a math problem: the Twelve Tribes of Israel multiplied by 12,000 marked people from each tribe equals 144,000. Symbolically, then, the 144,000 represents the incalculable number of Israelites who will be saved. In Heaven, there is room for everyone!

The Book of Revelation is full of numerology or number symbolism. The number 6 symbolizes imperfection. What do you think multiple 6s mean?

Perhaps the most well-known number from Revelation is 666, also referred to as the mark of the beast (see 13:18). The book itself tells us that it stands for a person. Because the number 6 symbolizes imperfection, three 6s in a row can also mean the "most imperfect" one.

In Greek language, they associate each letter of the alphabet with a number. You could take the Greek letters in a person's name, add together the numerical values of those letters, and come up with a single number representing the person's name. Therefore, 666 represents someone's name at the time the Book of Revelation was written. Scholars have identified Caesar Nero, the Roman emperor of the time, as one possibility, because the numerical total of the letters in his name equals 666. Nero blamed Christians for the burning of Rome and started a Christian persecution that resulted in the deaths of many Christians. He is remembered as one of the worst—or perhaps *the* worst—persecutors of the early Church.

Number	Symbolic Meaning
3	divine perfection, Trinity
4	necessary time, completeness (four winds or four directions)
6	something incomplete or evil (1 less than 7)
7	number of perfection
12	religious completeness (Twelve Tribes of Israel, Twelve Apostles)
1,000	a very large number, too big to count

Another symbolic element in Revelation is the use of colors. We will look briefly at two colors: red and white. Red is the color of blood. It symbolizes death, which is why it is the color of a horse ridden in war (see Revelation 6:4). Red also symbolizes the faith and bravery of those Christians who died for their faith, the martyrs. This is why priests wear red vestments to celebrate the feast days of martyrs. White is the color of purity. It is associated with the saints in Heaven, which is why the elders (see 4:4) and the 144,000 (see 7:9) are all wearing white robes. 🌟

UNIT 4

HMMMMMM. . . How does the use of signs and symbols affect our understanding of the Book of Revelation?

Article 51

An Overview of Revelation

When you read the Book of Revelation from beginning to end, as you should read any book you hope to understand, you may well find yourself confused. Instead of a well-developed plot that moves steadily along, you find yourself immersed in a series of images that begin to blend into one another. The events that are described when the seven seals are opened seem almost indistinguishable from the events that are described when the seven bowls are poured. You will be better able to keep track of what the author is teaching if you have an overview of the book.

The Setting: The Heavenly Court

The Book of Revelation describes seven visions of the heavenly court. Each vision will precipitate events on Earth. From the heavenly court:

1. The seven letters will be sent (see 2:1–3:22).
2. The seven seals will be opened (see 6:1–8:1).
3. The seven trumpets will be blown (see 8:2–11:19).
4. The battle between the devil and the woman will take place (see 12:1–18).
5. The seven bowls will be poured (see 15:1–16:21), and Babylon (a symbol of Rome) will fall (see 17:1–19:10).
6. The Word will go forth to fight the final battles (see 19:11–20:15).
7. The final victory of good over evil will be revealed (see 21:1–22:21).

Part of the message of hope in the Book of Revelation rests on the heavenly court as the setting. The Lamb of God is victorious in Heaven and is worshipped by the martyrs. The hoped-for and promised victory of good over evil is already accomplished in Heaven. Though the battle has not yet completely played out on Earth, its outcome is predetermined. The hope offered is not that Jesus will overcome evil but that Jesus *has* overcome evil. One must simply remain faithful to share in his victory.

UNIT 4

Description of Present Suffering

During the second vision (see Revelation 4:1–11), God is pictured holding a sealed scroll. An angel asks, "Who is worthy to open the scroll and break its seals?" (5:2). (In Revelation, when seals are opened it means the end-time is present.) At first it seems that no one is worthy to open the seals. However, an elder tells John, "The lion of the tribe of Judah, the root of David, has triumphed, enabling him to open the scroll with its seven seals" (verse 5). Only Jesus is worthy to open the seals because only Jesus is able to reveal God's plan and to initiate the events that bring his plan to fulfillment.

As each seal is opened, something terrible happens on Earth. Through symbols, the author is describing the kinds of suffering his audience is presently enduring. The horsemen (first, second, third, and fourth seals) represent conquest, war, famine, and death. The martyrs under the altar (fifth seal) are told that the people's suffering is not quite over (see Revelation 6:11). At the opening of the sixth seal, a great earthquake erupts. The seventh seal precipitates another vision of the heavenly court and the blowing of the seven trumpets. Again cataclysmic events are unleashed. With the opening of the seals, one quarter of the Earth is affected. With the blowing of the trumpets, one third of the Earth is affected. Things will get worse before they get better.

UNIT 4

Through the symbolism of the seven seals, the author of Revelation is describing the suffering of the people of his time.

MAKE IT SO

Though the imagery in the Book of Revelation can seem scary, the goal is not to instill fear in our heart. Revelation is meant to give us hope—the hope of everlasting life with God, the hope that comes with keeping our eyes on God. So many things in this world fight for our time. Do not be distracted, or you may lose your focus on God. The things that distract us from God aren't necessarily bad, but when they get in the way of our focus on God, they can become a problem. Make a mental note of which of the following are potential distractions for you: money, media, relationships, schoolwork, hobbies.

The Fall of Babylon and Final Victory

Although all the episodes resemble one another a great deal, there is some forward movement in the plot. The images change from describing persecution to describing judgment and then salvation. With the pouring of the seven bowls (see Revelation 16:1–21), Babylon is destroyed (see 16:19–18:24). *Babylon* is code for *Rome* because both empires destroyed the Temple in Jerusalem, Babylon during the Babylonian Exile (587–537 BC), and Rome in AD 70.

The book ends with the final victory of good over evil not only in Heaven but also on Earth. In his final vision (see Revelation, chapters 20–21), John is shown the **New Jerusalem**, another name for Heaven. New Jerusalem is described in glowing terms. Everything is made of precious stones and gold, and all its features are described in multiples of twelve. There is no sun in the New Jerusalem, "for the glory of God gave it light, and its lamp was the Lamb. The nations will walk by its light" (21:23–24). But in this new creation, the most

---

New Jerusalem ➤ In the Book of Revelation, a symbol of a renewed society in which God dwells; a symbol of the Church, the "holy city," the assembly of the People of God called together from "the ends of the earth"; also, in other settings, a symbol of Heaven.

moving promise is this: "[God] will wipe every tear from their eyes, and there shall be no more death or mourning, wailing or pain [for] the old order has passed away" (21:4). When nations walk by the light of Christ, peace will reign on Earth as it does in Heaven. ✳

In the final vision in Revelation, John is shown the New Jerusalem, another name for Heaven.

UNIT 4

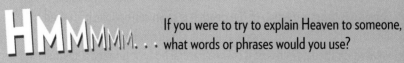

HMMMMMM. . .

If you were to try to explain Heaven to someone, what words or phrases would you use?

Article 52

Four Last Things

Logan and his friend Carly were discussing what happens to us when we die. "I don't think anything happens," said Carly. "We're just gone. That's it, nothing else." "I can't accept that," said Logan. "It just seems right that there's more to come after this life. I believe there is a God, Jesus rose from the dead, and Jesus promised that we too would live with him in Heaven." "Well, prove it," replied Carly. "I can't prove it to you scientifically," Logan answered. "but it makes so much sense. We all long for something greater, something more, and Heaven is the answer. And without Hell, bad people get away with horrible things in this life without any consequences. I know in the end that believing in God and Heaven is a matter of faith, but prove to me that they don't exist!"

Scripture and Tradition have a lot to say about what comes after this life. We've seen the references to Heaven and Hell in the Book of Revelation. The Church calls death, judgment, Heaven, and Hell the **four last things**. Let's take a closer look at what has been revealed about each of them.

I DIDN'T KNOW THAT!

Do you know what will happen to your body after the Final Judgment? The Bible tells us that when Jesus returns to Earth, he will physically raise all those who have died, giving them back the bodies they lost at death. But our resurrected bodies will not die and, for the righteous, they will transform into a glorified state, freed from suffering and pain.

When we live here on Earth, our bodies are corruptible; that is, they are susceptible to disease, deformity, and death. But when we are raised, our bodies will be incorruptible. Paul explains this in First Corinthians: "So also is the resurrection of the dead. It is sown corruptible; it is raised incorruptible. It is sown dishonorable; it is raised glorious. It is sown weak; it is raised powerful. It is sown a natural body; it is raised a spiritual body. If there is a natural body, there is also a spiritual one" (15:42–44).

UNIT 4

---

four last things ➤ The Church refers to death, judgment, Heaven, and Hell as the four last things.

Death

When we die, it is more than just a heartbeat stopping or brain waves ceasing. As Christians, we define death as the separation of our body and soul. When that occurs, our time on Earth is over. When we die, we are called to God, and we enter into everlasting life. That life may be the joy of Heaven or the pain of separation from God in Hell. We are not **reincarnated**, so this life is our only chance to discover God's love for us and accept his grace. Knowing we have a limited time on Earth, we should have a sense of urgency about following Jesus and sharing in his mission of love and mercy. It also means we need to prepare ourselves spiritually for our own death.

On Ash Wednesday, we receive ashes on our forehead.

UNIT 4

This is why we receive the ashes on our forehead and hear these or similar words on Ash Wednesday: "Remember that you are dust, and unto dust you shall return." It is also why every time we pray the Hail Mary, we ask Mary to "pray for us now and at the hour of our death."

reincarnation ➤ The belief that our soul can be reborn into a new body.

As Christians, we are also called to help others when they are facing their own death. Perhaps you have a grandparent or older relative who is sick and nearing death. It can be hard to stay at their bedside in the hospital or nursing home and watch them suffer. However, your presence is a way of sharing God's love with them when they need it most. You may think that you don't know what to say, but sometimes being silent and holding their hand is all they need. To help yourself through the difficult time, keep reminding yourself of our hope in resurrection. You will see your loved one again when you are reunited in Heaven!

Judgment

When we die, we will have to take responsibility for our choices in this life. This happens through two different types of judgment. The first is the **Particular Judgment**. At the moment of our death, we will face Christ, the judge of the living and the dead. The Particular Judgment has three possible outcomes.

One outcome is that we can be welcomed immediately into Heaven. This happens when we die united in friendship with God and are perfectly purified from all sin. Another outcome is that we can be sent to Purgatory. This happens if we are ultimately destined for Heaven but are not yet pure enough to enter. **Purgatory** is a state of final purification or cleansing that allows us to achieve the holiness needed to experience the eternal joy of Heaven. The third outcome is that we can be sent to Hell as a result of rejecting God's grace.

The second judgment is the **Final Judgment**. This occurs at the end of time, after the resurrection of all the dead, when the graves are all opened, and our souls are united with our **incorruptible** bodies. Revelation 21:11–15 describes this as the "**Last Day**."

UNIT 4

Particular Judgment ➤ The judgment that occurs immediately at the time of our death, when our immortal souls will be judged as worthy or unworthy of Heaven.

Purgatory ➤ A state of final purification or cleansing, which one may need to enter following death and before entering Heaven.

Final Judgment ➤ The judgment of the human race by Jesus Christ at his second coming. It is also called the Last Judgment.

incorruptible ➤ In reference to our bodies, not subject to decay or dissolution.

Last Day ➤ Described in the Book of Revelation, on the Last Day, all will stand before the One True Judge, Jesus Christ. Everything in our lives that is hidden, both good and bad, will be brought to light and we will be judged according to our deeds.

At the Last Day, all will stand before the One True Judge, Jesus Christ. Everything in our lives that is hidden, both good and bad, will be brought to light and we will be judged according to our deeds. Being at the end of time, this includes the farthest effects of our actions. Like a stone that is dropped in the middle of a still pond makes ripples all the way to the edges, our actions have effects that travel outward affecting others.

When has your sinful behavior had consequences that affected others?

Hell

The Book of Revelation tells us of the devil being sent to place of "fire and sulfur" (20:10). This symbolic language describes a place of utter torment, a place where there is no peace or love. Ultimately, Hell is being totally separated from God.

Because God gave us the gift of free will, he never forces us to be good or to do the right thing. We must freely choose to do so for ourselves, for the only way to be in communion with God is to freely choose to love him. When we choose evil, we reject the love, grace, and redemption God offers to us, and instead choose Hell, the "state of definitive self-exclusion from communion with God and the blessed" (*CCC*, number 1033). Those in Hell are eternally separated from God; this is Hell's chief punishment.

God does not send anyone to Hell. Rather, through our own choices, we can send ourselves there. By rejecting God's grace, we can condemn ourselves to separation from God for all eternity.

Heaven

Having examined death, judgment, and Hell, we have saved the best for last: Heaven. Those who die in God's grace and friendship and are perfectly purified go to Heaven. The *Catechism (CCC)* defines *Heaven* in various ways: as "communion of life and love with the Trinity, with the Virgin Mary, the angels, and all the blessed" (number 1024); as "the ultimate end and fulfillment of the deepest human longings, the state of supreme, definitive happiness" (number 1024); and as "the blessed community of all who are perfectly incorporated into Christ" (number 1026).

Though these definitions give us some glimpse into the reality of Heaven's glory, we cannot really know what Heaven is like until we are there. In fact, the idea of Heaven stretches the limits of human imagination and language. For this reason, Sacred Scripture uses metaphors in an effort to give us some sense of it. These metaphors include "life, light, peace, wedding feast, wine of the kingdom, the Father's house, the heavenly Jerusalem, paradise" (*CCC*, number 1027). ✳

UNIT 4

HMMMMM. . . How might your understanding of the four last things affect how you live today?

Article 53
Faith: Our Response to Revelation

We started this chapter asking about what the Book of Revelation tells us. Some Christians interpret it in a way that instills fear. They talk about tribulation and the antichrist and try to get people to change in fear of God and God's judgment. But most Catholics see the Book of Revelation as a book of hope. Yes, we are caught in a battle between good and evil, between God and the Devil. But Revelation promises that good will always triumph in the end, that Christ will overcome Satan. This brings us to an interesting question: Do we make our choices based on fear of Hell or on the hope of Heaven? In other words, is our life here on Earth motivated by fear of God's just judgments or out of love for God?

When we consider all of God's Revelation, it might seem like the answer is a mix of both. However, the Gospels make it clear that Jesus Christ does not want us to live in fear. One of his most frequent sayings after his Resurrection is, "Do not be afraid!" God has revealed to us that he loves us and calls us to love him. If we accept this, we need not have any fear. Consider this passage from the First Letter of John:

> God is love, and whoever remains in love remains in God and God in him. In this is love brought to perfection among us, that we have confidence on the day of judgment because as he is, so are we in this world. There is no fear in love, but perfect love drives out fear because fear has to do with punishment, and so one who fears is not yet perfect in love. We love because he first loved us. (4:16–19)

Our response to this central truth of Divine Revelation—that God loves us without condition—is faith. When we have faith in Jesus Christ, we become his disciples, or followers. First, this means we seek to imitate the words and actions of Jesus. Through faith we try to make Jesus' values, attitudes, and priorities our own. Furthermore, we seek to treat people as Jesus treated everyone during his earthly life—with dignity, compassion, and love. Second, when we become disciples of Christ, we fully recognize and accept Jesus as the Second Person of the Blessed Trinity, the Eternal Son of God. In order to unite us with God, he took on human flesh, died to liberate us from sin, and opened a path to new life for us through his glorious Resurrection and Ascension.

UNIT 4

As disciples, we accept with grateful hearts the gift of grace that, through the power of the Holy Spirit, makes us adopted children of God the Father and therefore brothers and sisters of Jesus and of one another.

Love Spreads

If we love God, it only makes sense that we would want others to know about God and the amazing things he has done. If that weren't enough, Christ commanded his disciples to continue his mission by sharing the Good News with all people. No one comes to faith all by themselves. We all need to hear the Good News from someone. When we proclaim our faith in Jesus Christ and the Good News of his life, death, and Resurrection through words and deeds, we call this **evangelization**.

Students at Father Lopez Catholic High School in Daytona, Florida, demonstrate solidarity with their brothers and sisters in Burkina Faso, West Africa, by packing sustainable meals to help them survive drought conditions.

evangelization ➤ The proclamation of the Gospel of Jesus Christ through word and witness.

We can witness our faith through both our words and deeds in many ways. For example, we can actively participate in the liturgical and sacramental life of the Church and invite others to do the same. We can use our talents to proclaim and to share with others what God has revealed for our salvation. We can actively engage in acts of charity and works of justice. We can live "in a way worthy of the gospel of Christ" (Philippians 1:27) so that others may be drawn to faith through our example. In these ways, we can do our part to bring others to place their faith in Jesus Christ. ✳

CATHOLICS MAKING A DIFFERENCE

Holy men and women of the Church are often depicted as serious and completely absorbed by rules and doctrine. Saint Pope John XXIII, who served as Pope from 1958 to 1963, defied that stereotype at every turn. His congenial nature and tendency to use humor to relate to the people, rather than preaching homilies or quoting Scripture, drew people close to the Church. Once he was asked by a journalist, "Your Holiness, how many people work at the Vatican?" Pope John paused and replied, "About half of them." His sense of humor seemed to flow from his joyful nature. He was comfortable enough to laugh at himself, poke fun at his office, and invite others to see the world with humor. When holy men and women of the Church are joyful, they can bring others to Christ just by being themselves.

UNIT 4

HMMMMM. . . How can love help us on our journey toward Heaven?

1. What is the Book of Revelation about?

2. Describe the characteristics of apocalyptic literature.

3. Why does the author of the Book of Revelation use signs and symbols?

4. What is the symbolic meaning of the numbers 3, 7, 12, and 1,000?

5. What two empires does *Babylon* refer to in the Book of Revelation?

6. Describe the two judgments that take place after death.

7. Why do we say that God does not "choose" who goes to Hell?

8. What is the greatest motivator for doing God's will?

9. What is evangelization?

UNIT 4

ART STUDY

SIGNS AND SYMBOLS IN REVELATION

This piece of artwork is densely packed with many detailed images from Revelation.

1. Think about the signs and symbols you read about in this chapter. Which ones do you see represented in this piece of artwork?

2. How do you feel after carefully examining the different elements of the piece?

UNIT 4 HIGHLIGHTS

CHAPTER 11 **Acts of the Apostles: The Church Spread throughout the World**

The Work of the Holy Spirit

Images: vecteezy.com

The Holy Spirit guided and empowered the first Christians to boldly proclaim the Good News.

The Church is revealed in the Book of Acts through the descent of the Holy Spirit upon the Apostles during Pentecost.

The Early Church, with the guidance of the Holy Spirit, found a way to welcome Gentiles into the community.

Christ plants (establishes) the Church.

Key Events in the Growth of the Church

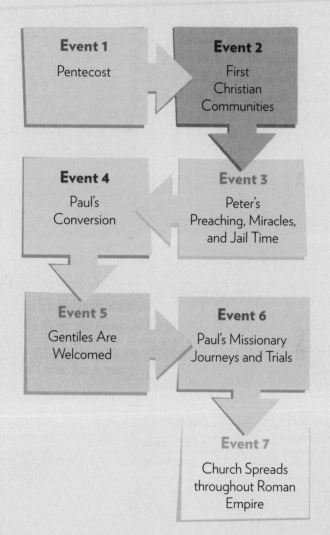

Event 1

Pentecost

Event 2

First
Christian
Communities

Event 4

Paul's
Conversion

Event 3

Peter's
Preaching, Miracles,
and Jail Time

Event 5

Gentiles Are
Welcomed

Event 6

Paul's Missionary
Journeys and Trials

Event 7

Church Spreads
throughout Roman
Empire

UNIT 4

CHAPTER 12 The Early Church Responds
to Challenges

The Pastoral Letters

In the Pastoral Letters, the author instructs Timothy and Titus on caring for new Christian communities. He emphasizes the characteristics of those who would lead the communities.

- Irreproachable
- Married only once
- Temperate

- Self-controlled
- Decent
- Hospitable
- Able to teach

Early Church Leaders Confront Social Injustice

Second Letter to Timothy

- Christian leaders must develop the endurance to serve the faithful over a lifetime.
- Christian leaders must be persistent and put up with hardships.

Letter of James

- Your faith shows itself by your actions.
- Pray for and anoint the sick.

Letter to Philemon

- Paul encourages a slave owner to accept a slave as a brother in Christ.
- The Church must confront injustices.

Images: vecteezy.com

CHAPTER 13   Revelation: Christ's Ultimate Triumph

Learning from the Seven Churches' Struggles

Persecution

Christians from the seven churches were imprisoned and even killed for remaining true to their faith.	Christians still suffer from persecution. They are forced from their homes, and their businesses and churches are vandalized and burned. Thousands have been killed.

False Teachings

Three of the seven churches were being tested by false teachers, posing as apostles. These people tried to pass their opinions along as God's truth.	We must be polite and respectful but not let falsehoods and injustices go unchallenged. We must speak the truth and help others grow in the faith.

Complacency

The people in some of the seven churches had let their love for God diminish. They were going through the motions, but their heart was not in it.	Like the seven churches, each of us can have struggles with our own faith. If we have grown complacent in living out our faith, we must rekindle the fire of true faith.

UNIT 4

Four Last Things in the Book of Revelation

Death

When we die, we are called before God and enter into everlasting life. We are not reincarnated. This life is our only chance to discover God's love for us and accept his grace.

When we die, we will have to take responsibility for our choices and actions in this life. We will stand before Jesus Christ in two judgments: our Particular Judgment and the Final Judgment.

Judgment

Heaven

Heaven is eternal communion of life and love with the Trinity, the Virgin Mary, the angels, and all the blessed. Heaven is fulfillment of the deepest human longings.

When we choose evil, we reject the love, grace, and redemption God offers to us. Hell is the state of definitive self-exclusion from eternal communion with God.

Hell

UNIT 4
BRING IT HOME

WERE THE FIRST CHRISTIANS THAT DIFFERENT FROM US?

FOCUS QUESTIONS

MATT
Providence Catholic High School

The early Christians were very similar to us. They had the teachings of the Apostles, communal life, breaking of the bread, and prayer. The early Christians were persecuted for publicly professing their faith. Though this may not be the case anymore, we still experience criticism for having faith. People may be judgmental when we say we are Christian, but it is in these times that we need to stay strong and keep the faith.

UNIT 4

REFLECT

Take some time to read and reflect on the unit and chapter focus questions listed in the facing page.

- What question or section did you identify most closely with?

- What did you find within the unit that was comforting or challenging?

318

UNIT 5
Following Jesus

WHAT DOES IT MEAN TO FOLLOW JESUS?

LOOKING AHEAD

UNIT 5

Following Jesus means I study Jesus' teachings and try to apply them to my life, not verbatim, but the real meaning behind what he says in the Bible. It means taking what he says and really believing in it, not just saying it. It means taking his teachings to heart, following him and trying my best to live my life according to him, with marginal errors along the way.

IFE
Mater Dei High School

CHAPTER 14
Our Call to Holiness

CAN I BE HOLY?

SNAPSHOT

Article 54

Letters of John: Living in Union with God

Tina, Dana, and Karen were best friends in eighth grade. They did everything together. During the summer, you never saw one of them without the other two by her side. Their families even went on vacation together. It seemed like nothing could split up these friends. But something changed when they started high school. Dana didn't seem as interested in hanging out with Tina and Karen. She had made some new friends and was spending all her time with them. It made Tina and Karen wonder if they had done something wrong. Had they really changed that much since high school started? Why do friends grow apart?

The Letters of John tell of people in the community parting ways and taking different paths. This often happens when we reach a crossroads in our lives. What changes have you experienced in your group of friends since you started high school?

Friends can part ways for many reasons. When it happens, it often leaves one or both sides wondering what happened. Many times it is just part of growing up and developing different interests. Other times, it can be more difficult, especially if one person is on a path of bad decisions that the other friends cannot support. In the three Letters of John, we find that some people in the community have parted ways to go down a dangerous path, leaving those who are staying true to Jesus' teaching wondering what happened.

© Twinsterphoto / Shutterstock.com

UNIT 5

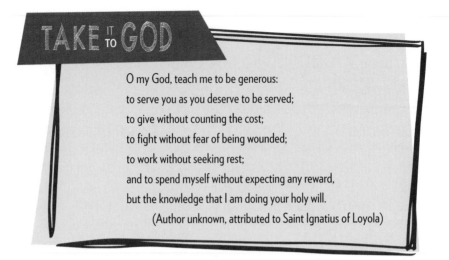

TAKE IT TO GOD

O my God, teach me to be generous:

to serve you as you deserve to be served;

to give without counting the cost;

to fight without fear of being wounded;

to work without seeking rest;

and to spend myself without expecting any reward,

but the knowledge that I am doing your holy will.

(Author unknown, attributed to Saint Ignatius of Loyola)

John's Letters Point Us toward Holiness

All three of John's letters seem to address the same Christian community that the Gospel of John addresses. Remember, when the Gospel was written, the community was wondering why they had been kicked out of the synagogue over their belief in Jesus' divinity. In the letters, the community appears to be past that concern, now facing another issue. Some of their members have departed because of a difference in belief about Jesus' humanity (see 1 John 2:19–23). They downplay Jesus' humanity and do not take seriously the need for Christians to avoid sin. The letter is addressed to those who remain in the community. The author offers guidance to help them stay true to their call to be in union with God and to live lives of **holiness**.

As in the Gospel of John, the letters use the theme of light and darkness to talk about God and good and evil (see John 1:5). The light represents God, and the Christians are called to be in the light, which means living a life of holiness. To be in the darkness means to go against God's will and to live a life of sinfulness. The author of John sees those who leave the community as being in darkness (see 1:5–10, 2:18–23). In believing that Jesus' humanity is not that important, these people also believe that what they do in the flesh is not important. This leads them to think that some sinful acts are okay (see 1 John 3:4–10; 2 John, verse 7).

---

holiness ➤ The state of being holy. This means to be set apart for God's service, to be devoted to God and united with him and his Church, to live a morally good life, to be a person of prayer, and to reveal God's love to the world through acts of loving service.

First John makes it clear that Jesus' humanity is very important, because it makes Jesus a model for our actions. John writes, "This is the way we may know that we are in union with him: whoever claims to abide in him ought to live [just] as he lived" (2:5–6). Thus, if we are truly in union with Christ, we must avoid sin, and if we do sin, we must acknowledge it and repent.

The letter makes it clear that our ability to be in the light—to live a life of holiness—is connected to how we love our neighbor. John states, "Whoever says he is in the light, yet hates his brother, is still in the darkness" (1 John 2:9). This means you cannot claim to be a Christian and then harbor feelings of hatred toward others. That would be like going to Mass, fully participating, and then talking on the car ride home about how much you can't stand one of your classmates.

The letter uses beautiful language to help us understand the meaning of love even more clearly.

> Beloved, let us love one another, because love is of God; everyone who loves is begotten by God and knows God. Whoever is without love does not know God, for God is love. In this way the love of God was revealed to us: God sent his only Son into the world so that we might have life through him. In this is love: not that we have loved God, but that he loved us and sent his Son as expiation for our sins. Beloved, if God so loved us, we also must love one another. No one has ever seen God. Yet, if we love one another, God remains in us, and his love is brought to perfection in us. (1 John 4:7-12)

John reminds us that Jesus gave us the example of how we are to love one another: "The way we came to know love was that he laid down his life for us; so we ought to lay down our lives for our brothers" (1 John 3:16). This sets a high bar for us as followers of Jesus.

UNIT 5

Living the Call to Holiness

Following Jesus and living a life of holiness is rarely about the big moments. It is in the small day-to-day moments that we live out our call to holiness. Holiness is first about our devotion to the glory of God. But it is also about service to our neighbor. John illustrates this when he asks a rhetorical question: "If someone who has worldly means sees a brother in need and refuses him compassion, how can the love of God remain in him?" (1 John 3:17).

What does it mean to you to live your "call to holiness"?

Although John specifically mentions money ("worldly means") in his question, we can apply his question to other needs as well. If you see someone in need of emotional help, the call to holiness directs you to respond. Being holy means reaching out to someone when you see that person expressing loneliness. It means finding ways to include a classmate when you see them being excluded. For holiness is ultimately about love: "Charity is the soul of holiness to which we are all called" (Catechism, number 826). United with Christ and sanctified by him, we will find our own specific calling and state of life to live a life of holiness. ✳

OVERVIEW of the Letters of John

- **Intended audience:** This is the same community to whom the Gospel of John is addressed.
- **Major theme:** Jesus is our model for behavior, and we are called to walk in the light and avoid sin.
- **Reason for writing:** Some members have left the community over a disagreement about Jesus' humanity and a Christian's need to avoid sin. John seeks to help those who have remained true to the faith.

HMMMMMM. . . How do John's letters help us to understand our call to holiness?

Article 55

Jesus and Prayer

Tina sat on her bed crying as she talked with her mother. Tina was feeling overwhelmed and confused. She missed her friend Dana, who stopped hanging out with her once school started. Her other friends, including Karen, wanted to spend time with her, but her part in the school play was taking up all of her free time. Her schoolwork was piling up and stressing her out. It was just too much for Tina to handle. Her mom has a strong faith, and is always encouraging Tina to pray about things.

But when her mom suggested it this time, Tina blew up. "Mom! I am too busy. Besides, I tried praying before and nothing happened!"

Tina's confusion about prayer is not uncommon. Perhaps you have even felt this way at times. But don't give up on prayer! Prayer is an essential part of a life of holiness. Fortunately, just as John's letters teach us that Jesus is the model for our holiness, the Gospels teach us that Jesus is the model for our prayer life. The Gospels have numerous accounts that teach us about prayer through Jesus' words and actions.

When have you felt that your prayers were not being answered?

Praying Like Jesus

Tina's feelings of frustration and confusion have led her to question the importance and effectiveness of prayer. So, let's first look at the importance of prayer in Jesus' life. From the Gospels, we learn that during his earthly life, Jesus often takes time alone to pray (see Matthew 14:23; Mark 1:35, 6:46; Luke 5:16, 6:12). Sometimes he takes time to pray before making important decisions (see Luke 4:1–14, 9:24–28, 23:34). In the Gospel of Luke, he spends the night in

UNIT 5

prayer before he chooses the Twelve Apostles (see 6:12–16). He also spends time in prayer the night before he dies on the cross, seeking to do the Father's will. "After withdrawing about a stone's throw from them and kneeling, he prayed, saying, 'Father, if you are willing, take this cup away from me; still, not my will but yours be done'" (Luke 22:41–42).

Jesus spends an anguished night in prayer before he is arrested and crucified.

However, Jesus does not save prayer just for the big moments in his life. We see that prayer was part of his regular days too. For example, the Gospel of Mark recounts the actions of Jesus after a busy day of teaching and healing in the town of Capernaum: "Rising very early before dawn, he left and went off to a deserted place, where he prayed" (1:35). Sometimes life got busy for Jesus as he ministered to the needs of others, but he still found time for prayer.

In Mark's Gospel, in the account of the Feeding of the Five Thousand (see 6:30–44), Jesus asks the Apostles to come away with him "to a deserted place and rest a while" (verse 31). However, crowds of people follow them, and Jesus, moved with compassion, teaches them and feeds them. When the people at last disperse, Jesus goes off by himself "to the mountain to pray" (6:46). Luke's Gospel also tells us that despite the great crowds that came to listen to Jesus and to be healed by him, Jesus would make the effort to "withdraw to deserted places to pray" (5:16). These Gospel accounts make clear that Jesus needed prayer to sustain him in his ministry. He consciously made time for prayer, often by getting up very early and finding a place where he could be alone. We lead busy lives, full of activities, work, school, and people who demand our time and attention. It can be challenging to find a time and a place to pray. But can you imagine Jesus not praying? Of course not! Prayer is a necessity, not a luxury, to following Jesus and living a life of holiness. Prayer is the strong foundation on which all the other aspects of our lives can rest—studies, activities, work, and relationships. Without prayer, our daily lives can become overburdened or meaningless. With prayer, our every thought, word, and deed can be directed toward following God's will in our life.

CATHOLICS **MAKING** A DIFFERENCE

Saint Monica (332-387) relied on prayer to see her through life's most challenging moments. When she was young, she was in an arranged marriage to a Roman soldier who had a violent temper. They had three children together, and he hindered her efforts to raise them as Christians. Monica's faith never wavered. She prayed for her husband and her children. A year before his death, her husband converted. Two of her children entered religious life, but her son Augustine tried to find satisfaction in everything but religion. Monica continued to pray without ceasing. After many personal trials, Augustine converted to Christianity and would become one of the Church's greatest saints, Saint Augustine of Hippo (354-430). On her deathbed, Monica told Augustine all her hopes in the world had been fulfilled.

UNIT 5

Prayer Challenges

Tina said she tried prayer once and nothing happened. Jesus taught an interesting parable about persistence in prayer (see Luke 11:5–8) that helps address Tina's concern. This parable is about a man who has an unexpected guest arrive at midnight. Completely unprepared, the man goes to a friend's house and asks to borrow three loaves of bread so he might extend hospitality to his guest by offering him a meal. Jesus says that although the friend may be annoyed at being disturbed in the middle of the night, "if he does not get up to give him the loaves because of their friendship, he will get up to give him whatever he needs because of his persistence" (verse 8).

Jesus uses this story to teach us that our prayers should be persistent and courageous. For our prayers to be effective, we should not just ask once, wait a few minutes for an immediate response, and then give up. We are called to continually bring our needs before God, day or night. Like the friend who responds to the man in need of bread, we know that God will likewise always respond to our needs with merciful love.

When Jesus was teaching his disciples about prayer, he even offered the promise that God hears and answers our prayers. In Matthew, Jesus assures us, "Ask and it will be given to you; seek and you will find; knock and the door will be opened to you" (7:7). Jesus compares the love and **fidelity** of his Divine Father to the love of a human father for his children. If a human father knows how to provide for his children, then "how much more will your heavenly Father give good things to those who ask him?" (verse 11). Jesus teaches us that we should spend time in prayer, persistently present our needs to God, and have faith that God will hear our prayers. ✳

MAKE IT SO

When do you pray to God? Do you pray daily, or do wait until you really need help? God is so much more than the "God of the 911." Yes, God wants us to call on him when we are in need. But God really wants prayer to be a regular part of your daily life. Think of prayer as an ongoing conversation between you and God. Tell him how you feel, what you think, what you need, and who you are worried about. Pray often for the needs of other people, both in your local community and across the world. Pray in private and in public. Keep a gratitude journal of the good things in your life so you can thank God for his gifts. And also take time to listen. Take time to be silent in God's presence, meditate, sit in adoration, and listen to what God has to reveal to you.

HMMMMM. . . How is Jesus a model for your prayer life?

fidelity ➤ Faithfulness.

Article 56

Growing in Prayer

Despite her frustrations about prayer, Tina tried praying, and over time, things in her life began to settle down. Her friends even came to see her perform in the school play and were amazed at Tina's acting ability. Once the play ended and her evenings were less busy, Tina's homework became more manageable. However, as she prayed, other questions about prayer arose for Tina. She wondered why her mom seemed to get those "warm fuzzy" feelings when she prayed, because Tina never really felt anything. She also wondered why sometimes it seemed like God answered her prayers, and other times it seemed like God was ignoring her. This made Tina wonder if she was even praying in the right way.

What is the most comfortable way for you to pray?

UNIT 5

Start with Humility

In the Parable of the Pharisee and the Tax Collector, Jesus teaches his disciples there is a right way and a wrong way to approach God in prayer (see Luke 18:9–14). Like many of Jesus' parables, this one contains a narrative twist, or surprise. The parable concerns two men who go to the Temple area to pray— one a Pharisee, a strictly observant Jew; the other a tax collector, a hated agent of Rome. Jesus' listeners would have assumed that the person worthy of holiness and respect would be the Pharisee. But Jesus overturns their expectations. It is the tax collector who, with eyes cast down and beating his breast, prays: "O God, be merciful to me a sinner" (verse 13). Jesus concludes with the statement: "I tell you, the latter went home justified, not the former; for everyone who exalts himself will be humbled, and the one who humbles himself will be exalted" (verse 14).

It is interesting to note the specific audience to whom Jesus addresses this parable: "those who were convinced of their own righteousness and despised everyone else" (verse 9). Could we be like the Pharisee, overly convinced of our own honesty and righteousness? Like the Pharisee, are we overly confident in our own superiority, certain that our thoughts and actions are pleasing to God? If so, we have fallen into the same trap as the Pharisee in the parable, who prays, "O God, I thank you that I am not like the rest of humanity— greedy, dishonest, adulterous—or even like this tax collector" (verse 11). All human beings sin. We all need the infinite mercy of God to flood our hearts and heal our souls. The tax collector, who stands at a distance and prays with humility, knows this. So Tina, who wonders if she is "doing it right," first needs to make sure she approaches her time with God with a healthy sense of humility.

I DIDN'T KNOW THAT!

Talk about feeling God's presence when you pray. Saint Joseph of Cupertino (1603–1663) sometimes got more than he expected. The seventeenth-century Franciscan was known to begin floating during prayer! In fact, during his beatification, witnesses testified that he levitated seventy different times during prayer, including once in the presence of the Pope. No wonder he is the patron saint of airplane pilots.

God's Presence in Prayer

Tina also wondered about not feeling anything during her time in prayer. If you have ever had someone share with you their story of a powerful prayer experience and you have not had one, it can make you question your prayer life. But don't worry; prayer is much more than a feeling. God is our Father, whom we approach through prayer because he loves us as his own children. Yes, God sometimes graciously offers us the gift of feeling his presence in some way, but that is not the only sign of God's love and interest in our prayers.

Our prayer life can often go through a dry spell, where we may feel like God is not there. It can make praying difficult, but those are the times that God is calling us to something deeper in our prayer life. It may mean that we need to change how we are praying. We need to avoid being so repetitive that we become bored with prayer. The dry spell can be God's way of telling us to do things differently. You might try:

How have you used music, Scripture, time in nature, or a journal to help you pray?

- reading a daily reflection
- reading and reflecting on Scripture
- keeping a gratitude journal or a prayer request journal
- meditating before the Blessed Sacrament
- a prayer walk

Remember God is always present to you, even if you do not feel him.

© Kamira / Shutterstock.com

UNIT 5

Finally, Tina questioned whether God was listening to her. There are two parts to this concern. The first thing Tina should probably ask is, "Am I listening to God?" Sometimes we are so busy talking to God that our prayers can become monologues. But prayer is not a monologue; it is a dialogue. This means that we talk to God in prayer, but we also have to be still and listen. If we want to live a life of holiness following God's will, we need to listen when he speaks in our hearts telling us what his will is for us. For many of us, simply being still and listening can be the most challenging part of prayer, but it can also be the most rewarding.

The second thing Tina should probably ask is, "How do I expect God to answer my prayers?" We have noted several times that Jesus taught us to be faithful and persistent in our prayer, to never lose heart or become weary. In fact, when we pray, Jesus intercedes for us , not only as the Son of God, but as a man who took our sins upon himself. He holds our prayers and intercessions in his own heart, sharing them with his Father. For what one Person of the Holy Trinity knows and cares for, all three Persons share.

So, what about the times when our prayers seem to go unanswered? Is God the Father not listening? Is he just being slow in responding? Or is something else going on?

Approaching prayer with a sense of humility means that we should not view our prayer requests as specific demands that God must answer in exactly the way we want him to. He is indeed faithful to our prayers and petitions, but sometimes his answers are not what we expect or desire. Sometimes God's answer is "no." Perhaps what we have asked of God may not be in our best interest. Or his plan is different from what we ask for or want—a plan that gradually unfolds and becomes clear over time. If we follow the advice of Saint Paul and "pray without ceasing" (1 Thessalonians 5:17), we will grow in our ability to trust in God's goodness and grace. Even when our prayers seem to go unanswered, we will come to understand that God never fails to embrace us in our time of need, offering us his gentle mercy and abundant compassion. ✳

HMMMMM. . . What advice would you give a friend who tells you that prayer does not work for them?

Article 57
The Theological Virtues

In this chapter, we have discussed our universal call to holiness. In the First Letter of John, we discovered the essential connection between love and holiness. Then we looked at prayer as an important spiritual discipline in becoming a holy person. Now let's consider another important grace God provides for our holiness, the Theological Virtues.

In Paul's First Letter to the Corinthians, he discusses love as one of three essential **virtues** needed to live a life of holiness (see 13:1–13). You probably have heard this passage before. It begins, "Love is patient, love is kind . . . " (verse 4). What are the other two virtues besides love? Faith and hope. Paul didn't use this term, but today we refer to faith, hope, and love as the **Theological Virtues.**

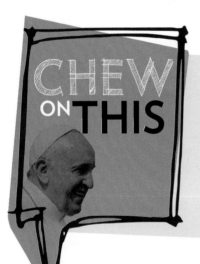

Before all else, the Gospel invites us to respond to the God of love who saves us, to see God in others and to go forth from ourselves to seek the good of others. Under no circumstance can this invitation be obscured! All of the virtues are at the service of this response of love.

(Pope Francis, *The Joy of the Gospel*, number 39)

UNIT 5

---

virtue ➤ A habitual and firm disposition to do good.

Theological Virtues ➤ The name for the God-given virtues of faith, hope, and love. These virtues enable us to know God as God and lead us to union with God in mind and heart.

A virtue is a good habit, a continual and firm disposition to do good. When the term *virtue* appears in the Bible, it generally indicates moral goodness. We develop virtues by working on them and asking God to strengthen them within us. We use the term *theological* to indicate that these three particular virtues focus on God and our relationship with him. They come from God, they are about God, and they lead us to God. The three theological virtues—faith, hope, and love (also called charity)—enable us to respond to God's Revelation and live a life of holiness.

Faith, hope, and love are the Theological Virtues. Why might they be considered the foundation for a person's spiritual life, regardless of their faith?

Faith

Faith enables us to believe what God has revealed. It allows us to respond to Revelation by uniting ourselves to Christ as living members of his Body, the Church. As disciples, we must profess our faith with confidence, bearing witness to it in the words and actions of our daily lives. We saw this earlier with Tina's mom. Tina knew about her faith because her mom spoke of it and did not hide it. Her mom was devoted to her prayer life, and she encouraged Tina to do the same.

Hope

Hope invites us to trust in the love of God the Father, the promises of Christ, and the grace of the Holy Spirit. This is especially important in our lives when we feel discouraged, abandoned, or disheartened, like Tina. Through the virtue of hope, we trust that our destiny is to share in the life of the Blessed Trinity and the joys of Heaven. By focusing on Heaven, we are able to keep our trials in life in proper perspective. We can strengthen our hope by reflecting on the times that God has worked in our lives and in the lives of others. When we recall these times, our faith is uplifted and our hope is renewed.

© Andrea Haase / Shutterstock.com

UNIT 5

---

faith ➤ In general, the belief in the existence of God. For Christians, the gift of God by which one freely accepts his full Revelation in Jesus Christ. It is a matter of both the head (acceptance of Church teaching regarding the Revelation of God) and the heart (love of God and neighbor as a response to God's first loving us); also, one of the three Theological Virtues.

hope ➤ The Theological Virtue by which we trust in the promises of God and expect from God both eternal life and the grace we need to attain it; the conviction that God's grace is at work in the world and that the Kingdom of God established by and through Jesus Christ is becoming realized through the workings of the Holy Spirit among us.

Love

Love, also referred to as charity, is the virtue that helps us follow the Greatest Commandment Jesus taught to his disciples: "You shall love the Lord, your God, with all your heart, with all your soul, and with all your mind. This is the greatest and the first commandment. The second is like it: You shall love your neighbor as yourself" (Matthew 22:37–39). This love is more than "I love the shirt you are wearing." In Greek, the word for this type of love is *agape*. *Agape* love is best seen in what Jesus did for us on the cross. *Agape* love is the complete giving of yourself to God and others. This love always wants what is best and right for our neighbor. As Paul points out in First Corinthians, chapter 13, *agape* love binds all the other virtues and without it, everything else is worthless. ✳

Love is also referred to as charity. This love always wants what is best and right for our neighbor.

UNIT 5

HMMMMM. . .
How can the Theological Virtues help you fulfill your call to holiness?

love ➤ Also called charity, the Theological Virtue by which we love God above all things and, out of that love of God, love our neighbors as ourselves.

1. How can we grow in holiness?

2. According to the First Letter of John, how are love and holiness connected?

3. Describe Jesus' prayer life and why it was a vital part of his ministry.

4. What does Jesus' Parable of the Pharisee and the Tax Collector teach us about holiness?

5. What is one thing we might try if we feel that our prayer life is going through a dry spell or it seems that God is not answering our prayers?

6. List and explain the Theological Virtues.

7. What is *agape* love, and who is the best example of it?

Holiness in Our Everyday Lives

Take some time to examine the word cloud. Look up
any words that are unfamiliar to you.

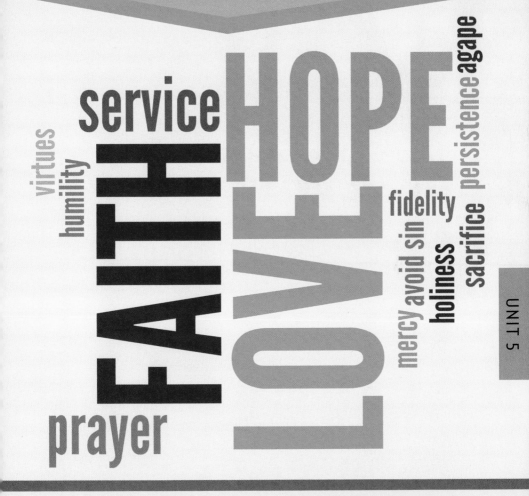

1. Which words are most challenging for you on your daily journey toward holiness?

2. What words would you add that are important in your own journey toward holiness?

CHAPTER 15
Our Call to Serve

WHAT DOES CHRISTIAN SERVICE MEAN?

SNAPSHOT

Article 58
Paul Models Committed Service

It can seem that the opportunities we have to serve others aren't always at convenient times. If you are volunteering to build homes for the financially disadvantaged, you will probably have to be on the job site early on a Saturday morning. If you are tutoring, any chance of hanging out with your friends, playing video games, or taking a nap after school are pretty much gone. However, teens are logging hundreds of service hours every year. Why are they willing to sacrifice their time (and sleep!) to help others?

What type of service do you enjoy?

UNIT 5

Those who are in need gratefully receive food, clothing, shelter, medical care, tutoring, and many other services to help them. If you were to ask the volunteers who are providing this help, they would more than likely tell you that they are the ones who have received a blessing. Serving others is at the essence of Christ's teachings. For some guidance on serving others well, we can look again to Saint Paul.

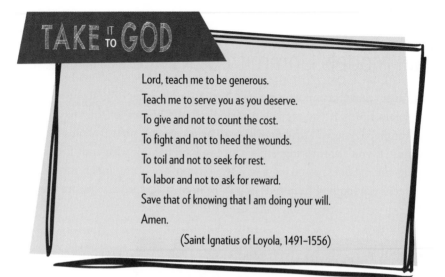

TAKE IT TO GOD

Lord, teach me to be generous.

Teach me to serve you as you deserve.

To give and not to count the cost.

To fight and not to heed the wounds.

To toil and not to seek for rest.

To labor and not to ask for reward.

Save that of knowing that I am doing your will.

Amen.

(Saint Ignatius of Loyola, 1491–1556)

Keys to Serving Others Well

Paul was a tent maker, a writer, a traveler, and an evangelizer; but even while doing all these things, he was also doing something else. He was working to help the poor in Jerusalem. You may have noticed the reference to this when you read Acts of the Apostles:

© GL Archive / Alamy Stock Photo

> At that time some prophets came down from Jerusalem to Antioch, and one of them named Agabus stood up and predicted by the Spirit that there would be a severe famine over all the world, and it happened under Claudius. So the disciples determined that, according to ability, each should send relief to the brothers who lived in Judea. This they did, sending it to the presbyters in care of Barnabas and Saul. (11:27–30)

Saint Paul offers practical advice for how to be of service to others.

UNIT 5

We know from historians that a famine happened during this time. The people of Judea, the area around Jerusalem, were severely affected. Note how the Church gathers to address the need and then sends Barnabas and Saul (Paul) to address the problem. In Paul's Second Letter to the Corinthians (see chapters 8 and 9), he directly addresses his work of raising money to help the poor in Jerusalem. From this discussion, we learn three important points for understanding how to serve others well.

Finish What You Start

"And I am giving counsel in this matter, for it is appropriate for you who began not only to act but to act willingly last year: complete it now, so that your eager willingness may be matched by your completion of it out of what you have" (2 Corinthians 8:10–11). The first point is Paul's encouragement to the Corinthians to finish what they have started and with the same enthusiasm they had when they began.

Originally, the Corinthians had given money cheerfully to help the poor in Jerusalem. Then it appeared they needed an additional push from Paul to continue. Admittedly, they may have had other things they wanted to spend their money on, but they had already promised Paul they would help. It is like telling your elderly neighbor that you will mow their lawn, and halfway through you get a text from a friend asking if you want to go out to eat. Do you stop mowing the lawn and leave the yard half done? Or do you finish what you started?

CATHOLICS MAKING A DIFFERENCE

A saint who laughs all the time and gets along with everyone? Does such a saint exist? Meet Saint Philip Neri, known for his remarkable happiness and great sense of humor. In fact, he is the patron saint of laughter, humor, and joy. His cheerful heart made him popular with the poor of Rome. His positivity attracted others to him, making him a sought-after confessor. People wanted to participate in the Sacrament of Penance and Reconciliation with Father Neri because he related to people and their everyday struggles. His unconventional prayers, popular preaching style, and perpetual joy continue to make him a prime example of a cheerful giver.

UNIT 5

Give from Your Surplus

"Not that others should have relief while you are burdened, but that as a matter of equality your surplus at the present time should supply their needs, so that their surplus may also supply your needs, that there may be equality" (2 Corinthians 8:13–14). Paul is not asking the Corinthians to put themselves in poverty to help others out of poverty. He is asking them to look honestly at what they have and to give away their surplus. Saint Basil the Great, a fourth-century bishop, put it this way: "When someone steals another's clothes, we call them a thief. Should we not give the same name to one who could clothe the naked and does not? The bread in your cupboard belongs to the hungry; the coat unused in your closet belongs to the one who needs it; the shoes rotting in your closet belong to the one who has no shoes; the money which you hoard up belongs to the poor." Today is a good day to take an inventory at home and donate any "surplus" to the poor.

© Makistock / Shutterstock.com

Have you ever thought of your extra clothes "belonging" to a person who needs them?

Give Cheerfully

"Each must do as already determined, without sadness or compulsion, for God loves a cheerful giver" (2 Corinthians 9:7). Paul reminds us that attitude is everything. If we whine and complain while serving others, they feel like they are a burden. If we feel forced to serve others, it will show in our attitude and work. On the other hand, when we give freely of our time, talent, or treasure, possibilities to make change manifest themselves. Paul encourages us to be cheerful givers and to see what happens, not just in the lives of those we are serving but in our own lives as well.

Paul makes a commitment to help the poor people in Jerusalem who need money to buy food, a commitment he takes seriously. As you read in the Acts of the Apostles, Paul knows that going to Jerusalem to deliver the collection is dangerous; even his friends encourage him not to go (see 21:7–14). Paul goes anyway and ends up getting arrested, eventually traveling to Rome for his trial and execution. Paul risks his life and dies, not only for proclaiming the Good News but also for serving the poor in Christ's name. ✳

HMMMMM. . . How might you choose to use your time serving others?

UNIT 5

Article 59

Serving Others: A Requirement or Nice to Do?

We saw how important serving the poor was for Saint Paul. You probably agree that serving other people is a good thing to do. But is it just something nice to do when we have the time or the inclination, or should it go deeper than that and become an ongoing commitment expressed in our daily life? A careful reading of the Bible makes it clear that it is indeed a deeper call, a commitment that should permeate all aspects of who we are.

Created to Serve

"Then God said: Let us make human beings in our image, after our likeness" (Genesis 1:26). If you truly believe this line from the first chapter of Genesis, then your whole life is affected. It means that every single human being, no matter who they are, where they live, or what they believe, is a reflection of God. Every person on Earth has infinite worth and dignity. When someone's life or dignity is threatened, we have a responsibility to come to their aid.

© Vitalinka / Shutterstock.com

Every single human being is created as a reflection of God. What better reason is there for serving one another?

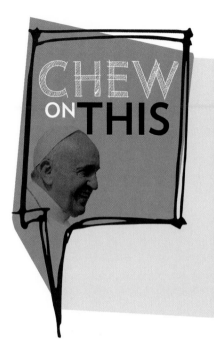

But to all of you, especially those who can do more and give more, I ask: Please do more! Please give more! When you give of your time, your talents, and your resources to the many people who struggle and who live on the margins, you make a difference. It is a difference that is so desperately needed, and one for which you will be richly rewarded by the Lord. ("Address of His Holiness Pope Francis to the Young People of Santo Tomas University," January 18, 2015)

Genesis then tells us that God created Adam and Eve to live together and help one another (see 2:18–24). We were not created to live in isolation from one another. Just like the life of the Trinity we discussed in chapter 9, we are to reflect the loving and serving relationship we see in the Trinity. From the very beginning, we were made to serve one another.

Jesus teaches us even more about being fully human. He teaches us that to be fully human means to accept and become the person God created us to be. To help us do this, we are all created with special gifts that reflect the image of God within us: immortality, intellect, free will, and the ability to love. It is our choice as to how we use these gifts. When we use these gifts well by serving others, we reflect God's love more and more. Jesus models this perfectly for us, as when he takes on the role of a servant to wash his disciples' feet (see John 13:1–20).

Service and the Final Judgment

Here's the thing: Jesus does not just say that serving one another is a nice thing to do. He is clear that how we spend eternity depends upon it. If you have not done so, take a moment now to read Matthew 25:31–46, Jesus' powerful parable about the Final Judgment. Do you notice how shocked the goats are at being told they have not served Jesus? They can't imagine that they missed seeing Jesus in their lives. If Jesus had been in the room, surely they would have helped him. Jesus points out their sad misunderstanding. Jesus is always

UNIT 5

The Corporal Works of Mercy are clear examples of service we are called to perform for others.

in the room, and he can be found in the faces of the people around us. We are called to look for him there. We are called to serve Jesus by serving everyone who is in need.

Jesus gives us clear examples of the service we are expected to perform: feed the hungry, give drink to the thirsty, welcome the stranger, clothe the naked, care for the sick, and visit the imprisoned. We refer to these as the Corporal Works of Mercy. Notice that most of these works involve serving **marginalized** people, the people most of society ignores or even looks down upon. Jesus makes it clear that society's view is wrong. The marginalized are our concern no matter who they are or what their circumstances. They are our concern because they are human, made like us in God's image and likeness. ✳

HMMMMM. . . Why are serving and showing mercy so important?

marginalized ➤ Those who are relegated to an unimportant or powerless position within a society or group.

UNIT 5

Article 60

Concern for the Common Good

Donating resources and volunteering our time to feed hungry people is a good thing to do, but it is not enough. Our call to service also challenges us to correct the inequalities and violence that cause hunger and starvation. This type of service is sometimes called the work of **social justice**. For some, Jesus' call to serve by working for social justice can feel overwhelming. How can one person end the causes of world hunger? The answer is that one person cannot. This type of change happens only when many people work together to change social injustices.

As followers of Jesus Christ, we are all called to work with others for justice and peace. Another way to say this is that we are all called to promote the **common good**. Look at how Jesus defines his own ministry as a call to proclaim the Good News, and serve the common good:

> The Spirit of the Lord is upon me,
>   because he has anointed me
>   to bring glad tidings to the poor.
> He has sent me to proclaim liberty to captives
>   and recovery of sight to the blind,
>   to let the oppressed go free,
> and to proclaim a year acceptable to the Lord.
>   (Luke 4:18–19)

If promoting the common good is at the center of Jesus' own ministry, then as followers of Jesus, it must also be at the heart of who we are. The members of the Catholic Church have been serving the common good for over two thousand years. Let's look at the principles that guide us in this work.

UNIT 5

---

social justice ➤ The defense of human dignity by ensuring that essential human needs are met and that essential human rights are protected for all people.

common good ➤ Social conditions that allow for all citizens of the Earth, individuals and families, to meet basic needs and achieve fulfillment.

Catholic Social Teaching

The Church teachings that guide our efforts to create a more just and peaceful world are called Catholic social teaching. Catholic social teaching is guided by seven key principles. Together, these principles are a guide for how we can be involved in working for justice and serve the common good.

1. **Life and Dignity of the Human Person.** All human life is sacred and must be respected and protected at all times. This means that people, young and old alike, are always more important than things. In our daily life, this may be as simple as putting down our cell phones during a meal and fully participating in the conversation. We can visit with elderly residents at the local nursing home, or volunteer at a local crisis pregnancy center. There isn't a cost to treating people with respect and dignity.

© Pressmaster / Shutterstock.com

Putting down your phone and giving others your full attention is a way to show respect. What is another way you can treat others with respect and dignity?

UNIT 5

2. **Call to Family, Community, and Participation.** We must be concerned about not only our own success and well-being but also the common good of all people, especially those most in need. Notice that this principle mentions family first. We are called to build up and support members of our own family. This may mean babysitting a younger sibling or taking the time to call our grandparents. But we mustn't stop there. The community is important as well. You could volunteer at your parish, offer tutoring at school, or participate in programming sponsored by your local community center. Maybe you could even be a teen representative to the committee that makes decisions about the service programs your parish offers.

How can you build up and support the members of your own family?

© Pressmaster / Shutterstock.com

UNIT 5

3. **Rights and Responsibilities.** We all have the right to life and to access life's basic needs, such as food, shelter, and health care. We also have the responsibility to ensure that these rights are always protected. All people have a right to participate in the cultural, economic, and political life of society. As a teen, you may need to speak up in class when these issues are being discussed. You can register to vote and exercise that right when you turn eighteen. If you do not speak up or vote, your silence can be interpreted as agreement when these basic rights are violated.

One way for you to ensure that human rights are protected is to participate in the voting process.

4. **Preferential Option for the Poor and Vulnerable.** The needs of the poor must have first priority in how we spend our time, money, and other resources. Imagine two kids walking down the street with their mom. One child falls down and skins his knee. What does the mom do? She stops and bends down to help the child with the skinned knee. Does this mean she loves that child more than the child who did not skin his knee? No, she loves them both, but at that moment, she has a "preferential option" or special focus for the one in need. Even as a teenager, you can aid the poor and vulnerable. You can purchase fair-trade products, or even ask your student government association to host a fair-trade event at the school. You can also volunteer for a school or parish mission trip to serve economically distressed people.

I DIDN'T KNOW THAT!

Did you know that the Catholic Church in the United States provides humanitarian aid all over the globe? Through the ministry of Catholic Relief Services (CRS), Catholics in the United States seek to end poverty, hunger, and disease. CRS works in 112 countries, reaching more than 121 million people. Though CRS is an international organization, it helps Catholics in parishes, dioceses, and schools to live their faith by supporting programs and activities that promote human dignity and respond to human needs around the world. Their focus is both charity and justice; they address urgent, immediate needs, but they also develop solutions to help vulnerable people survive and thrive in the long term.

5. **The Dignity of Work and the Rights of Workers.** Workers have a right to a fair wage and to decent working conditions. Workers have the right to organize and join unions and to go on strike when their basic rights are not being respected. We can support the dignity and rights of workers by tipping fairly and by not shopping at stores and businesses that pay their workers poorly or treat them unfairly. Notice that the Church also refers to the "dignity" of work. That is because from a faith perspective "Work is more than a way to make a living; it is a form of continuing participation in God's creation" (USCCB, "Seven Themes of Catholic Social Teaching"). Take some time to think about what kind of work you might want to do that would give you a sense of fulfillment and dignity, rather than just working to pay bills.

6. **Solidarity.** We must support and care for one another as brothers and sisters in one global human family. Governments are obligated to protect human life and human rights, promote human dignity, and build the common good. We must see ourselves in solidarity with all people around the world, our global family. When our brothers and sisters are displaced from their homes due to war or natural disasters, you can do something! Your family could sponsor a refugee family through your parish. You could collect food, clothing, toiletries, and medical supplies to donate to those who no longer have a home.

UNIT 5

7. **Care for God's Creation.** We must protect the resources of our planet, preserving them for future generations. Anytime questions about taking care of creation arise, the guiding question should always be, "Who owns the Earth?" The answer is God. He is the Creator, and he has given us the task of helping care for his creation. We are his stewards, charged with protecting life and using creation respectfully. In keeping with that calling, start with your own home. How does God's yard look? Think about your school. Does your school have a recycling program so as not to don't waste God's resources? You can participate in local beach, river, or park clean-ups. Educate yourself about environmental issues, and raise awareness by talking to your parents, teachers, and friends. Just remember, how we treat the Earth is a reflection on how we respect the owner, God. ✳

How can you support the dignity and rights of workers, even if you don't have a job or can't vote yet?

UNIT 5

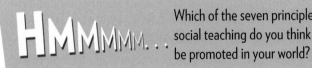

HMMMMM. . .

Which of the seven principles of Catholic social teaching do you think most needs to be promoted in your world?

Article 61
Young Saints Serving Others

Savannah climbed in the car after Mass and complained to her mom: "Mom, I am so tired of Deacon Steve's homilies. If I hear one more story about his trip to a developing Third-World country, I am going to scream!" Savannah's mom replied: "Savannah, that does not sound like you. What is really bothering you about his homilies?" Savannah sighed and said: "Mom, he keeps saying we have to do something, but I am just a kid. I don't have any money, and I can't just jump on a plane and go overseas to help people. So what difference can I make? I'm glad Deacon Steve is helping people, but it doesn't really have anything to do with me."

The Time Is Now

Have you ever felt like Savannah? As a teenager, finding concrete ways to help others can be overwhelming. You may feel hesitant to boldly answer the call to serve. However, many holy men and women found the courage to imitate Jesus through their bold service. Some of these saints made the decision to serve when they were teenagers, or even younger!

Saint Aloysius Gonzaga (1568–1591) was born into a wealthy political family in Italy. When he was only nine years old, he decided on a commitment to religious life. Unfortunately, kidney disease prevented him from participating in normal activities as a young boy. However, Aloysius did not let his illness sideline him from dedicating his time to prayer and devotions. His studying led him to begin teaching other children about the faith.

Lilies are associated with Saint Aloysius Gonzaga (1568–1591), symbolizing his innocence.

© silvionka / Shutterstock.com

UNIT 5

When Aloysius turned eighteen, he decided to become a Jesuit priest. As a priest, he was well known for giving spiritual guidance to those seeking help. Saint Aloysius died serving the sick who had the plague, after he contracted the deadly disease and died from it. His life is an amazing example of serving others, especially when you consider how young Aloysius was when he started.

Saint Dominic Savio (1842–1856) is different from Saint Aloysius, in that he grew up in a poor family. His parents could not read, nor could they afford to send Dominic to school. It was their deepest desire that Dominic receive an education and commit his life to Jesus. Fortunately, Dominic met Saint John Bosco (1815–1888), who ran a school for poor boys. Father Bosco invited Dominic to enroll. The invitation meant that Dominic would have to move away from home. His parents gave their permission in order for Dominic to have this opportunity that they could not provide for him.

Away at school, Dominic became more religious. He went to church several times a day, and sometimes even skipped meals so he could pray. When other students teased Dominic for his commitment, Father Bosco told him that the way to holiness was to be happy and to help others find happiness. So he joyfully helped other students with their studies and chores. Sadly, Dominic became sick and died at the age of fourteen. He is one of the youngest people, who wasn't a child martyr, to be declared a saint. We can all imitate his simple acts of daily service.

MAKE IT SO

So you think you are too young to give money to charities, right? Could you save just $1 a week of the money you use for snacks or fast food? That's about $5 per month, or $60 per year. If you were to put that money in the Catholic Relief Services' Rice Bowl during Lent, you would feed a family in a developing country for a couple of months or help them buy two or three sheep to raise, making a huge difference in the quality of their life. Start now and make it a lifelong commitment!

Saint Chiara Luce Badano (1971–1990) was a miracle baby for her parents. After more than ten years of praying and hoping for a baby, they welcomed Chiara into the world. Even as a little girl, she already seemed aware of the needs of others. She began her service to others at the young age of four. She was known to give away her extra toys to the poor. She would invite people who were in need to her house for holiday meals. She even visited the sick. Chiara was popular. She played sports, and she loved to sing and dance. She tried to bring her friends to Jesus, not with her words but rather by the example of how she lived her life. When she was just seventeen, she was

Saint Chiara Luce Badano (1971–1990)

diagnosed with bone cancer and became bedridden. Yet even from bed, she would take the time and effort to write letters of encouragement to others about their faith journey. She even refused pain medication, as it would have made her too sleepy to live her life as she wished to. She gave all of her savings to a friend who was becoming a missionary in Africa. Saint Chiara shows us that age and even illness are no barriers to finding ways to serve others.

These are only three of the countless young saints that have shown us how we can all answer Jesus' call to love and serve those around us. Though they each had a different calling, they all made service a central part of their life. They chose to say yes. Are you willing to also boldly answer this call? ✳

UNIT 5

HMMMMM...

If someday the Church declares you a saint, what do you think your story of bold service will be?

1. Explain how the Book of Genesis sets the expectation that we are to serve others.

2. What three important points can we learn from Saint Paul about our call to service?

3. Why are the goats surprised in Jesus' Parable of the Last Judgment? What have they missed?

4. What does it mean for us to be fully human, and what gifts have we received to help us achieve our potential?

5. What are the seven principles of Catholic social teaching?

6. Choose one of the three young saints mentioned in this chapter and explain how they answered God's call to serve.

7. In what specific way can the young saints mentioned in this chapter help you on your journey to follow Christ?

UNIT 5

(left) © Art Collection 3 / Alamy Stock Photo; (center) INTERFOTO / Alamy Stock Photo; (right) © 2018 Fondazione Chiara Badano

UNIT 5

Think back to the stories of these three young people who committed themselves to a life pleasing to God, even in small and simple ways.

Saint Dominic Savio, pray for us.

Saint Aloysius Gonzaga, pray for us.

Saint Chiara Luce Badano, pray for us.

Young saints of service, inspire us.

CHAPTER 16
Our Call to Witness

WHAT DOES IT MEAN TO WITNESS?

SNAPSHOT

Article 62

First Peter: Give Witness to Your Faith

In late March 1966, seven monks from the Atlas Abbey of Tibhirine, in Algeria, were kidnapped and eventually executed by the Armed Islamic Group (GIA). You might assume that was death brought on by conflict between Christians and Muslims. This assumption would be false. In fact, the monks lived peacefully for many years working side by side with their Muslim neighbors.

© mauritius images GmbH / Alamy Stock Photo

Cistercian monks

Br. Jean Pierre Schumacher was one of two monks who survived the attack. In an interview with a Spanish publisher in 2010, he explained the role of the monks in the local community. "We worked in the fields and the garden. We lived on the mountain and our relations with them (our Muslim neighbors) were positive and very fraternal. We were like a family. . . . We attended religious services and funerals, whatever the people wanted. We have very good relations with them" (in *Catholic News Agency*, January 17, 2011).

Brother Jean Pierre gave insight to the daily life of the monks and their neighbors: "We had a small gardening association together with four parents who worked with us. Each one had a small plot and sold their crops. At the end of the year, we shared the sales. It was a beautiful way of living together as a family. We didn't talk about religion much, but we had good relations, and it was a way for us to communicate with their family" (in *Catholic News Agency*, January 17, 2011). Based on Brother Jean Pierre's account, it would be hard to imagine that the monks were living in a hostile environment.

UNIT 5

TAKE IT TO GOD

Dear Jesus,

You call us to witness to our faith in you.

Please give me the courage to share my faith.

So often I feel uncomfortable talking about you with my friends,
   afraid they may think that I am weird or strange.

In those times, let my words be inspired by the Holy Spirit
   so that I can share my beliefs.

Give me wisdom and strength
   so that my actions do not contradict what I say.

Amen.

However, much like the early Christian community of Peter's letters, the monks would learn that the monastery and the surrounding community were the targets of extremist groups. The situation became dangerous as the extremists advanced and the Algerian government tried to use the monks as pawns. The monks' decision to remain with their neighbors was not an easy one. None of them wanted to put themselves at risk of martyrdom. However, in the end, they decided not to leave the monastery. Their decision to stay with their Muslim neighbors, and their willingness to die for what they believed to be right and true, is one of the most powerful modern-day examples of Christian witness that Saint Peter described in his letters.

Witness to Your Faith

The Letters of Peter show us that Christians have been struggling with living out their faith in the world since the time of the early Church. Peter's two letters are written to a Gentile Christian community that is apparently surrounded by nonbelievers. The nonbelievers frequently ridicule the Christians for not participating in their activities. Peter's advice is advice we all need to hear.

First Peter points out the special dignity that comes with being a Christian. The letter describes Christians and their purpose as "'a chosen race, a royal priesthood, a holy nation, a people of his own so that you may announce the praises' of him who called you out of darkness into his wonderful light" (1 Peter 2:9). As followers of Jesus, we have a unique perspective. Why do we have to look at things differently? Jesus Christ has united us to God through his Incarnation and by his death and Resurrection. Through Baptism, we have become the free adopted children of the Father. Through our words and actions, we are called to witness to our faith in Jesus Christ. Sometimes, when we choose to witness to our faith, others may ridicule us for doing so. Peter was aware of this problem as well. He writes, "If you are insulted for the name of Christ, blessed are you, for the Spirit of glory and of God rests upon you" (4:14).

Following Jesus means that we have to make choices. Sometimes the choices are difficult ones that set us apart from our friends and the people around us. For example, a group of teens chooses to attend a pro-life rally on a Saturday morning. They could be at the beach or hanging out with friends, but because of their commitment to their faith, they participate in a function they feel passionate about. We may encounter resistance to our choices and faith practices when those around us don't understand them, but we must be brave and bold, like the Trappist monks and the early Christians.

First Peter also makes it clear that when we witness to our faith, we must make sure that we are living morally. "Maintain good conduct among the Gentiles, so that if they speak of you as evildoers, they may observe your good works and glorify God on the day of visitation" (1 Peter 2:12). In other words, be good no matter what, so that others cannot use your bad example against you. ✳

These teens are taking part in the March for Life, held every year in Washington, DC. They are marching to protect the dignity of all life, especially the lives of unborn children threatened by abortion.

UNIT 5

HMMMMM. . . How should the unique dignity of Christians affect the choices they make?

Article 63

Living Morally: Excerpts from Paul's Letters

In this course, we have been learning about Jesus Christ and what it means to be one of his disciples. To be an authentic witness for Jesus Christ we must live the faith. That means making good choices and avoiding sin every day. Making good choices and avoiding sin every day can be a challenge for a person of any age. However, God gives us gifts to prepare us to deal with temptation and ridicule. Through our faith, Jesus Christ redeems us and gives us his grace so that we can choose the good according to God's will, and resist sin and its effects. Jesus invites us to believe in him, to invite him into our hearts, and to follow him and his teaching as the path that leads to life, for he is "the way, the truth, and the life" and is worthy of our belief, adoration, and love.

How can we live out that faith? By building up the Kingdom of God with our words and deeds. "Preach the Gospel at all times. When necessary, use words." This inspiring statement has been attributed to both Saint Augustine and Saint Francis. We return God's love by loving one another. In our actions of service and kindness, we demonstrate to others what it is like to have Jesus in our lives.

Jesus Christ reveals the way to repentance and conversion, teaching us to leave sin behind and to live a new life of holiness. He gives us the spiritual power and grace to overcome evil; he also teaches us about God's forgiveness. Knowing that life is full of temptations, Jesus shows us and teaches us how to be single-hearted in our desire for God, to offset the disordered affections and divided hearts with which we live.

UNIT 5

I DIDN'T KNOW THAT!

One of the Apostles was Simon the Zealot, and another was Matthew the tax collector. The zealots were Jews who advocated overthrowing Roman rule over Palestine. The tax collectors collaborated with Rome to help maintain Rome's dominance over Palestine. The zealots and the tax collectors despised each other. Isn't it just like Jesus to bring members of these two groups together as members of his inner circle? What an amazing witness they must have been to the people of their time, showing them how to see beyond their differences and recognize their common dignity.

Sometimes life comes at us so fast we can forget what we learned and end up feeling exhausted and depressed. The important thing to do is get back up, focus on what we have learned, and try again. Saint Paul offers us some images that can inspire us to persevere in living out our faith commitments.

Pottery, Buildings, and Armor

Our first image comes from Saint Paul's Letter to the Romans. Paul uses the image of God as a potter, and we are the clay he is molding (see 9:20–21). Paul is building on an image from the prophet Isaiah:

Saint Paul uses the image of God as a potter and we as the clay.

> We are the clay and you our potter:
> we are all the work of your hand.
> (64:7)

Paul asks if the clay has a right to ask the potter why he shaped the clay the way he did. When you are frustrated by your own sinfulness and can't seem to do the right thing, remember this image. God is like the potter using his hands to work out the lumps on a bowl he is making out of clay. The lumps are the parts of our lives that are not in line with God's will. When there is sin in your life and you can't seem to get free of it, imagine that God is at work in your life, slowly and gently molding you to reach your true potential.

In the First Letter to the Corinthians, Paul uses the metaphor that we are all building a church and Jesus Christ is the foundation:

> For we are God's co-workers; you are God's field, God's building.
>
> According to the grace of God given to me, like a wise master-builder I laid a foundation, and another is building upon it. But each one must be careful how he builds upon it, for no one can lay a foundation other than the one that is there, namely, Jesus Christ. (3:9–11)

Through our choices, we determine how and what we add on top of that foundation. Our positive, moral choices add beautiful and sturdy materials to that foundation: brick, gold, and precious stones. On the other hand, our

UNIT 5

sinful actions add straw and inferior materials that will not stand up to the Holy Spirit's purifying fire. The next time you are faced with a difficult moral choice, ask yourself what you want your contribution to Christ's saving work to be—something beautiful and lasting or something weak and fleeting.

Finally, in his Letter to the Ephesians, Paul gives us an image about clothing to help guide our decisions as followers of Jesus (see Ephesians 6:10–18). He isn't talking about any ordinary pair of jeans and a T-shirt. Paul tells us to put on the "armor of God," which includes the breastplate of righteousness, the shield of faith, the helmet of salvation, and the sword of the Spirit.

Paul is comparing a life of faith to a spiritual battle. However, this battle is not waged through violence; it is waged through living faithfully and virtuously. It is fighting against our inclination to sin and battling against falsehood and injustice. When you are losing hope and feel like you are ready to give up, imagine putting on the armor of God. With God's protection, we can accomplish many things. ✳

THE ARMOR OF GOD

Saint Paul compares living a life of faith to a spiritual battle, and our armor is faith, righteousness, salvation, and the Holy Spirit!

UNIT 5

HMMMMM. . . Which of Paul's images do you relate to the most and why?

Article 64

The Apostles: Models of Witness

The crucifixion of Saint Peter

Can you imagine being crucified upside down? This is how Saint Peter died. An ancient tradition says that Peter requested to be crucified upside down because he was unworthy to die like Jesus Christ. And it wasn't just Peter who was martyred, all but one of the Apostles died witnessing to their faith. Their courage and humility has a lot to teach us about witnessing to our faith in Jesus Christ, the Second Person of the Blessed Trinity.

CATHOLICS **MAKING** A DIFFERENCE

Saint Ignatius of Antioch proclaimed: "Let me be food for the wild beasts, for they are my way to God. I am God's wheat and shall be ground by their teeth so that I may become Christ's pure bread." Talk about a bold commitment to faith! Saint Ignatius of Antioch was an early Church Father who was martyred in AD 107. He was an outstanding example of bravery and faithfulness. Thankfully, most of us will never have the need to express our commitment by welcoming martyrdom. Still, Saint Ignatius's willing sacrifice challenges us to embrace the fears and hardships we may encounter while following God's call.

UNIT 5

Witnesses of Divine Revelation

Consider all that the Apostles learned from Jesus as he fulfilled Divine Revelation. They were there during the Sermon on the Mount, listening and learning along with the crowd (see Matthew, chapters 5–7). The Sermon on the Mount (the Sermon on the Plain in the Gospel of Luke) is a long speech by Jesus. In addition to teaching the **Beatitudes**, the **Law of Love**, and the Golden Rule, this speech covers many of his key teachings on prayer, forgiveness, judging others, loving your enemies, and other attitudes necessary for growing in goodness and holiness. It is kind of like a cheat sheet for how to live as a disciple of Christ. Teachings like the Sermon on the Mount and the parables helped the Apostles (and helps us!) rethink their attitudes and behaviors as well as the norms of their society.

© Zvonimir Atletic / Shutterstock.com

The Apostles and other followers learned from Jesus through his Sermon on the Mount, the Beatitudes, his parables, and his attitudes and behaviors.

UNIT 5

Beatitudes ➤ The teachings of Jesus that begin the Sermon on the Mount and that summarize the New Law of Christ. The Beatitudes describe the actions and attitudes by which one can discover genuine happiness, and they teach us the final end to which God calls us: full communion with him in the Kingdom of Heaven.

Law of Love ➤ Divine Law revealed in the New Testament through the life and teaching of Jesus Christ and through the witness and teaching of the Apostles. The Law of Love perfects the Old Law and brings it to fulfillment. Also called the New Law.

The Apostles were there when the rich man asked Jesus, "Good teacher, what must I do to inherit eternal life?" (Mark 10:17). They learned that to follow Jesus and be his witness, we must be willing to give up everything (see verses 17–22). The Apostles also heard Jesus sum up the Law and echo the prophets with the simple, yet challenging command to love God and our neighbor. They were present when Jesus taught that he will be there at the end of time to judge us on how we have treated the most vulnerable people among us (see 25:31–46). Having experienced so much in their encounters with Christ, the Apostles' lives were profoundly changed. They became amazing models of how to witness to the faith. Their faith became so strong that they even embraced persecution and death to continue Jesus' mission. According to ancient traditions, this is how most of the Apostles were martyred:

Apostle	Where He Traveled	Death Tradition
Peter	Rome	crucified upside down
Andrew	Western Greece	scourged and crucified
Philip	Asia and Egypt	scourged and crucified
James the Greater	Spain	killed with a sword by King Herod
John	Ephesus and Asia Minor	was not martyred
Bartholomew	India	beaten and crucified or in other accounts skinned alive and beheaded
Thomas	Greece and India	run through with a spear
Matthew	Mediterranean	stabbed in the back with a sword
James the Less	Jerusalem	beaten with a club and stoned to death
Judas Thaddeus	Turkey and Greece	crucified
Simon the Zealot	Africa and England	crucified
Matthias	Cappadocia and the coasts of the Caspian Sea	beheaded

UNIT 5

The beauty of their stories is that they not only listened to Jesus' words but, strengthened by the Holy Spirit, also followed his example. As they did, they grew in holiness and in their confidence to witness to the faith. They left behind their jobs, their financial security, and their homes. They left a life they knew for something completely unknown. Living our faith and witnessing to it can be like that at times. When we face fear and nervousness in following God's plan, we can look to the Apostles and realize that when we follow God's calling, it leads to an adventure, one in which God is by our side.

Where Did They Get Their Courage?

After his Resurrection, Jesus appeared to his Apostles and made this promise: "But you will receive power when the holy Spirit comes upon you, and you will be my witnesses in Jerusalem, throughout Judea and Samaria, and to the ends of the earth" (Acts 1:8). The Apostles waited in Jerusalem, along with some of the women disciples, for the Spirit that Jesus had promised. Acts of the Apostles 2:2–8 recounts the events of Pentecost, when the Apostles were filled with the Holy Spirit. Emboldened by the Holy Spirit, they began preaching to the crowds gathered for the Pentecost festival. No longer were they timid, fearful, or filled with doubt; the Holy Spirit strengthened their faith, filled them with courage, and made their mission clear.

© jozef sedmak / Alamy Stock Photo

The Holy Spirit strengthened the Apostles and filled them with courage at Pentecost.

The Church was revealed to the world on the day of Pentecost. The Church was founded by Christ, in his preaching, in his healing, and in the saving work of his death, Resurrection, and Ascension. But at Pentecost the Spirit that had anointed Jesus was now poured onto the entire Church. The Church became Christ's presence in the world. We are living in the age of the Church, a time when Christ continues his ministry, not as a historical man living in a particular place and time, but rather through the Church, which is now his true Body.

The Apostles Shared Our Imperfections Too

As Christ lives and acts in and with his Church, remember that he chose to work through those who had faults, weaknesses, and imperfections. Even the Apostles, who were wonderful, faithful followers of Jesus, were not perfect, especially at the beginning of their time with Jesus. For example, they argued amongst themselves about which one of them would be the greatest in the kingdom (see Mark 9:33–37). Afterward, Jesus pointed out their pride and taught them that witnessing to the faith is about service and humility. Recall when they were in the boat after they had just seen Jesus multiply the loaves and fish. They were worrying about not having bread (see 8:14–21)! Even they sometimes needed to be reminded of Jesus' amazing power, and that witnessing to the faith means calling upon that power.

What about us? Do you wonder if you are worthy or have the gifts to share in Christ's mission? Are you afraid of what others might think or where his call will lead you? If so, you are not alone. Remember that the Apostles had to deal with fear and doubt. Despite their weaknesses, their faith grew and so did their ability to witness to the faith. We are called, in our own weakness, to follow their footsteps and grow in witnessing to our faith. ✳

UNIT 5

HMMMMM. . . How did the Apostles witness to their faith?

Article 65

A Great Cloud of Witnesses

Have you ever felt tired and discouraged when trying to succeed in a difficult task? Maybe it's learning to play a new instrument or taking a challenging class or learning a new hobby. It often helps when others who are going through the same thing can support one another with tips and encouraging words. In a similar way, the Church provides role models who can inspire and encourage us to excel in living our call as disciples of Jesus Christ.

The Letter to the Hebrews refers to these models of faith as a "great cloud of witnesses" (12:1). Another name we give these models of faith is the **Communion of Saints**. In the most general sense, a saint is someone who has been baptized and is living a life in union with God through the grace of Christ. The Communion of Saints includes all saints, living and dead, who are united by our shared faith in Christ. The Communion of Saints includes people from both Testaments of the Bible, as well as the saints and martyrs throughout the Church's history.

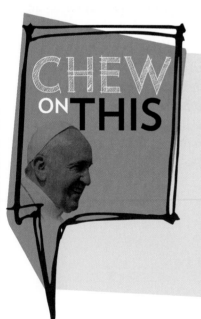

CHEW ON THIS

Jesus did not say: "One of you go," but "All of you go": we are sent together. Dear young friends, be aware of the companionship of the whole Church and also the communion of the saints on this mission. . . . Jesus did not call the Apostles to live in isolation, he called them to form a group, a community. ("Homily of His Holiness Pope Francis at the Holy Mass on the Occasion of the XXVIII World Youth Day," July 28, 2013)

Communion of Saints ➤ This phrase refers to two realities: (1) the communion of spiritual goods that Christ has shared with the Church, such as the sacraments (especially the Eucharist), charisms, helping those in material need, and our love for one another, and (2) the spiritual union of all the redeemed, those on Earth and those who have died.

Great Witnesses: The Old Testament

The Old Testament is filled with examples of people whose faith led them to bravely answer God's call, especially in difficult circumstances. They can inspire our own faith and desire to give witness to our faith. Earlier in the course, when you read Hebrews, chapter 11, you may have noticed that the author calls to mind several ancestors in the faith. The letter mentions Noah, Abraham, and Moses. Here are a few more we can learn from.

Ruth

Ruth's deep faith leads her to care for her mother-in-law, Naomi, after both women have become widows. Ruth promises Naomi:

> Wherever you go I will go,
> wherever you lodge, I will lodge.
> Your people shall be my people
> and your God, my God.
> (Ruth 1:16)

Ruth risks everything, even living in poverty, for love of her mother-in-law. They live together in Naomi's hometown, Bethlehem, until Ruth remarries. Ruth eventually becomes the great-grandmother of King David, and an ancestor of Jesus. Ruth shows us the power of self-sacrifice, and how God can use us to witness to his greatness, no matter where we live or where we come from.

Ruth risked everything to support her mother-in-law, Naomi. She is a witness to loving self-sacrifice.

Esther

Esther is an orphaned Jewish girl who marries a pagan king and becomes queen. She learns of a top official's plot to trick the king into killing all the Jews in the kingdom. Esther risks her status as queen, and even her life, to change the king's mind. Her courage saves God's people, and is celebrated today within Judaism during the Feast of Purim. Esther witnesses to the courage we need to live our faith and to stand up for what is right.

Queen Esther took a big risk in challenging the king's decision. She is a witness to courageous love.

Jeremiah

Jeremiah is terrified when God asks him to become a prophet. He tells God he is too young to speak for him and wouldn't know what to say. Nevertheless, in faith, he trusts in God's will and does what is asked of him. Jeremiah becomes one of the greatest prophets of the Old Testament, bravely risking his reputation, and even his life, to speak God's Word. Jeremiah helps us recognize that whatever is lacking in our abilities, God will provide for us to fulfill his purposes.

More Great Witnesses: The New Testament

The New Testament also abounds with examples of holy men and women who freely surrender to God's call, even when it requires great personal sacrifice.

Mary, Mother of Jesus

The Virgin Mary most perfectly embodies the "obedience of faith." She freely offers "yes" in response to her role in God's plan of salvation as the Mother of Jesus. She stays by Jesus as he suffers and dies on the cross. She is there among the other disciples after Jesus' Resurrection. She is truly our greatest example of faith.

UNIT 5

Mary Magdalene

Mary Magdalene is one of the women from Galilee who leaves home to accompany Jesus during his ministry. In all four Gospels, she is among the first of the faithful witnesses of the resurrected Lord Jesus. Jesus entrusts her with the mission of proclaiming the Good News to the other disciples. Mary Magdalene reminds us that faith can lead us anywhere, and the reward in the end is worth the effort.

In John's Gospel, Jesus entrusts Mary Magdalene with the mission of proclaiming the Good News of his Resurrection to the other disciples.

Priscilla and Aquila

Priscilla and Aquila are a Jewish couple from Rome who have been exiled to Corinth. When Saint Paul comes to Corinth, he stays with them, and it is likely that they become Christians while he is with them. In future letters, Paul refers to them as "my co-workers in Christ Jesus, who risked their necks for my life" (Romans 16:3–4). We learn in Acts 18:18–19 that they accompany Paul to Ephesus and teach and minister with him there for three years. Even in a male-dominated society, Priscilla is given equal footing to her husband in ministering to the community. According to tradition, they were martyred upon their return to Rome, probably around the same time as Paul.

Priscilla and Aquila were dear friends of Saint Paul who were martyred for their faith.

UNIT 5

© ASP Religion / Alamy Stock Photo

© ASP Religion / Alamy Stock Photo

Saints and Martyrs: Lives of Faith

The lives of the saints, some of whom were also martyrs, are a rich resource of inspiration for us to excel in living our faith. The Church's saints and martyrs show us how to maintain and grow our faith, especially during our most trying times.

Saint Ignatius of Loyola (1491–1556)

Saint Ignatius of Loyola is a soldier who puts all of his trust in God's Revelation. While resting from an injury he had sustained on the battlefield, he fervently studies the faith. He seeks out books about Jesus and the saints. He also begins practicing **spiritual exercises**. This combination of prayer, contemplation, and meditation is designed to help one grow closer to God, and discern God's will in one's life. He begins practicing these exercises with several others. These people become the first members of a new religious order, the Society of Jesus, or **Jesuits**. Saint Ignatius witnesses to the power of studying our faith and working on our relationship with God.

Saint Catherine of Siena (d. 305)

© bubutu / Shutterstock.com

Saint Catherine of Siena enjoys her quiet life at home helping her family, but God has bigger plans for her. God calls her to enter the political world to help the Church and serve the poor. Catherine is outspoken, particularly for a woman in that time. She confronts Pope Gregory XI, the last of seven successive popes to reside in Avignon, France, rather than in Rome. With the Pope far from the capital of the Roman

Saint Catherine of Siena (1347–1380)

Empire, the Church grows out of touch with the needs and living conditions of its members. She urges him to return to the holy city of Rome. You might

UNIT 5

---

spiritual exercises ➤ Originally established by Saint Ignatius of Loyola, spiritual exercises are prayers, meditations, reflections, and directions for retreat. Their purpose is to regulate one's life in such a way that no decision is made under the influence of attachment to anything other than God.

Jesuits ➤ The name of the members of the Society of Jesus. This order was founded by Saint Ignatius of Loyola in 1534. The Jesuits engage in teaching, missionary, and parish work and also conduct retreats.

even say she chastises him into returning when she says, "Be manly in my sight, and not timorous." Perhaps to her great surprise, he listens to her. Saint Catherine's life reminds us that God's plan may move us out of our comfort zone as we witness to the world.

Saint Maximillian Kolbe (1894–1941)

Saint Maximillian Kolbe was a Polish-born Conventual Franciscan Friar living during World War II. Using the monastery as a hospital, he helps hide countless Jews from Nazi persecution. He is eventually arrested by the Nazis and taken to Auschwitz, the infamous concentration camp. In July of 1941, three prisoners appear to have escaped from the camp. As a result, the commander orders ten men to be starved to death as a warning to the other prisoners. When one of the selected men cries out that he has a family, Father Kolbe volunteers to take his place, even though he doesn't know the man. He leads the starving men in prayers and hymns to Mary before they die. His life, or more important his death, is a powerful witness that can encourage us when we are confronted with the opportunity to sacrifice ourselves for the good of others.

Saint Maximillian Kolbe (1894–1941) was a Franciscan Friar who was martyred in a concentration camp during World War II.

UNIT 5

The examples of these and countless other holy women and men who have gone before us show us how to live a life of faith and witness to others. They teach us how to dedicate our whole selves—mind, heart, and spirit—to sharing God's love and mercy with others. ✳

HMMMMM. . . How do the stories of other people's faith help your own faith and your ability to witness to it?

Article 66

The Call to Evangelization

When we see a good movie or hear a great song, we want to share it with others. We want others to experience the same joy we feel. It is natural to want to share something exciting and wonderful. Throughout this course, we have discussed something far greater than a good movie or song. We have delved into the New Testament, which reveals the mystery of our God and his plan for our salvation. We have studied the life, death, and Resurrection of God's beloved Son, Jesus Christ, who revealed God's New Covenant with the whole human race. We have seen how God the Holy Spirit continues to guide the Church and strengthen individuals seeking holiness and eternal life. We have discussed how faith in Christ, our Savior, saves us from sin and death and saves us for holiness and happiness. This information—better yet, this Great News—is far too amazing to simply keep to yourself. You need to share it!

As baptized Christians, we have received the mission of sharing the Good News of Jesus Christ with all those we meet. Proclaiming the beauty and truth of Christ through our words and our actions is called **evangelization**. *Evangelization* comes from the Greek word *euangelion*, which means "good news." The life, death, and Resurrection of Jesus is truly Good News for all humanity.

Jesus and the Mission of the Disciples

We can see the roots of our own call to evangelize in the mission Jesus gives to his disciples. For example, in the Gospel of Luke (see 10:1–20), Jesus sends out seventy-two disciples in pairs. He directs them to various cities and towns, asking them to teach and heal in his name. When his disciples return from their mission, they rejoice at all they have been able to accomplish. In the same way, in the Gospel of Matthew, the Risen Christ commissions the eleven Apostles with these famous words: "Go, therefore, and make disciples of all nations, baptizing them in the name of the Father, and of the Son, and of the holy Spirit, teaching them to observe all that I have commanded you. And behold, I am with you always, until the end of the age" (28:19–20). In carrying out their mission, the Apostles appoint successors as their own deaths draw near. Thus, the work of evangelization can continue "until the end of the age" (verse 20).

---

evangelization ➤ The proclamation of the Gospel of Jesus Christ through word and witness.

Jesus has entrusted us with the same mission of evangelization as the original disciples. We must give authentic witness to our faith in Jesus today in our own part of the world. We hope that this witness may lead others to faith in him. For example, we can pray regularly; share generously, especially with the poor; speak freely and without embarrassment of our Christian faith; and bring God's revealed truth to discussions on current issues. Just as he gave courage and wisdom to the original disciples, God will surely give us the same, so that we may become light to the world.

MAKE IT SO

What's holding you back from telling other about Jesus? Are you afraid that you won't know the right things to say? Are you afraid of being rejected? Maybe you think it's someone else's job? Don't hesitate. There are plenty of ways you can evangelize in your everyday life:

- Set time apart for God through prayer and meditation. Don't be afraid to share with others what you are doing.
- Be a disciple of Christ by volunteering, praying, fasting, and putting your own money in the collection basket.
- Keep Sundays holy. Attend Mass and try to reserve the day for your family.
- Invite a friend to church or youth group.
- Be friendly and cheerful.
- Speak out when you see something happening that is clearly wrong.

UNIT 5

Evangelizing, Not Proselytizing

In some Christian denominations, the mission to evangelize has become distorted by **proselytism**, the active, even aggressive, seeking of converts to one's own religious faith, often away from another religion. Usually with the best of intentions (the salvation of souls), proselytizers will sometimes relentlessly pursue people, even individuals who have never shown interest in their message.

The Catholic approach to evangelization is different. Recall what Peter wrote about explaining our faith, that we must always do it with "gentleness and reverence" (1 Peter 3:15). As Catholics, we take that to heart. We recognize that God calls each person to an authentic relationship with him. We can't bully someone into seeing our point of view, much less bully them into falling in love with God. Therefore, we must respect people's basic freedom to accept or reject the Gospel message. This does not mean that we are to be passive. We are looking "for opportunities to announce Christ by words addressed either to nonbelievers with a view to leading them to faith, or to the faithful" (*Decree on the Apostolate of Lay People [Apostolicam Actuositatem]*, number 6). Note that our call to evangelize is directed toward unbelievers and fellow Catholics as well. Everyone can benefit from having their faith encouraged by others.

© Steve Debenport / iStockphoto.com

We are called to evangelize in what we say and in what we do.
How can you, in your daily routine, encourage others in their faith?

proselytizing ➤ The practice of inducing someone to convert to one's faith.

When you do evangelize, be patient. In a world with 24-hour news and instant access on the internet, we are used to getting results immediately. This is not the case with matters of faith. Faith is ultimately about building a relationship. So do not be surprised or disheartened if the witness of your own faithful life does not have any immediate visible effect on another person. Our role is to simply plant the seeds of faith, and leave the growth up to God. God is always at work, in ways we cannot fully understand. Two thousand years of growth have shown that the Gospel is spreading throughout the world. It is time to do your part to help spread the Good News. ✳

OVERVIEW of the Letters of Peter

- **Intended audience:** Gentile Christians who were alienated and treated as evil for living the Gospel.

- **Theme:** Christians must accept suffering, ignore false teaching, and hold on tightly to their faith.

- **Reason for writing:** To give support and encouragement to the community being persecuted by outsiders for not participating in pagan activities.

HMMMMM... How would you describe the Catholic Church's approach to evangelization?

UNIT 5

1. What words does Peter use in First Peter to describe our Christian dignity?

2. What is one similarity between the early Christian communities described in Peter's letters and Christian communities today?

3. What must we do in order to be authentic witnesses to Jesus Christ?

4. What are two ways we can witness to our faith through our actions?

5. How do the lives of the Apostles inspire us to excel in living out our faith?

6. What are three images Saint Paul uses in his letters to help us remember to follow Jesus, to live morally, and to keep the faith?

7. How did Saint Maximillian Kolbe witness to his faith?

8. Give one example of when the Apostles learned from Jesus about the faith and living it out in their daily lives.

9. Name two people covered in this chapter, and explain how their lives were a witness of faith.

10. Explain the difference between evangelizing and proselytizing.

© Noah Pascua Gutierrez

ART STUDY

COMMUNION OF SAINTS

Take some time to review this modern depiction of the Communion of Saints.

1. What characteristics or elements of this piece of art appeal to you?

2. How many of the saints depicted here can you easily identify?

3. Are there any saints depicted here that you want to learn more about? Why?

UNIT 5 HIGHLIGHTS

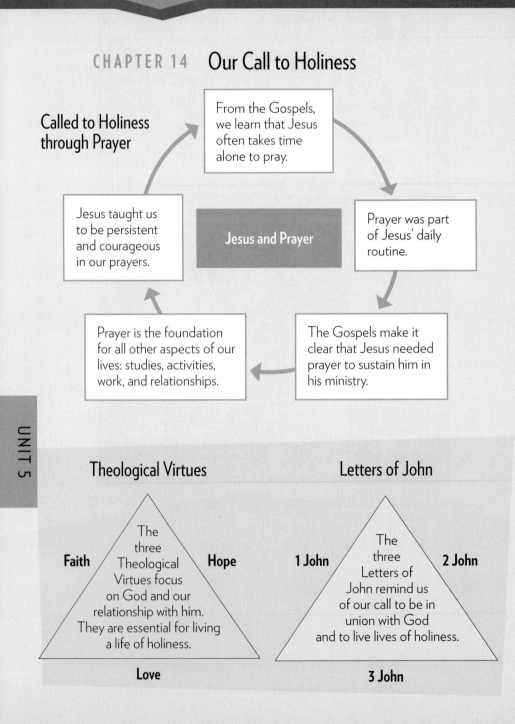

CHAPTER 14 **Our Call to Holiness**

Called to Holiness through Prayer

From the Gospels, we learn that Jesus often takes time alone to pray.

Jesus and Prayer

Jesus taught us to be persistent and courageous in our prayers.

Prayer was part of Jesus' daily routine.

Prayer is the foundation for all other aspects of our lives: studies, activities, work, and relationships.

The Gospels make it clear that Jesus needed prayer to sustain him in his ministry.

Theological Virtues

Faith

Hope

The three Theological Virtues focus on God and our relationship with him. They are essential for living a life of holiness.

Love

Letters of John

1 John

2 John

The three Letters of John remind us of our call to be in union with God and to live lives of holiness.

3 John

CHAPTER 15 **Our Call to Serve**

Paul's Points for Serving Well

Finish What You Start

Give from Your Surplus

Give Cheerfully

The Creation account in Genesis makes it clear that God created us to live together and to help one another. In Jesus' powerful parable about the Final Judgment, he tells us that how we spend eternity depends on how we serve one another.

The Principles of Catholic Social Teaching

The Church teachings that guide our efforts to create a more just and peaceful world are called Catholic social teaching. These principles are a guide for how we can work for justice and serve the common good.

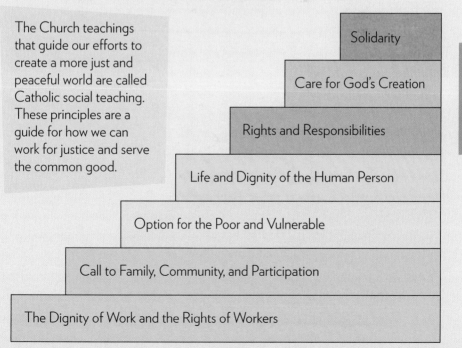

Solidarity

Care for God's Creation

Rights and Responsibilities

Life and Dignity of the Human Person

Option for the Poor and Vulnerable

Call to Family, Community, and Participation

The Dignity of Work and the Rights of Workers

UNIT 5

CHAPTER 16   Our Call to Witness

Peter and Paul's Images Inspire Us to Live Out Our Faith

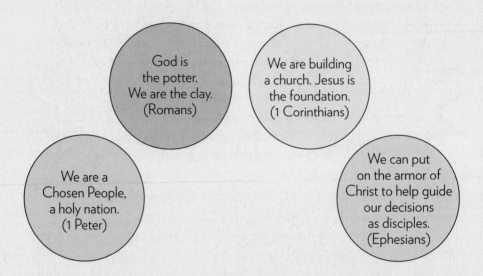

God is
the potter.
We are the clay.
(Romans)

We are building
a church. Jesus is
the foundation.
(1 Corinthians)

We are a
Chosen People,
a holy nation.
(1 Peter)

We can put
on the armor of
Christ to help guide
our decisions
as disciples.
(Ephesians)

Paul gives us images that can inspire us to persevere in our call to discipleship.

We can also draw inspiration from the models of discipleship of those who have come before us.

The Apostles

Martyrs

The Communion
of Saints

Giving Witness

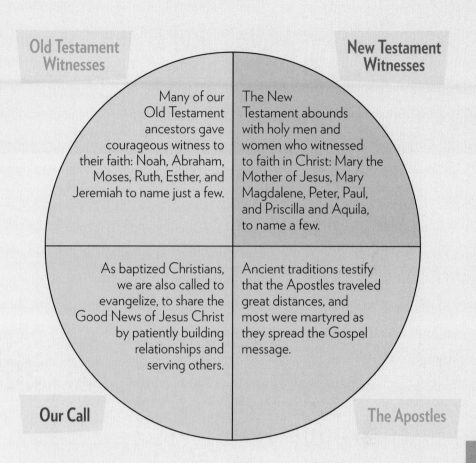

Old Testament Witnesses

Many of our Old Testament ancestors gave courageous witness to their faith: Noah, Abraham, Moses, Ruth, Esther, and Jeremiah to name just a few.

New Testament Witnesses

The New Testament abounds with holy men and women who witnessed to faith in Christ: Mary the Mother of Jesus, Mary Magdalene, Peter, Paul, and Priscilla and Aquila, to name a few.

Our Call

As baptized Christians, we are also called to evangelize, to share the Good News of Jesus Christ by patiently building relationships and serving others.

The Apostles

Ancient traditions testify that the Apostles traveled great distances, and most were martyred as they spread the Gospel message.

Where Did They Get Their Courage?

They were inspired by Jesus' words and strengthened by the Holy Spirit to follow his example.

UNIT 5

UNIT 5
BRING IT HOME

WHAT DOES IT MEAN TO FOLLOW JESUS?

FOCUS QUESTIONS

CHAPTER 14 Can I be holy?

CHAPTER 15 What does Christian service mean?

CHAPTER 16 What does it mean to witness?

IFE
Mater Dei High School

Following Jesus means applying not only Jesus' teachings but also his lifestyle. We're supposed to follow his pattern of prayer, calling on God not only when we need help but also when we're happy, or sad, or just want to talk. It means making personal sacrifices, because Jesus did. Following Jesus isn't about trying to become a carbon copy of him; rather, it means taking his teachings and understanding them and why they really matter, and then applying them.

UNIT 5

REFLECT

Take some time to read and reflect on the unit and chapter focus questions listed on the facing page.

• What question or section did you identify most closely with?

• What did you find within the unit that was comforting or challenging?

APPENDIX
Challenge Questions

The content of this course will raise some important questions for those who think seriously about their faith. This is especially true today, when many people are asking hard questions about religious beliefs. We are not afraid of these hard questions, because an honest search for answers will deepen our faith and understanding of what God has revealed. Here are some common questions with some key points for how to answer them. The references to paragraphs in the *Catechism of the Catholic Church (CCC)* are for further reading if you want to explore these questions more deeply.

QUESTION 1: Does God really exist?

First, we need to be clear that God's existence cannot be proven like a math problem or science theory. Science and math deal with physical reality; religion and faith deal with spiritual reality. Although the two realities are connected, we use different approaches and different criteria when we discuss the truth and reality of each. Put slightly differently, we cannot prove in a scientific way that God exists, but there are several convincing arguments that together prove that it is very reasonable to believe in the truth of God's existence.

Even if we did not have the Bible and Divine Revelation, our experiences of the world around us and the use of our own reason reveal the existence of God (see *CCC*, numbers 36–39, 50, 156–159). Have you ever been out in nature and found yourself in awe of its beauty? Perhaps the delicate details of a spiderweb or the wondrous majesty of tall rock formations have taken your breath away. When we stop to think about these experiences of creation, we begin to see God's presence (see *CCC*, numbers 156–159). The breathtaking order and beauty found in all of creation point us to its origin and creator, God (see number 295). This beautiful and complex creation did not happen by chance. Recent efforts by scientists support this. Their calculations result in extremely small probabilities that life as we know it could emerge spontaneously. Throughout history, the Church has taught that something had to be behind it, and that something we call God (see numbers 156, 295).

Another spiritual reality to consider is the longing of the human heart for something more. Why do we long to love and be loved? Why do we long for eternal life and grieve over death? These longings point to the spiritual truth that we are more than just material objects and point to God's existence. We are spiritual beings, connected to a larger reality than just the things we can see and touch. A connected reality is natural law, the moral law that can be understood by all people through the use of human reason. Why do all human beings have this innate sense of right and wrong, unless it comes from God, our common Creator? Each and every person has this God-given ability to understand what it means to be in right relationship with God, other people, and the world—another reality pointing to the existence of God. The natural law is written upon every human heart, another longing for God that points to God's existence (see *CCC*, numbers 1954–1960).

Just as our reason and experience can point us to God, they can also teach us to accept the word of other believers (see *CCC*, number 39). Think of all the times you have accepted the word of a friend or family member because you trust that person. Just like believing a trusted family member, we can trust the believers who have passed on God's Revelation through the centuries. This starts with the Apostles and the biblical saints and martyrs (see numbers 823, 828, 857, 946, 1258, 2473), whose testimony comes to us through Scripture and Tradition (see numbers 50–53, 74–83). The saints, martyrs, and great teachers of the Church have witnessed to the power of God through their amazing lives. We can also look to the faith of people we know today: the Pope and the bishops in union with him; priests, nuns, and deacons; parents, grand-parents, and other family members; teachers and catechists; the witness of fellow Catholics as well as the witness of non-Catholic believers (see numbers 85, 1655–1658). If you allow the courageous love of these many people to touch your heart, you must at least allow for the possibility of the God who inspires their actions.

A final spiritual reality that points to God's existence is harder to explain. Jesus touches on this several times in the Gospels when he says things like: "Are your hearts hardened? Do you have eyes and not see, ears and not hear?" (Mark 8:17–18). The spiritual truth that Jesus is pointing to is that our ability to experience and know God comes through an openness to believe. When people close their minds and hearts to the possibility of God, they will not experience him. It is through our willingness to take the leap of faith, to accept the grace that God offers when we ask for it, and our willingness to approach God in prayer and meditation, that we grow in the knowledge of the reality of God and his existence (see *CCC*, numbers 143, 153–159).

QUESTION 2: How can people say that God is good if suffering and evil are present in the world?

This is another difficult but very important question. In response to this question, we must consider two things. First, all creation is in process; it has not yet reached the perfection that God intends it to have. This is why we know in our hearts that things are not as they should be during times of suffering and experiences of evil. This is verified in the accounts of Creation and of Adam and Eve's Original Sin. Until the time comes when God ushers in the New Heaven and the New Earth, evil and suffering will be part of our reality.

Second, God is not the immediate cause of suffering and evil. Even though God is the creator of all that is, the suffering that exists in the world is not something he caused or sends to us. God brings about only what is good, for he is goodness itself. When there is evil and suffering, God does not cause it, but sometimes he does permit it for reasons we cannot now know or understand (see *CCC*, numbers 1500–1501). Evil is a reality and a mystery; that is, it is hard to understand the *why* of it (see numbers 309–314).

However, some causes are clear. Some evil and suffering are a result of the work of the Devil or Satan, the fallen angel who works against God's will (see *CCC*, number 395). And much of our suffering is the result of human sin. God gave us free will, but our misuse of this gift creates the evil and suffering we experience, the consequences of our sinful choices (see numbers 1849, 1852–1853).

The Passion and death of Jesus can help us to see beyond suffering and remind us that God is present with us in our suffering, pain, and death. Scripture can help us to understand suffering: the Psalms, the story of Job, and the prophets offer insights and consolation. The Resurrection of Jesus can help us to see beyond suffering to hope and to eternal life (see *CCC*, numbers 638–655). Through faith, when we unite our own personal suffering with Jesus' suffering, our suffering even becomes redemptive for ourselves and others (see number 1851).

In the face of suffering, even suffering caused by natural disasters, we need to remember that God always wants what is best for us (see *CCC*, numbers 374–379). Natural disasters can be understood in part as a consequence of Original Sin. The harmony God intended between humanity and nature has become broken, and nature is now at times "alien and hostile" (see number 400). We must trust in God's wisdom and goodness, which allows "the existence of the more perfect alongside the less perfect, both constructive and destructive forces of nature" (*CCC*, number 310). In other words, the world is not yet as God intends. It is also journeying toward ultimate perfection. We must not take this as a sign of God's displeasure or a punishment from God.

QUESTION 3: How can we say that God loves us when there is so much suffering in the world?

This question is closely related to the question of why God allows evil in the world. But let's approach this from a different perspective. Let's consider the overwhelming evidence pointing to God's love for us and list the many ways we may experience God's love:

- We can discover God's love through creation (see *CCC*, number 54). God created the world, not because he had to, but out of love (see *CCC*, number 295).

- Our ability to give and receive love is another sign that God is love. Because he created us in his own image and likeness, with our desire to love and to be loved, then how much more true is that of God (see numbers *CCC*, 1700–1706).
- We experience God's love through the love of other people and the events of our lives. Many people love us, and we love them in return: family, friends, coaches, teachers, ministers, and so on. Even though their love is imperfect (and unfortunately, sometimes lacking), it points us to the perfect love that God has for us.
- Ultimately, it is the suffering and death of Jesus Christ that shows and proves the amazing depth of God's love for us (see *CCC*, numbers 599–623). As the Second Person of the Divine Trinity, Jesus Christ took our suffering upon himself for our sake (see number 1505). Out of love, God the Father sent his Son to redeem everyone from sin so that all can share a life of love eternally with him in Heaven (see numbers 599–605).
- Jesus lives now and establishes a relationship based on love with each and every one of us, particularly through the sacramental life of the Church. In the sacramental liturgies, Christ is present to us through the Liturgy of the Word, speaking through the Scripture readings. He is present in the person of the sacramental minister and in the people gathered to sing and pray. He is especially present through his Body and Blood in the Eucharist (see *CCC*, numbers 662–664, 1084–1090). We are lovingly and continually called by God into union with him and his Son through the Holy Spirit by means of a life of holiness (see numbers 1091–1109).
- We also know of God's love because of the efforts he's made to reveal his loving plan to save us. He tells us in Scripture, the living Word of God. God is the ultimate author of the Bible, speaking through the words of the human authors of Scripture. The Bible is the living Word of God, which is never out-of-date or irrelevant. Through the words of Scripture, God communicates his saving love to every age and to every generation (see *CCC*, numbers 80–82).
- We also have evidence of God's loving plan for our salvation in the liturgy of the Church. In every liturgical celebration, we listen to the words of Scripture, which tell the story of salvation history. As we go through the liturgical year, we hear God's plan unfold in the readings of Sunday Mass, beginning with Christ's birth and ending with Christ proclaimed as Lord and King of all creation. In all the sacraments, we experience his saving power, equipping us with the grace needed to live as his disciples. This is especially true in the Eucharist as we remember and make present Christ's sacrifice and the saving power of his Passion, Death, and Resurrection. Participation in the Eucharist brings us into closer communion with God and with one another, giving us a foretaste of the full communion we will share with God in Heaven (see numbers 1067, 1324–1327).

- Finally, God tells us he loves us through the ministry of the Church and the loving community of believers we are called to be part of. "As I have loved you, so you also should love one another" (John 13:34). God loves you through those who belong to the Church, including bishops, priests, Confirmation sponsors, catechists, your family, and so many others. These people share in Christ's mission and want the best for you. You can go to them when you are struggling, when you are hurting, when you need help and guidance. When you are united with them, Christ is never far away. (see *CCC*, numbers 785–786).

QUESTION 4: Does God really want us to be happy?

God most definitely wants us to be happy! From the beginning of Creation, God has created us to be happy both in this world and in the next. We know that our desire for happiness comes from God. He has placed that desire within our hearts. In the Creation accounts in the Book of Genesis, we see the state of happiness that God originally intended for us. Before Original Sin occurs, Adam and Eve live in harmony with God, with one another, and with nature in a state of holiness and justice.

Then Adam and Eve cause their own unhappiness when they choose not to listen to God (see *CCC*, numbers 374–379). Unfortunately, this continues today, as people continue to make choices contrary to God's will, rejecting the path to happiness revealed in the life and teachings of Jesus Christ. Fortunately, God the Father sent his only Son, Jesus Christ, so that we might be saved. Our confident hope in the salvation gained for us by Christ is the cause for happiness. Our faith in Christ can bring happiness even when we are suffering (see numbers 599–605). At the Last Supper, Jesus Christ even points out that his teachings are aimed at helping everyone share in his joy: "I have told you this so that my joy may be in you and your joy may be complete" (John 15:11). This passage and many others in Scripture show us again and again God's desire for our happiness (see *CCC*, numbers 736, 1832).

A final answer to this question are the Beatitudes, a central aspect of Jesus' teaching (see Matthew 5:3–11, Luke 6:20–26). The word beatitude is derived from a Latin word meaning "happy, fortunate, or blissful." The Beatitudes give us a blueprint for true discipleship and happiness (see Matthew 5:2–10; *CCC*, numbers 1716–1718). It may seem odd that the Beatitudes characterize being poor, persecuted, or meek as qualifications for happiness. This is the challenging vision of the Kingdom of God. True happiness does not lie in money, possessions, power, or prestige. Our joy and happiness are found when we show mercy, fight for righteousness, and make peace.

One final consideration is that in the Bible true joy is the mark of the followers of Christ (see Philippians 4:4). This is one of the reasons Jesus established his Church—to help people find true happiness and joy (see *CCC*, number 1832).

QUESTION 5: How can we be sure that what the Church teaches comes from God?

Some people dismiss God's Revelation. They say that the beliefs and doctrines taught by the Church are simply made up by members of the Church. These people would insist that mistaken beliefs are handed down from one generation to another and the members of the Church just accept them without question. This is an important question, because if these people are right, there are a whole lot of gullible people in the Church putting their faith in empty beliefs.

Let's cut straight to the point. What these people are really questioning is if God really does reveal himself to humanity. If you believe there is a God, and if you believe that God wants to make himself known to humanity, there is plenty of evidence supporting the Church's trusted role in this process.

We can be sure that what the Church teaches has come from God because of Apostolic Tradition and Apostolic Succession (see *CCC*, numbers 888–892, 861–862, 858–860). What was revealed in and through Jesus Christ was entrusted to Saint Peter and the Apostles, who were taught directly by Jesus. They in turn passed on those beliefs through those who succeeded them (see numbers 81, 84). Through the centuries, popes and bishops, the successors of Saint Peter and the Apostles, have carefully taught the people in their charge the truths revealed and taught by Jesus Christ (see numbers 96, 171, 173, 815).

To help the Church protect his teachings from falling into error, Christ has also given the Church a share in his own infallibility—that is, the gift of teaching the revealed truths related to faith or morals without error (see *CCC*, numbers 889–892). This is the responsibility of the Pope and of the bishops (see article 10 in chapter 2 for a description of how infallible doctrines are taught). Because of the Church's infallibility, all Catholics throughout time, whether in the third century or the twenty-first, whether in Korea or Ethiopia or Honduras, believe the same divinely revealed truths that go all the way back to Christ himself. The God who, in Jesus Christ, promised to be with us "until the end of the age" (Matthew 28:20) has guaranteed that all of us will continue to have access to the truth until Christ comes again in glory.

QUESTION 6: Why do Catholics pray to Mary? How could Mary remain a virgin when the Gospels talk about the brothers and sisters of Jesus?

The question about Catholics praying to Mary is most often based on a misunderstanding. First, it is important to know that Catholics do not worship Mary. Our worship belongs to God alone. Catholics venerate Mary and the saints. To venerate means to show respect for someone or something. The Mother of God is certainly worthy of our respect!

Catholics understand that Mary does not have the power to answer prayers on her own. God alone has that power. Just like when we ask a friend to pray for us, our prayers to Mary are asking for her intercessory help. Because Mary is already in Heaven, she will know better than us how to offer praise and prayer to God. When people pray to the Blessed Mother, they are asking her in turn to offer the same prayer for them to God. When Mary and the saints lived on Earth, they cooperated with God to do good for others. Now from their place in Heaven, they continue to cooperate with God by doing good for others, those who are in need here on Earth and those who are in Purgatory.

The question about the brothers and sisters of Jesus is really a question about the proper interpretation of the Bible. Recall that one of the principles of good interpretation is to consider the cultural beliefs and practices of the human authors of the Bible's books. In first-century Palestine, people lived in very close-knit family groups. Aunts and uncles were a second set of parents, and cousins were just as close as brothers and sisters. In fact, people referred to their cousins as their brothers and sisters. Therefore, it is likely that the people referred to as Jesus' brothers and sisters were, in fact, his cousins. Or perhaps they could have been his half-brothers and half-sisters, if Joseph had been a widower with children. They would not have been the sons and daughters of Mary.

From the earliest days of the Church, Mary has been revered as ever-virgin. She was a virgin before Jesus' birth and remained a virgin afterward. This is the revealed truth of Sacred Tradition.

GLOSSARY

A

adoration ➤ The prayerful acknowledgment that God is God and Creator of all that is.

Advocate ➤ Another name for the Holy Spirit. The Third Divine Person of the Blessed Trinity, the personal love of Father and Son for each other. Also called the Paraclete and the Spirit of Truth.

Annunciation ➤ The biblical event that includes the angel Gabriel's visit to the Virgin Mary to announce that she is to be the Mother of the Savior, Mary's "yes" to God, and Christ's conception through the power of the Holy Spirit.

apocalyptic literature ➤ A literary form that uses dramatic events and highly symbolic language to offer hope to a people in crisis.

apostate ➤ One who denies or renounces one's faith.

Apostolic Succession ➤ The uninterrupted passing on of authority from the Apostles directly to all the bishops. It is accomplished through the laying on of hands when a bishop is ordained in the Sacrament of Holy Orders as instituted by Christ.

Arianism ➤ A heretical movement that claimed Jesus was a creature who, although begotten by God the Father, lacked a divine nature. Arius denied that Christ was consubstantial with God the Father.

Ascension ➤ The "going up" into Heaven of the Risen Christ forty days after his Resurrection.

Assumption ➤ The dogma that recognizes that the body of the Blessed Virgin Mary was taken directly to Heaven after her life on Earth had ended.

B

Beatitudes ➤ The teachings of Jesus that begin the Sermon on the Mount and that summarize the New Law of Christ. The Beatitudes describe the actions and attitudes by which one can discover genuine happiness, and they teach us the final end to which God calls us: full communion with him in the Kingdom of Heaven.

Beloved Disciple ➤ In the Gospel of John, an unnamed disciple who may have been the Apostle John.

blasphemy ➤ Speaking, acting, or thinking about God in a way that is irreverent, mocking, or offensive. It is a sin against the Second Commandment.

C

canon of Scripture ➤ The books of the Bible officially recognized by the Church as the inspired Word of God.

charity ➤ The Theological Virtue by which we love God above all things and, out of that love of God, love our neighbor as ourselves.

Christological ➤ Having to do with the branch of theology called Christology. Christology is the study of the divine and human natures of Jesus Christ, the Son of God and the Second Divine Person of the Trinity, and his earthly ministry and eternal mission.

Christology ➤ Literally the study of Christ; the systematic statement of Christian beliefs about Jesus Christ, including his identity, mission, and saving work on Earth.

Church Fathers ➤ Church teachers and writers of the early centuries whose teachings are a witness to the Tradition of the Church.

Code of Canon Law ➤ The collected body of rules and regulations used to govern the Church in its mission toward the salvation of souls.

common good ➤ Social conditions that allow for all citizens of the Earth, individuals and families, to meet basic needs and achieve fulfillment.

Communion of Saints ➤ This phrase refers to two realities: (1) the communion of spiritual goods that Christ has shared with the Church, such as the sacraments (especially the Eucharist), charisms, helping those in material need, and our love for one another, and (2) the spiritual union of all the redeemed, those on Earth and those who have died.

complacency ➤ A state of self-satisfaction, especially when accompanied by unawareness of actual dangers or deficiencies; unaware or uninformed self-satisfaction.

concupiscence ➤ The tendency of all human beings toward sin, as a result of Original Sin.

consubstantial ➤ Having the same nature or essence.

conversion ➤ A profound change of heart, turning away from sin and toward God.

Corporal Works of Mercy ➤ Charitable actions by which we help our neighbors in their bodily needs.

creed ➤ An official profession of faith, usually prepared and presented by a council of the Church and used in the Church's liturgy. Based on the Latin credo, meaning "I believe."

cult ➤ A small religious group that is not part of a larger and more accepted religion and that has beliefs regarded by many as extreme or dangerous.

D

Deposit of Faith ➤ The heritage of faith contained in Sacred Scripture and Sacred Tradition. It has been passed on from the time of the Apostles. The Magisterium takes from it all that it teaches as revealed truth.

disciple ➤ Follower of Jesus.

discourse ➤ An authoritative speech or presentation.

Divine Revelation ➤ God's self-communication through which he makes known the mystery of his divine plan. Divine Revelation is a gift accomplished by the Father, Son, and Holy Spirit through the words and deeds of salvation history. It is most fully realized in the Passion, death, Resurrection, and Ascension of Jesus Christ.

Docetism ➤ A heretical movement that claimed Jesus' humanity was a sort of disguise—he looked like a human and acted like a human, but he was only divine, lacking a human nature.

doctrine ➤ An official, authoritative teaching of the Church based on the Revelation of God.

E

Ecumenical Council ➤ A gathering of the Church's bishops from around the world convened by the Pope or approved by him to address pressing issues in the Church and in the world.

elites ➤ A select group that has the most power and influence in a society, typically because of their wealth and social status.

episcopacy ➤ The position or office of a bishop.

evangelization ➤ The proclamation of the Gospel of Jesus Christ through word and witness.

evangelizers ➤ Those who proclaim the Gospel of Jesus Christ through word and witness.

exalt ➤ To raise someone to a higher rank or character; to dignify or make someone noble.

F

faith ➤ In general, the belief in the existence of God. For Christians, the gift of God by which one freely accepts his full Revelation in Jesus Christ. It is a matter of both the head (acceptance of Church teaching regarding the Revelation of God) and the heart (love of God and neighbor as a response to God's first loving us); also, one of the three Theological Virtues.

fidelity ➤ Faithfulness.

filial ➤ Having to do with the relationship between a child and his or her parent.

Final Judgment ➤ The judgment of the human race by Jesus Christ at his second coming. It is also called the Last Judgment.

four last things ➤ The Church refers to death, judgment, Heaven, and Hell as the four last things.

free will ➤ The gift from God that allows human beings to choose from among various actions, for which we are held accountable. It is the basis for moral responsibility.

fruits of the Holy Spirit ➤ When we cooperate with the grace and gifts we receive from the Holy Spirit, we see the effect of the Holy Spirit's presence in our lives in special qualities and attitudes that we develop as we grow in faith. The twelve fruits of the Holy Spirit are love, joy, peace, patience, kindness, goodness, generosity, gentleness, faithfulness, modesty, self-control, and chastity.

G

Gentile ➤ A non-Jewish person. In Sacred Scripture, the Gentiles were the uncircumcised, those who did not honor the God of the Torah. Saint Paul and the other evangelists reached out to the Gentiles, baptizing them into the family of God.

genuflect ➤ To kneel on one knee as a sign of reverence for the Blessed Sacrament.

Gifts of the Holy Spirit ➤ At Baptism, we receive seven Gifts of the Holy Spirit. These gifts are freely given to us to help us live as followers of Jesus and to build up the Body of Christ, the Church. The seven gifts are wisdom, understanding, right judgment or counsel, fortitude or courage, knowledge, piety or reverence, and fear of the Lord or wonder and awe.

Gnosticism ➤ A heretical movement that claimed that only a select, elite group could attain salvation, by acquiring special, secret knowledge from God.

Gospel ➤ Most basically, "the good news" of the Revelation of God in and through the Word Made Flesh, Jesus Christ, proclaimed initially by him, then by the Apostles, and now by the Church; also refers to those four books of the New Testament that focus on the person, life, teachings, suffering, death, and Resurrection of Jesus.

grace ➤ The free and undeserved gift that God gives us to empower us to respond to his call and to live as his adopted sons and daughters. Grace restores our loving communion with the Holy Trinity, lost through sin.

H

handmaid ➤ A term of humility and respectful self-deprecation in the presence of God; a woman who is in servitude to another.

Heaven ➤ A state of eternal life and union with God, in which one experiences full happiness and the satisfaction of the deepest human longings.

Hell ➤ Refers to the state of definitive separation from God and the saints, and so is a state of eternal punishment.

heresy ➤ The conscious and deliberate rejection by a baptized person of a truth of faith that must be believed.

High Priest ➤ This person led the religious services and conducted animal sacrifices held at the Temple in Jerusalem. The High Priest was appointed by the Jewish king with the approval of the Roman governor.

holiness ➤ The state of being holy. This means to be set apart for God's service, to be devoted to God and united with him and his Church, to live a morally good life, to be a person of prayer, and to reveal God's love to the world through acts of loving service.

hope ➤ The Theological Virtue by which we trust in the promises of God and expect from God both external life and the grace we need to attain it; the conviction that God's grace is at work in the world and that the Kingdom of God established by and through Jesus Christ is becoming realized through the workings of the Holy Spirit among us.

hypostatic union ➤ The union of Jesus Christ's divine and human natures in one Divine Person.

I

idolatry ➤ The worship of other beings, creatures, or material goods in a way that is fitting for God alone.

Immaculate Conception ➤ The Catholic dogma that the Blessed Virgin Mary was free from sin from the first moment of her conception.

Incarnation ➤ From the Latin, meaning "to become flesh," referring to the mystery of Jesus Christ, the Divine Son of God, becoming man. In the Incarnation, Jesus Christ became truly man while remaining truly God.

incorruptible ➤ In reference to our bodies, not subject to decay or dissolution.

indentured servant ➤ A person who is under contract to work for another person for a period of time, usually without pay; often considered a form of slavery.

infallibility ➤ The gift given by the Holy Spirit to the Church whereby the Magisterium of the Church, the Pope, and the bishops in union with him, can definitively proclaim a doctrine of faith and morals without error.

inspired ➤ Written by human beings with the guidance of the Holy Spirit to teach faithfully and without error the saving truth that God willed to give us.

intercede ➤ To intervene on behalf of another.

interreligious dialogue ➤ The efforts to build cooperative and constructive interaction with other world religions.

J

Jesuits ➤ The name of the members of the Society of Jesus. This order was founded by Saint Ignatius of Loyola in 1534. The Jesuits engage in teaching, missionary, and parish work and also conduct retreats.

justice ➤ The Cardinal Virtue concerned with rights and duties within relationships; the commitment, as well as the actions and attitudes that flow from the commitment, that ensure we give to God and to our neighbor, particularly those who are poor and oppressed, what is properly due them.

justification ➤ God's act of bringing a sinful human being into right relationship with him. It involves removal of sin and the gift of God's sanctifying grace to renew holiness.

K

kerygma ➤ This refers to the initial Gospel proclamation designed to introduce a person to Christ and to appeal for conversion.

L

Last Day ➤ Described in the Book of Revelation, on the Last Day, all will stand before the One True Judge, Jesus Christ. Everything in our lives that is hidden, both good and bad, will be brought to light and we will be judged according to our deeds.

Last Judgment ➤ The judgment of the human race by Jesus Christ at his second coming. It is also called the Final Judgment.

Law of Love ➤ Divine Law revealed in the New Testament through the life and teaching of Jesus Christ and through the witness and teaching of the Apostles. The Law of Love perfects the Old Law and brings it to fulfillment. Also called the New Law.

Levites ➤ Members of the Hebrew tribe of Levi, from whom came the priests who performed the sacrifices and led the worship in the Jewish Temple.

love ➤ Also called "charity," the Theological Virtue by which we love God above all things and, out of that love of God, love our neighbors as ourselves.

M

Magisterium ➤ The Church's living teaching office, which consists of all bishops, in communion with the Pope, the bishop of Rome. Their task is to interpret and preserve the truths revealed in both Sacred Scripture and Sacred Tradition.

marginalized ➤ Those who are relegated to an unimportant or powerless position within a society or group.

martyr ➤ A person who voluntarily suffers death because of his or her beliefs. The Church has canonized many martyrs as saints.

Messiah ➤ Hebrew word for "anointed one." The equivalent Greek term is Christos. Jesus is the Christ and the Messiah because he is the Anointed One.

miracle ➤ A special manifestation, or sign, of the presence and power of God active in human history.

missionary ➤ A person sent to preach the Gospel, or to help strengthen the faith of already professed, among people in a given place or region.

Monophysitism ➤ A heretical movement that claimed Jesus' divinity fully absorbed his humanity, so that, in the end, he was only divine and not human.

monotheism ➤ The belief in one God instead of many gods.

N

natural law ➤ The moral law that can be understood by all people through the use of human reason. It is our God-given ability to understand what it means to be in right relationship with God, other people, the world, and ourselves. The basis for natural law is our participation in God's wisdom and goodness because we are created in the divine likeness.

Nestorianism ➤ A heretical movement that claimed there were actually two Persons joined together in Christ, one divine and the other human.

New Covenant ➤ The covenant or law established by God in Jesus Christ to fulfill and perfect the Old Covenant or Mosaic Law. It is a perfection on Earth of the Divine Law. The law of the New Covenant is called a law of love, grace, and freedom. The New Covenant will never end or diminish, and nothing new will be revealed until Christ comes again in glory.

New Jerusalem ➤ In the Book of Revelation, a symbol of a renewed society in which God dwells; a symbol of the Church, the "holy city," the assembly of the People of God called together from "the ends of the earth"; also, in other settings, a symbol of Heaven.

New Testament ➤ The twenty-seven books of the Bible, which have the life, teachings, Passion, death, Resurrection, and Ascension of Jesus Christ and the beginnings of the Church as their central theme.

Nicene Creed ➤ The formal statement or profession of faith commonly recited during the Eucharist.

O

Old Covenant ➤ The covenant between God and the ancient people of Israel established in the Sinai Covenant with Moses; also called the Old Testament.

Old Law ➤ Divine Law revealed in the Old Testament, summarized in the Ten Commandments. Also called the Law of Moses.

oral tradition ➤ The stage in the formation of the Gospels by which the Good News was spread by "word of mouth" prior to being written down.

Original Sin ➤ The sin by which the first humans disobeyed God and thereby lost their original holiness and became subject to death. Original Sin is transmitted to every person born into the world, except Jesus and Mary.

P

pantheon ➤ All of the gods of a people or religion collectively.

parable ➤ Generally a short story that uses everyday images to communicate religious messages. Jesus used parables frequently in his teaching as a way of presenting the Good News of salvation.

Parousia ➤ The second coming of Christ as judge of all the living and the dead, at the end of time, when the Kingdom of God will be fulfilled.

Particular Judgment ➤ The judgment that occurs immediately at the time of our death, when our immortal souls will be judged as worthy or unworthy of Heaven.

Paschal (Mystery) ➤ The work of salvation accomplished by Jesus Christ mainly through his Passion, death, Resurrection, and Ascension.

Passion ➤ The suffering of Jesus during the final days of his life: his agony in the garden at Gethsemane, his trial, and his Crucifixion.

Passover ➤ The night the Lord passed over the houses of the Israelites marked by the blood of the lamb, and spared the firstborn sons from death. It also is the feast that celebrates the deliverance of the Chosen People from bondage in Egypt and the Exodus from Egypt to the Promised Land.

Pastoral Letters ➤ The Pastoral Letters are three books of the New Testament: First Timothy, Second Timothy, and Titus. They are addressed to the pastors in the early Church, and they offer advice for dealing with false teachers and the roles of Church leaders.

patriarchal ➤ Describes a society, government, or religion in which the positions of power are held by men and important decisions are made by men.

Pentecost ➤ The fiftieth day following Easter, which commemorates the descent of the Holy Spirit on the Apostles and Mary.

persecution ➤ The act or practice of harassing or abusing those who differ in origin, religion, or social outlook.

pharaoh ➤ A ruler in ancient Egypt.

Pharisees ➤ This group of Jews was well-known for its strict adherence to all the laws of the Old Testament. The Pharisees believed in the resurrection of the dead.

philosophy ➤ In Greek, this word literally means "love of wisdom." It refers to the study of human existence using logical reasoning.

polytheism ➤ The belief in many gods.

preeminence ➤ Surpassing all others.

presbyter ➤ A synonym for elder in the Acts of the Apostles and an alternative word for priest today.

Promised Land ➤ In the Bible, the land of Canaan, which was promised to Abraham and his descendants.

proselytizing ➤ The practice of inducing someone to convert to one's faith.

providence ➤ God's divine care and protection.

Purgatory ➤ A state of final purification or cleansing, which one may need to enter following death and before entering Heaven.

R

Real Presence ➤ The doctrine that Jesus is really or substantially present in the Eucharist, not merely symbolically or metaphorically.

Redeemer ➤ One who frees others from distress, harm, captivity, or the consequences of sin; specifically, Jesus Christ.

redemption ➤ From the Latin redemptio, meaning "a buying back," referring, in the Old Testament, to Yahweh's deliverance of Israel and, in the New Testament, to Christ's deliverance of all Christians from the forces of sin. As the agent of redemption, Jesus is called the Redeemer.

reincarnation ➤ The belief that our soul can be reborn into a new human body.

Resurrection ➤ The passage of Jesus from death to life on the third day after his death on the cross; the heart of the Paschal Mystery and the basis of our hope in the resurrection of the dead.

S

Sabbath ➤ A day of religious observance and abstinence from work, kept by Jews from Friday evening to Saturday evening, and by most Christians on Sunday.

Sacred Tradition ➤ This word (from the Latin meaning "to hand on") refers to the process of passing on the Gospel message. Tradition, which began with the oral communication of the Gospel by the Apostles, was written down in Scripture, is handed down and lived out in the life of the Church, and is interpreted by the Magisterium under the guidance of the Holy Spirit.

sacrifice ➤ A ritual offering made to God by a priest on behalf of the people as a sign of adoration, gratitude, and communion. The perfect sacrifice was Christ's death on the cross.

Sadducees ➤ This group of Jews consisted largely of the elite, wealthy class; many were chief priests. They did not believe in the resurrection of the dead.

salvation ➤ From the Latin salvare, meaning "to save," referring to the forgiveness of sins and assurance of permanent union with God, attained for us through the Paschal Mystery—Christ's work of redemption accomplished through his Passion, death, Resurrection, and Ascension. Only at the time of judgment can a person be certain of salvation, which is a gift of God.

salvation history ➤ The pattern of specific events in human history in which God clearly reveals his presence and saving actions. Salvation was accomplished once and for all through Jesus Christ, a truth foreshadowed and revealed throughout the Old Testament.

sanctify ➤ To purify or make holy.

Sanhedrin ➤ The highest council of the ancient Jews, consisting of seventy-one members exercising authority in religious matters.

Savior ➤ One who brings salvation; specifically, Jesus Christ.

scribes ➤ These people were scholars and teachers of the Jewish Law and Scripture. They were associated with both the chief priests and the Pharisees.

second coming ➤ The second coming of Christ as judge of all the living and the dead, when the Kingdom of God will be fulfilled. Also called the Parousia.

slippery slope ➤ A course of action that seems to lead inevitably from one action or result to another, with unintended consequences.

social justice ➤ The defense of human dignity by ensuring that essential human needs are met and that essential human rights are protected for all people.

solidarity ➤ Union of one's heart and mind with those who are poor or powerless or who face an injustice. It is an act of Christian charity.

spiritual exercises ➤ Originally established by Saint Ignatius of Loyola, spiritual exercises are prayers, meditations, reflections, and directions of retreat. Their purpose is to regulate one's life in such a way that no decision is made under the influence of attachment to anything other than God.

Spiritual Works of Mercy ➤ Actions that guide us to help our neighbors in their spiritual needs.

synagogue ➤ The building where a Jewish assembly or congregation meets for religious worship and instruction.

synoptic Gospels ➤ From the Greek for "seeing the whole together," the name given to the Gospels of Matthew, Mark, and Luke, because they are similar in style and content.

T

tenant farmer ➤ A farmer who works someone else's land, paying the landowner a percentage of the crops or animals raised.

Theological Virtues ➤ The name given for the God-given virtues of faith, hope, and love. These virtues enable us to know God as God and lead us to union with God in mind and heart.

Torah ➤ A Hebrew word meaning "law," referring to the first five books of the Old Testament. It can also refer to the Law of Moses.

Trinity ➤ Often referred to as the Blessed Trinity, the central Christian mystery and dogma that there is one God in three Persons: Father, Son, and Holy Spirit.

V

virtue ➤ A habitual and firm disposition to do good.

W

written tradition ➤ The stage during the formation of the Gospels when the human authors, under the inspiration of the Holy Spirit, drew upon the oral tradition and earlier writings to create the four Gospels we have today in the Bible.

Z

Zealots ➤ These people believed that God wanted Israel to be an independent nation again, free from foreign rule. They preached a violent overthrow of the Roman occupiers.

INDEX

Note: Charts and maps are indicated with "C" and "M," respectively.

ACKNOWLEDGMENTS

The scriptural quotations in this publication are taken from the *New American Bible, revised edition* © 2010, 1991, 1986, 1970 Confraternity of Christian Doctrine, Inc., Washington, D.C. All Rights Reserved. No part of this work may be reproduced or transmitted in any form or by any means, electronic or mechanical, including photocopying, recording, or by any information storage and retrieval system, without permission in writing from the copyright owner.

The excerpts throughout this publication marked *CCC* are from the English translation of the *Catechism of the Catholic Church* for use in the United States of America, second edition. Copyright © 1994 by the United States Catholic Conference, Inc.—Libreria Editrice Vaticana (LEV). English translation of the *Catechism of the Catholic Church: Modifications from the Editio Typica* copyright © 1997 by the United States Catholic Conference, Inc.—LEV.

The excerpt on page 25 is from "Address of His Holiness Pope Francis to Participants in the General Chapter of the Society of the Catholic Apostolate," October 10, 2016, at *http://w2.vatican.va/content /francesco/en/speeches/2016/october/documents/papa-francesco_20161010_capitolo-pallottini.html*. Copyright © Libreria Editrice Vaticana (LEV).

The quotation on page 52 is from *Dogmatic Constitution on Divine Revelation* (*Dei Verbum*, 1965), number 10, at *www.vatican.va/archive/hist_councils/ii_vatican_council/documents/vat-ii_const_19651118_dei-verbum_en.html*. Copyright © LEV.

The excerpt by Pope Francis on page 52 is from his "Ecumenical and Interreligious Meeting Address," Nairobi, Kenya, November 26, 2015, at *https://w2 .vatican.va/content/francesco/en/speeches/2015/november /documents/papa-francesco_20151126_kenya-incontro-interreligioso.html*. Copyright © LEV.

The excerpt by Pope Francis on page 72 is from his "Address to the Community of Christian Life (CVX)—Missionary Students' League of Italy," April 30, 2015, at *http://w2.vatican.va/content/francesco/en /speeches/2015/april/documents/papa-francesco_20150430 _comunita-vita-cristiana.html*. Copyright © LEV.

The excerpt on page 81 is from *Embracing a Generous Life: The Joyful Spirituality of Stewardship*, by Robert F. Morneau (New London, CT: Twenty-Third Publications, 2013), page 23. Copyright © 2013 by Robert F. Morneau.

The excerpt by Pope Francis on pages 92 and 260 are from "*The Light of Faith*" ("*Lumen Fidei*," 2013), numbers 22 and 51, at *http://w2.vatican.va/content /francesco/en/encyclicals/documents/papa-francesco_20130629_enciclica-lumen-fidei.html*. Copyright © LEV.

The excerpt by Pope Francis on pages 117 and 333 are from *Evangelii Gaudium* (2013), numbers 269 and 39, at *http://w2.vatican.va/content/francesco/en/ apost_exhortations/documents/papa-francesco_esortazione-ap_20131124_evangelii-gaudium.html*. Copyright © LEV.

The excerpt on page 133 is from a live radio broadcast of Holy Thursday Mass, April 13, 2017, on CNS News, Vatican City. For more of the broadcast, see *www.catholicnews.com/services/englishnews/2017 /pope-washes-feet-of-12-prison-inmates-at-holy-thursday -mass.cfm*.

The excerpt on page 141 is from "Address of Pope Francis at the Prayer Vigil with the Young People on the Occasion of the XXVIII World Youth Day," July 27, 2013, at *https://w2.vatican.va/content/francesco/en /speeches/2013/july/documents/papa-francesco_20130727 _gmg-veglia-giovani.html*. Copyright © LEV.

The excerpt on page 158 is from "Address of Pope Francis at the Meeting with the Leaders of Other Religions and Other Christian Denominations," September 21, 2014, at *https://w2.vatican.va /content/francesco/en/speeches/2014/september/documents /papa-francesco_20140921_albania-leaders-altre-religioni .html*. Copyright © LEV.

The excerpt by Pope Francis on page 180 is from his *Bull of Indiction of the Extraordinary Jubilee of Mercy* (*Misericordiae Vultus*, 2015), number 15, at *https://w2 .vatican.va/content/francesco/en/apost_letters/documents /papa-francesco_bolla_20150411_misericordiae-vultus .html*. Copyright © LEV.

The excerpt on page 195 is from *Rite of Baptism for Children* © 1969, International Commission on English in the Liturgy (ICEL), number 179, in *The Rites of the Catholic Church*, volume one, prepared by the ICEL, a Joint Commission of Catholic Bishops' Conferences (Collegeville, MN: The Liturgical Press, 1990). Copyright © 1990 by the Order of St. Benedict, Collegeville, MN. Used with permission of the ICEL. Texts contained in this work derived whole or in part from liturgical texts copyrighted by the International Commission on English in the Liturgy (ICEL) have been published here with the confirmation of the Committee on Divine Worship, United States Conference of Catholic Bishops. No other texts in this work have been formally reviewed or approved by the United States Conference of Catholic Bishops.

The quotations on pages 208 and 234 are from the English translation of *The Roman Missal* © 2010, International Commission on English in the Liturgy Corporation (ICEL) (Washington, DC: United States Conference of Catholic Bishops, 2011), page 139 and page 34, number 67. Copyright © 2011, USCCB, Washington, D.C. All rights reserved. Used with permission of the ICEL. Texts contained in this work derived whole or in part from liturgical texts copyrighted by the International Commission on English in the Liturgy (ICEL) have been published here with the confirmation of the Committee on Divine Worship, United States Conference of Catholic Bishops. No other texts in this work have been formally reviewed or approved by the United States Conference of Catholic Bishops.

The excerpt on page 206 is from Pope Francis's *Angelus*, Saint Peter's Square, May 22, 2016, at *https://w2.vatican.va/content/francesco/en/angelus/2016/documents/papa-francesco_angelus_20160522.html*. Copyright © LEV.

The quotation by Pope John XXIII on page 229 is from "Opening Remarks of the Second Vatican Council," October 11, 1962, at *https://w2.vatican.va/content/john-xxiii/it/speeches/1962/documents/hf_j-xxiii_spe_19621011_opening-council.html*. Copyright © LEV.

The excerpt by Pope Francis on page 227 is from his "Homily for the Inauguration of the Jubilee," December 8, 2015, at *http://en.radiovaticana.va/news/2015/12/08/pope_francis_homily_for_inauguration_of_the_jubilee/1192758*. Copyright © Vatican Radio.

The excerpt by Pope Francis on page 274 is from "Homily of Pope Francis at the Holy Mass and Conferral of the Sacrament of Confirmation," Saint Peter's Square, April 28, 2013, at *http://w2.vatican.va/content/francesco/en/homilies/2013/documents/papa-francesco_20130428_omelia-cresime.html*. Copyright © LEV.

The excerpt on page 295 is from Pope Francis's *Angelus*, Saint Peter's Square, November 1, 2013, at *http://w2.vatican.va/content/francesco/en/angelus/2013/documents/papa-francesco_angelus_20131101.html*. Copyright © LEV.

The excerpt on page 345 is from "Address of His Holiness Pope Francis to the Young People of Santo Tomas University," January 18, 2015, at *https://w2.vatican.va/content/francesco/en/speeches/2015/january/documents/papa-francesco_20150118_srilanka-filippine-incontro-giovani.html*. Copyright © LEV.

The quotation on page 351 is from "Seven Themes of Catholic Social Teaching," text drawn from *Sharing Catholic Social Teaching: Challenges and Directions* (Washington, DC: USCCB, 1998) and *Faithful Citizenship: A Catholic Call to Political Responsibility* (Washington, DC: USCCB, 2003).

The quotations by Br. Jean Pierre Schumacher on page 359 are from an interview with Spanish publisher Alfa y Omega in 2010, quoted in *The Catholic News Agency*, January 17, 2011.

The excerpt on page 370 is from "Homily of His Holiness Pope Francis at the Holy Mass on the Occasion of the XXVIII World Youth Day," July 28, 2013, at *http://w2.vatican.va/content/francesco/en/homilies/2013/documents/papa-francesco_20130728_celebrazione-xxviii-gmg.html*. Copyright © LEV.

To view copyright terms and conditions for internet materials cited here, log on to the home pages for the referenced websites.

During this book's preparation, all citations, facts, figures, names, addresses, telephone numbers, internet URLs, and other pieces of information cited within were verified for accuracy. The authors and Saint Mary's Press staff have made every attempt to reference current and valid sources, but we cannot guarantee the content of any source, and we are not responsible for any changes that may have occurred since our verification. If you find an error in, or have a question or concern about, any of the information or sources listed within, please contact Saint Mary's Press.

Endnote Cited in a Quotation from the *Catechism of the Catholic Church, Second Edition*

Chapter 12
1. *Sacrosanctum concilium* 73; cf. Codex Iuris Canonici, cann. 1004 § 1; 1005;1007; Corpus Canonum Ecclesiarum Orientalium, ca. 738.